RECONCEIVING LIBERALISM

Pitt Series in Policy and Institutional Studies

Oren M. Levin-Waldman

RECONCEIVING LIBERALISM

Dilemmas of Contemporary Liberal Public Policy

University of Pittsburgh Press

Published by the University of Pittsburgh Press, Pittsburgh, Pa., 15260

Manufactured in the United States of America
Printed on acid-free paper
10 9 8 7 6 5 4 3 2 1

Library of Congress Cataloging-in-Publication Data
Levin-Waldman, Oren M.
Reconceiving liberalism : dilemmas of contemporary liberal public policy / Oren M. Levin-Waldman.
p. cm.—(Pitt series in policy and institutional studies)
Includes index.
ISBN 0-8229-3937-1 (acid free paper).—ISBN 0-8229-5594-6 (pbk. : acid-free paper)
1. Liberalism—United States. 2. Values—United States. I. Title. II. Series.
JC574.2.U6L49 1996
320.5'13'0973—dc20 96-25190
CIP

A CIP catalog record for this book is available from the British Library.

For Renee

Contents

Preface

Why is it that the American public has such contempt for liberalism? Why has it become the dreaded L-word? It is supremely ironic that a doctrine so core to America's founding principles could come to be viewed as being so contrary to community values. This book isn't a history of how liberalism came to be so despised. It is an attempt to put forth a liberal vision that bridges the gap between liberal public policy and mainstream thought and opinion. Yet, the public that despises liberalism really knows little about it. The public has come to assume that liberals are those who "tax and spend," favor big government, and oppose family values. They are assumed to be antifamily because of their opposition to school prayer, abortion restrictions, and sexual constraints. These are simplistic characterizations to be sure, but they have nonetheless sufficed to cause most politicians to run for cover when confronted with a liberal label. Yet, liberalism is the basic philosophy contained in the

American Declaration of Independence, and its values underpin much of American constitutional structure. Liberalism, however, has evolved over the years, and much of the antagonism may stem from the appearance that liberalism today does not appear to be what it was then.

Contemporary liberalism is often conceived of as a public philosophy justifying the use of government to achieve certain social objectives. Under the banner of liberalism, government regulates the activities of corporations, as well as sponsors an array of social programs designed to achieve greater opportunity and, ultimately, greater equality. This liberalism is assumed to be different from its more classical version, which stressed that the role of government was to be limited to no more than the preservation of a framework in which individuals could pursue their own self-interests. Liberalism has clearly evolved from a public philosophy of limited government to one of active government, from a philosophy of the minimalist state to one of the positive state. The assumption, then, is that contemporary liberalism has repudiated its classical antecedent, at least with regard to the role of government in the marketplace. At the same time, liberalism is seen as being contradictory when it seeks to prohibit all government interference in people's personal lives. By the public's perception, big government is the norm in the marketplace, and complete liberty bordering on licentiousness is the norm in the bedroom.

As tempting as it would be to respond that the actions of economic actors aren't necessarily equivalent to the actions of actors in the privacy of their homes, it nonetheless fails to confront the public perception that liberalism as an ideology is really a web of contradictions. The conception that seems to have emerged, as evidenced in the nature of contemporary American politics, is that liberalism has gone so far afield that it is literally suspect. The liberalism of the past, which to a large extent has found expression in contemporary conservatism, is viewed as good, whereas the liberalism of the present is considered to be contrary to basic American values. Much of liberalism's problems may stem from the fact that there really isn't much of a consensus on what its core principles are. Liberalism has encompassed a broad spectrum of thought and opinion, and over the years it has consisted of several different strands emphasizing different principles. Yet, despite its various permutations, the theme of individual liberty unconstrained by arbitrary exercises of power and authority (state and other) has transcended each. The misperception is that what liberalism opposes today is not what it opposed in the past. On the contrary, what it opposes now is what it has always opposed—political absolutism and arbitrariness.

Liberalism is a political philosophy espousing the right of individuals to choose for themselves their own conceptions of *good* and to live their lives accordingly. Individuals are assumed to have moral agency, the capacity to reason for themselves what their own personal good is and to be able to act on it. No two persons are the same, but they are separate and distinct. Different individuals with different conceptions will naturally lead different lives. This then implies the need for political and social arrangements that respect and protect individual agency. It also precludes government from having its own conception of good apart from individual conceptions of it. Rather, government is exhorted to respect the integrity of each individual's good and to refrain from choosing one's conception over another's. Government, then, is to be neutral with regard to conceptions of good or life choices, and the best way it can do this is by being limited in its function and only intervening when absolutely necessary. It is by restricting its function that it can check itself against the possible use of arbitrary authority. In terms of political philosophy, the overriding concern of liberalism now, as before, is to defend against oppressive demands and intrusions of authority. As a political philosophy, liberalism seeks to secure those political conditions necessary for the exercise of personal freedom.

For most people, however, this is simply too abstract. How can a doctrine purporting to promote freedom on the basis of limited government also justify greater government, which to many suggests restrictions on freedom? Historically, liberalism was a response to the clericalism and absolutism of feudalistic societies in which political sovereignty was in the hands of the monarch who could claim rightful authority through divine right of kings. Individuals weren't entitled to their own conceptions of the good; rather, they were to subordinate their individual interests to the absolute authority of the king, the church, or both. Liberalism, as it developed during the seventeenth century, had the effect of liberating typical individuals from these constraints and enabling them to think for themselves and pursue their interests accordingly. It was a liberal ideology that John Locke ultimately used to justify the Glorious Revolution of 1688, and it was a liberal ideology that the American revolutionaries used to justify breaking off from the British in 1776. This freedom of conscience that often tends to find practical expression in a framework that enables individuals to pursue their self-interests—be it economic or other—is really the essence of liberal philosophy. So too has it been the essence of the American experience.

That liberalism now sees a greater need for government intervention than in the past isn't indicative of any less of a commitment to freedom. Rather, other forces aside from government can threaten it. Historically, liberals have always stood for personal freedom, the value core to American political identity. But it was also liberal ideology that the framers of the New Deal during the 1930s relied upon to justify an active government. It was the notion, as expressed by John Dewey, that liberalism would be a blueprint for social action, and that government should take "affirmative action" to see that the public interest was served. If government was to maintain its commitment to a liberal goal of protecting individual liberty, it would have to take steps in the form of policies and programs aimed at generating opportunities for personal growth. Liberalism as a public philosophy justifying greater government involvement to a large extent has responded to the new realities of a more complex society in which there are any number of forces beyond our control with the capacity to strip us of our own respective individual worth. In abstract terms, there would appear to be consistency. Government intervenes to prevent harm to others, as it always has. The critical difference is that harm is conceived more broadly than in the past. In an industrial economy, government regulates more because the actions of private actors are more likely to cause harm than would have been the case in an agrarian economy. Still, the actions of individuals performed in the privacy of their homes will not cause harm to others.

It seems easy to assert that, relative to the complexity of society, government is still limited and individuals enjoy the same basic freedoms they always have. That is, despite its evolution, liberalism's core commitments haven't changed, but objective social circumstances have. So why, then, the public antagonism toward liberalism? Why has it become the dreaded L-word, conjuring up images of big, intrusive government and licentiousness? In contemporary political discourse, liberalism is characterized by the slogan "tax and spend." Indeed, in the spirit of enhancing individual liberty, government actively pursued programs aimed at generating opportunities. These programs, as do all, cost money, and revenues had to be raised. Some programs may have worked, but any number failed. It isn't entirely clear why they failed, but the fact that they did has sufficed in the minds of many to call for a return to principles of free markets. And these calls have invoked the classical liberal theme that the government that governs best is the one that governs least. That any number of programs may not have had a chance because of inadequate funding—particularly in the face of the Vietnam War during the late 1960s and early 1970s—is irrelevant to most. The public has simply come to the view that liberalism with its government solutions to society's problems simply does not work. The liberal who says he or she cares about personal freedom simply isn't taken seriously. Care for personal freedom, the rejoinder goes, means reducing the scope of government and eliminating its intrusions into people's lives.

I began writing this book shortly after the 1992 Republican National Convention where right-wing commentator Patrick Buchanan proclaimed that the presidential election was tantamount to a religious war in which the forces of God and morality would triumph over those of liberal atheism, promiscuity, and immorality. At the time it may have appeared that this public embrace of the right was a contributing factor to the Republican party's defeat for reelection. Yet, this was by no means an aberration. On the contrary, this type of demagoguery was merely another episode in a continuum. It worked quite successfully for George Bush against Michael Dukakis in 1988. By portraying Dukakis as a "liberal" out of touch with mainstream American values, Bush managed to position himself as the spokesperson for the common man. This was quite ironic given that Bush, scion of an old eastern patrician family, was anything but the common man. Yet Bush defeated Dukakis for the presidency in a landslide. Four years later, when Bill Clinton ran for president, he went out of his way to define himself as a new Democrat and not a liberal. And despite Bush's best efforts to paint Clinton with a liberal brush, Bush was defeated. Bush's defeat, however, cannot be considered a triumph for liberal resurgence. Clinton campaigned on a platform of change, and Bush was simply unable to understand what it was that was bothering most Americans.

One shouldn't be so complacent as to think that Clinton's election signifies any public reconsideration of liberalism. If anything, the public is as antiliberal as it ever was. Perhaps nothing dramatizes this more than the Republican sweep of 1994 where the Republicans for the first time in forty years took control of the House of Representatives and the U.S. Senate. To a large extent, the election was a repudiation of Clinton and his effort to reform the health care system. And yet, this repudiation was the rejection of what the public took to be a liberal plan by a liberal president. Moreover, the current Speaker of the House, Newt Gingrich, continues the assault on liberalism and often frames political battles in terms of "us" (that is, true Americans) against "them" (that is, the immoral liberal counterculture).

In this book I maintain that liberalism is largely misunderstood, but that this misunderstanding in part stems from a tendency to both formulate and measure policy in accordance with neutrality as opposed to other principles best represented by its civic tradition. That if policy, framed in the name of liberalism, were to be measured by these other principles, liberalism would end up being more consistent with community values. The liberal bashing in recent years certainly does make this book topical. But it is not a response to those demagogues on the Right who would distort and twist liberalism for their own partisan gain. Nor is it for that matter a defense of those on the Left who would defend all that has passed as liberal policy over the last thirty years, as though it is the only answer to society's problems. The problem is that it is too simplistic, as the Right might have one believe, to go back to the minimalist state. Society is by far too complex for that. At the same, liberal public policy hasn't always been cognizant of community values. Rather, this book represents an attempt to find the middle ground and reconcile liberalism with mainstream American values. In so doing, I seek to put forth a liberalism that, while it accommodates a positive state, maintains continuity with the past. The Left's portrayal of classical liberalism as rights-based, antigovernment, and ultimately anticommunity simply misses the mark. The Right's portrayal of liberalism as devoid of values also misses the mark. If anything, such characterizations only dramatize that liberalism is misunderstood. In part, the problem has arisen from the view that classical theorists like Locke were simply dated and bore no relevance to the contemporary world. This was a problem compounded by the misguided assumption that any application of classical theory to the modern world really aspires to a libertarian world view best exemplified by Robert Nozick's theory of the minimalist state in *Anarchy, State, and Utopia*. These theories, after all, were too simple for a vastly complex world, one that clearly bears no resemblance to the one Locke lived in. In this book, I show that this is not correct. But the other problem stems from the tendency to abstract liberal principles into the realm of high theory whereby the expression of individualism assumes the form of atomistic individualism unbounded by any types of community constraints. This has effectively placed the individual in a realm of privacy whereby one is free to do whatever one wants with total indifference to community sensibilities on the grounds that the state may not restrict personal actions in privacy because that would effectively be tantamount to the imposition of a good on others. But it is also on the grounds that one's actions in private cannot cause harm to others.

The point is that the assault on liberalism hasn't been only political but has been intellectual as well. The principal criticism is that liberalism, because it is centered on a conception of neutrality, fails to conceive of individuals as having any responsibility to their communities. The principal concern being that the liberal depiction of society consisting of atomistic individuals leads to individual alienation and, ultimately, anomie. People can wall themselves off from the community and wrap themselves in the language of rights. The result is that communitarian ends and purposes cannot be achieved. Unquestionably, liberalism in America has consisted of a strong tradition of rights. It isn't that these critics would necessarily do away with rights, but that they would like to see a greater balance between rights and obligations.

A number of attempts have been made in recent years to reconstruct liberal philosophy around a more civic conception, one that stresses the equal importance of the community to the individual. For instance, William Galston in *Liberal Purposes*, coming from a more communitarian perspective, has put forth a vision on the basis of liberal purposes centered on liberalism's two primary virtues of individualism and tolerance for diversity. From the more traditional rights-based perspective, Stephen Macedo in *Liberal Virtues* puts forth a vision stressing the virtues of citizenship and community. These ideals, he argues, can be located "in an ideal of constitutionalism sustained by a basic commitment to public reasonableness." His vision also emphasizes the virtue of tolerance, as that is essential to a peaceful community, and tolerance is achieved through public justification. Public justification aims to achieve respect for diversity while "forging a framework of common moral principles that all can understand, accept, and openly affirm before one another." Such acceptance ultimately forms the basis of a shared identity. And too, John Rawls, who best expressed the concept of liberal neutrality in *A Theory of Justice*, has put forth in *Political Liberalism* a liberal vision that in its commitment to neutrality on comprehensive moral doctrines, holds forth the proposition that social unity can be achieved through the idea of overlapping consensus. Social unity is the product of a broad consensus of reasonable comprehensive doctrines, and this only comes about through political cooperation yielded by democratic institutions.

As much as these visions place greater stress on the community, they by no means depart from traditional liberal emphases on human agency. Instead they stress the importance of community to the development and realization of that agency. But neglected, and most ironic, is that these visions fail to make reference to the principal architect of liberalism, John Locke. It is because the modern world is so vastly different from Locke's that there has been a tendency to abstract liberal principles to the point that they almost appear to be a repudiation of their classical antecedents. Yet, the vision that is often aspired to is really a Lockean one. This book departs from most attempts to reconstruct liberalism by arguing that there is a civic tradition of liberalism that emphasizes the community as much as the individual, and that this civic tradition can be located in liberalism's classical antecedents. Through a reconsideration of Locke, it is possible to locate a basis of community and derive a set of values that are relevant to the world in which we live.

Much of the material on Locke and my reinterpretation of him stems from my participation in a summer seminar sponsored by the National

Endowment for the Humanities at Princeton University during the summer of 1992. Through that seminar, led by Hans Aarsleff, we were supposed to understand that Locke's major contribution to intellectual history was the priority of methodological individualism over community. It was through my own individual project on Locke that I came to understand that while Locke certainly rejects a particular conception of community, he by no means rejects the whole concept. I thank Professor Aarsleff for the intellectually engaging experience and the NEH for its support. I would also like to thank William Brandon and Charles Whalen for reading parts of the manuscript and offering suggestions, as well as anonymous reviewers for their comments. They no doubt made this a better book, but I alone bear sole responsibility for any errors and omissions still remaining. Most of all, I would like to thank my family who as usual bore the brunt of this project. My wife, Renee, provided the love, support, and encouragement necessary to complete this project, and my two sons, Avi and Ariel, though too young to offer any substantive assistance, did provide the love and necessary distractions essential to keeping me going.

1. *Introduction*

IN contemporary American political discourse, liberalism is under siege. Liberalism, long the basis for a rich political tradition encompassed in the Declaration of Independence and the Constitution,[1] has become the dreaded "L-word" associated with heretical and perceived anti-American values.[2] Not only is liberalism viewed as being totally bereft of value, but worse, it sanctions licentiousness, which threatens the moral fabric of the community. Liberals are often portrayed as self-centered individualists who are atheistic, antifamily, and anticommunity. While they call upon government to intervene in people's daily lives when it comes to the marketplace, liberals also exhort government to respect the sanctity of personal privacy when it comes to social issues, regardless of how offensive it may be to the community's overall moral sensibilities.

At the 1992 Republican National Convention, this mythology

achieved a degree of prominence when commentator Pat Buchanan, who had challenged incumbent President Bush for the party's nomination, declared, "This election is about much more than who gets what. It is about what we stand for as Americans. There is a religious war going on for the soul of America. It is a cultural war, as critical to the kind of nation we will one day be—as was the cold war itself."[3] If the Democrats were to be returned to the White House, the liberal agenda of sexual liberty, family disintegration, and other values contrary to Americans' sense of right would be established. This was an election about the heart and soul of the nation in which the forces of good and virtue would triumph over those of evil and decadence. The evil and decadence the country were to fight against were assumed to be at the heart of liberalism. If the country were to build a new moral order, or at least reconstruct the one that appeared to have vanished, it would have to stamp out liberalism and all it stood for. Yet to do so would be to deny the very tradition that has been core to American identity.

How is it that a political philosophy so critical to American identity would appear to be so out of touch with mainstream American values? Why is there such a perceived difference between the ideals of liberalism and the public's perception of them? Why are liberal politics perceived to be out of the mainstream of public acceptance, when ironically they were intended to foster traditional American ideals—and liberal ones at that—contained in the Declaration of Independence? How are we to account for liberalism's apparent impoverishment? Has public policy in America lost sight of the values of community, tolerance, mutuality, and citizenship?

In part, the answer to these questions lies in the fact that liberalism's purposes and values aren't entirely clear. They often appear to be contradictory. Yet liberalism, contrary to popular misconceptions, does contain a moral vision of what constitutes the good life.[4] And in this vision are a set of principles that can serve as a good yardstick of whether public policy accords with the philosophic principles that underlie this society. These principles, as I hope to make clear throughout this study, have been obscured in large measure because of a reliance on neutrality as a measure of policy. One of the principal arguments of this book is that the apparent divergence between liberal policy and mainstream perceptions of traditional American values—they are often considered to be different—is caused by the tendency to formulate and evaluate policy within the confines of the neutrality principle.

Neutrality essentially exhorts government, when acting in any capacity, not to show preference for one group over another. It is the notion that government must not embrace any particular conception of the *good;* rather, it must be neutral on those questions of what constitutes the good life. If government is neutral on these questions, which are essentially about life choices or, as Rawls refers to them, comprehensive moral doctrines,[5] individuals are free to conceive of their own good according to liberal assumptions of human agency. If neutrality is the principle by which government governs, it assumes that individuals are equal and must therefore be accorded equal respect and treatment. A government that shows preference for group A over group B cannot be treating individuals equally.[6]

As a theoretical abstraction this may appear straightforward, but how can it realistically be implemented in the world, where conflicts emerge between individuals and groups and their conflicting conceptions of what constitutes the good life? The practical implication would be for a limited form of government that does nothing other than maintain a framework conducive to the pursuit of self-interests, when these interests represent individual expressions of good. Such a government would only mediate conflict and would only intervene when it is absolutely clear that such intervention is essential to the preservation of the framework. Action would be indicated once a situation reached the point of crisis. So why not use this as a yardstick for determining the appropriateness of government action? Indeed, this was the criterion during an earlier period when society was considerably more simple and the need for government action was seldom. This period is commonly referred to as laissez-faire, in which government functions were confined to that of a night watchman.

The problem with neutrality is that it suggests that government may not act, because any action will have the effect of embracing some comprehensive doctrine. After all, what is policy, if not some type of practical program for implementing a vision of good or some elements of it? Because policy in a liberal democratic society is the result of a competitive struggle between divergent groups in an open political system, the result in the end is that some vision of good will have been adopted. To then suggest that liberal policy can be neutral is chimerical, to say the least.

Moreover, the needs of an increasingly more complex modern society do require government to act. The modern society we live in is forced to address gripping social and economic issues. To talk about neutrality in politics when government is forced to make choices is to raise a contradiction in terms. Either government does nothing, or it honors every request because neutrality proscribes the making of choices. But given that resources are limited, honoring every request just isn't possible. Moreover, neutrality, in and of itself, can be said to represent a value choice. If government is to remain theoretically neutral and at the same time make the necessary choices, it is only inevitable that the door is open to power politics.

In his classic *The End of Liberalism: The Second Republic of the United States*, Theodore Lowi argues that a state predicated on neutrality is unable to order its priorities. Consequently, when groups come to government requesting different goods, it ends up distributing to each and all alike. The ranking of goods is not a question of which has a higher intrinsic value, but which has a stronger interest group lobbying for it. In attempting to accommodate the administrative state, liberalism became completely devoid of the principles it was initially predicated on. Those principles were commitment to the rule of law and protection against government arbitrariness. Because the tasks of the positive state were so immense, and the public increasingly came to look to the federal government for solutions to all of its problems, more power and authority were delegated to agencies and departments within the executive branch. Instead of lobbying Congress, as was the prescription in the Constitution and the very embodiment of liberalism, interest groups went directly to agencies and departments for their wares. The distribution of goods was no longer based on what best served the public interest, but which interest group in the most powerful iron triangle—a mutually reinforcing relationship—was able to prevail. The government could distribute goods and services to all who would come a'courting largely because those who were bearing the costs simply weren't visible.[7] What Lowi's analysis illustrates quite clearly is how the ends of the policy process were not neutral, as it effectively leads to even greater inequalities and inequities. But the irony is that the means theoretically were neutral. What becomes most clear is that a state that attempts to be neutral on all questions of good will ultimately appear to stand for nothing, especially at a time when people perceive core values to be under siege. In a time of crisis, how can we know what action to take, and by what criteria do we decide that it was in fact good action?

More than the stinging critique that it is, Lowi offers us the tantalizing prospect of reconceiving the administrative state along the lines of a juridical democracy in which policies and programs would be implemented according to known rules and the letter of the law.[8] While acknowledging the administrative state to be an essential component of modern industrial societies, Lowi essentially challenges us to reconcile this state with those principles underpinning the society in which it serves. The analysis, however, did not go far enough. While juridical democracy could be said to represent a criterion by which policy would be adopted, it didn't really speak to the issue of just how it would be evaluated. Moreover, as his critique called attention to the apparent impoverishment of liberalism, his prescriptions had more to do with ensuring administrative state accountability than to assuring how policy could accord with liberal purposes. In this vein, his critique could be said to fall within the liberal tradition of rights protection, as the object is to ensure that individual liberties will be protected from the arbitrary exercises of administrative power. Because the executive branch has received its power through congressional delegations of authority, it is no longer held in check by constitutional separation of powers. The emphasis was not on how to have the positive state better serve the needs of the community while remaining consistent with traditional liberal precepts. Yet, the impoverishment to which Lowi alludes is ultimately the by-product of a policy process operating (whether consciously or not) within the confines of neutrality.

The other problem with neutrality is that it tends to place greater emphasis on the rights of individuals to be protected from government, with less emphasis on individuals' commitments to their communities. As one is considered to be equal in the capacity to conceive one's own good, there can be no absolute or universal good. This, of course, presupposes that individuals can have goods that are separate from, and even contradictory to, the good of the community. The community, then, has no other good than perhaps the sum total of individual ones. As a result, what separates individuals is prior to what unites them.[9]

The central point of this book is to argue that the liberal state would do better to rely less on neutrality and look more toward other values within liberalism. Neutrality should be abandoned as the primary measure in favor of what could be said to constitute liberalism's core principles. Those principles, to an extent, accord with William Galston's conception of *purposive liberalism,* which is centered on liberalism's primary virtues of individualism and tolerance for diversity, and would require that content and specificity be given to liberalism's traditional distinction between public and private and its commitment to individual freedom.[10] And it also emphasizes mutuality and community as they are deemed essential to furthering the human project.

The ideal that I put forth in the next chapter and that forms the foundations for policy analysis can also be referred to as the *civic tradition of liberalism*, which will be referred to as the *Lockean ideal.* Although it prizes individualism, it equally prizes the community and its preservation. As much as the Lockean ideal holds each individual to be fully autonomous and that individual autonomy needs to be respected, it also expects each member to contribute to the good of the community. Certainly it stresses the maximization of human agency, but this agency is understood within the context of strong communities. The ideal is one of socially bounded individualism, which means that individuals who are part of communities are in fact shaped by their communities. Individual behavior, while in part a function of how each perceives the world, is principally a function of socialization.[11] In addition to the more commonly understood emphasis on individualism, the ideal also stresses the importance of tolerance, mutuality, and a common project. And if individuals share and participate in a common project, they can be said to be citizens of the community. What is important about this conception is that as much as individuals do have rights, they also have obligations. What emerges in the end, then, is what could be said to be a broadly inclusive community.

And yet, in claiming that these values form the core of the Lockean ideal, I am actually presenting a view of Locke that differs from how Locke has traditionally been understood. It is because of the profound influence that Locke has had on American political culture and the nature of American politics that it is essential to demonstrate how this ideal differs from the more traditional conception of Locke. One of the main arguments I wish to make is as follows: When Locke is reinterpreted and understood to be less libertarian and more community minded, it is then possible to move policy beyond the constraints of neutrality to a framework in which its evaluation will be more consistent with the values of the community. And in so doing, policy that is formulated in the name of liberalism will ultimately be in greater harmony with those communities—their values—that it is intended to serve.

To talk about obligations, however, isn't to diminish the importance of what liberalism has historically been opposed to—mainly arbitrary exercises of authority. Individuals can only be expected to do their fair share if they are regarded as equal members of the community and they are afforded the space to develop themselves as free-thinking human beings. This requires constitutional safeguards against the possibility of arbitrary exercises of power; the ideals put forth in this study assume that these safeguards will be in place. Hence, a degree of neutrality is assumed and must, in fact, be there. But we must move beyond it. It, alone, cannot be the sole criterion. Once these safeguards are in place, the community may legitimately ask that individuals give something back—that they work to further the common project of their communities. A common project can only develop if there is a sense of mutuality. At a minimum, this requires that each of us should respect the rights we would like to have respected. But it also requires each of us to contribute our fair share to society, to be a productive member of the community.

This does not mean that individuals are required to sacrifice to their communities, as modern fascist theories maintain, but that communities are equally as important as the individuals who comprise them, and that balance is the key. A central theme of this book is that individual characters are formed in communities—that is, they are shaped by their communities. The social context is vitally important to the concept. Contrary to those who hold liberalism to be impoverished, it is not a political philosophy about individual atomism, but a social theory that links individuals to their communities.

als to their communities. And in establishing the limits, as a theoretical underpinning for public policy, it strikes the balance between individuals and their communities.

In the end any policy that merely promotes individual interests at the expense of community ultimately undermines the liberal project. But why these principles as opposed to more neutral ones? One could argue that the neutral ones are those that are contained in Lockean liberalism, and thus maintain continuity with our past. Arguably, this is one way to read Locke, and perhaps the more traditional way, but it is not the only way. Lockean liberalism is really more social than is commonly attributed to him.[12] And yet, the emphasis on the neutral elements of his theory has only obscured the other principles that constitute the civic tradition of liberalism.

Political Theory in Policy

In establishing a theoretical framework it will also become clear why not only these principles specifically but also political theory generally serves as a better basis for policy analysis. The measurement of policy against liberal purposes obviously requires a new methodology of policy analysis. It requires nothing less than the application of political theory to the analysis of policy. Theory involves the discussion of values. Policy evaluation predicated on neutrality, however, has required the removal of values from evaluative criteria. Traditional policy analysis, similarly operating within the same confines of neutrality, has tended to rest on the assumption that facts—those that are clearly observable—can be separated from values—normative conceptions of how things ought to be. Though value may intuitively figure into policy construction, consideration of value is supposed to be absent during evaluation of policy effectiveness.

Using theory as a measure of public policy, I hope to demonstrate that theory and policy do go hand in hand—that there is a common project between the two.[13] If one considers under what circumstances liberalism in theory can seriously justify intervention, the empirical dimension becomes all that much more crucial for determining when objective circumstances are such that intervention intended to serve the public interest is necessary. To focus on empiricism to the exclusion of value is to ultimately distort the purpose of public policy, that it is essentially the vehicle for the attainment of communal ends.[14] If neutrality is to be deemphasized, then theory—which asks how we can make for better society—must replace the neutral evaluative criteria of cost-benefit analyses or input-output assessments or both. But this requires returning to the tradition.

What I am positing in this book is that an exploration of Locke ultimately demonstrates the interdependence between individuals and their communities, and that agency is in effect socially defined. Moreover, if policy analysts understood this relationship, they might find the classical critique to be more satisfying than the neutral measures they have relied upon thus far. Measuring policy against these principles would tell us whether policy is serving the larger interests of society and is in accord with its underpinning values, as opposed to whether policy merely works. If it does this, the gap between the goals of policy and the values of the community will effectively be narrowed. My framework for policy analysis rests on the premise that agency, while still critical to all permutations of liberalism, becomes completely meaningless unless strong communities exist to nourish it. Not only, then, does Lockean liberalism support strong communities and communal institutions, but without them, the more traditional conception of Locke's vision of individualism isn't even possible. The problem, however, is that because Locke has been so narrowly constructed—as the defender of individualism, private-property rights, and the accumulation of wealth—liberal policy, in its attempts to serve community interests, has had to achieve its legitimacy by repudiating Lockean liberalism. Modern liberal policy has artificially been conflated with modern liberalism, which has distinguished itself from its classical ancestor with the mythic notion that it repudiated Locke and in effect embraced the state.[15] Insofar as Lockean liberalism has been conceived narrowly as antistatist and a blueprint for limited government, this may be true. But modern policy did not divorce itself from neutral measures that did come from a particular reading of Locke. Rather, all it did was cast aside small government in favor of big government. The idea was that classical liberalism was antiquated and that, with its emphasis on limited government, it was ill-equipped to deal with the needs of modern society. But by repudiating its classical conception, modern liberal policy has undercut its legitimacy by divorcing itself from its philosophic roots. Had Locke been understood properly to begin with, it would have been possible to formulate policy in such a way that it would maintain its consistency with its philosophic roots.

Why These Principles?

My major argument in this book is that if American public policy were to be evaluated against these purposes, liberalism, as the underpinning philosophy of these policies, would be in greater harmony with contemporary public opinion and thought. Public policy must be measured against the criterion of whether it is working to foster a civil society consisting of equal and interested citizens and not a society that merely supports the rights of individual atomism. The error has been to assume that support for the positive state and its policies can only be found in neutrality. On the contrary, what we will find in the chapters that follow is that when we do evaluate policies in light of neutrality, they by no means further liberal purposes. In fact they may, ultimately, undermine the public interest. Yet, it is the public interest that the liberal state is supposed to serve.

At this point one might ask why we need to reconceive liberalism at all. Perhaps the question to ask is why neutrality is such a vaunted principle? Americans live by their tradition, and much of the tradition that Americans live by comes from their founding and indeed is born out of a sense that government is bad. Americans have a big antipathy toward big government, and when government oversteps its bounds, it isn't at all uncommon for Americans to retreat to so-called first principles in the form of what Samuel Huntington has referred to as creedal passion periods.[16] Or as political commentator Kevin Phillips notes, periods of overly "liberal" policy making are followed by a conservative backlash.[17] Neutrality obviously served the purpose of limiting government activity to those matters deemed essential to society's preservation, or so it did in a simpler age. Neutrality also served the purpose of protecting individual liberty from government, traditionally viewed as the locus of power. But because society is vastly more complex than it was a couple hundred years ago, government is required to act. Government must act not only to ensure that liberty will continue to be preserved, which does involve a measure of opportunity, but tolerance as well. When government acts, there can be no neutrality even if the procedures and mechanisms employed to act were indeed neutral and worked to ensure the equal respect and participation of individuals.[18]

The challenge for a reconstructed liberalism, in part, is to find the appropriate balance between public and private. The tension arises, however, because the needs of the modern state represent a divergence from an American tradition of limited government and antistatism, or so this has been the public perception. This, however, is a wrong assumption. On the contrary, the history of liberal policy making is a history of operating within the confines of the antistatist tradition.[19] And it is because of that tradition that we have neutrality as the principal measure. Rather if policy were to be formulated in light of the broader historical tradition of liberalism—which incorporates its classical permutations along with its modern ones—that tension that appears to animate much of American politics might be eliminated. It would be eliminated largely because those values that are core to that tradition would stand out and serve as a viable yardstick for the measurement of policy. Liberalism reconceived would bridge the gap between the necessities of modern society and those traditions that have shaped our identity. The result would be to maintain consistency between the present and past because the purposes of the liberal state would be clear and policies would be determined and evaluated in light of them.

In the chapters that follow, I intend to show how Locke traditionally understood has effectively restricted the scope of public policy, and that a broader reading of Locke would effectively lead to a set of principles by which policy can be measured in such a way that liberal public policy would be consistent with the community's values. These principles are to be found in a reinterpretation of Locke and can be substituted for the neutrality measure that usually flows from the more traditional conception. It is in chapter 2 that this framework of the Lockean ideal is established for the examination of policy issues in the remaining chapters. I lay out the traditional understanding of Locke and explain why Locke has been misunderstood. It is only by understanding the basis upon which neutrality is formed—that it comes from a particular conception of Locke—that it is also possible to understand why the same theory more broadly conceived will imply a different set of criteria for public policy. It then becomes possible to put forth his community credentials. Chapter 2 thus paves the way for a discussion and application of the Lockean ideal to public policy in the succeeding chapters. In chapter 3, I discuss a broad category of economic stabilization policies, ranging from regulation, monetarism, plant-closing policy, and corporatism. They are arrayed on a trajectory in order to show that as society grows more complex and perhaps requires more statist solutions, neutrality becomes less viable. As we move through the trajectory of stabilization policies, neutrality is progressively diminished. Such policies thus ultimately pose a dilemma: If society and the public interest are to be preserved, can this occur if policies are framed in accordance with neutrality?

The community's interest must be taken into account, which means government has an ongoing responsibility to include the community in defining it. When it comes to economic stabilization policies (that is, traditional fiscal and monetary policies aimed at boosting the economy during times of recession and slowing it during times of inflation), it isn't sufficient to simply adopt a neutral policy that may be in the form of tools implemented by an independent agency, with the effect being that the chips fall where they may. Neutral policies of arbitrarily drawing lines in the middle—regardless of who may get hurt—or throwing money at the problem do not solve the problem. Rather, there must be a clear sense of values that the community is trying to promote.

On the positive side of public policy, this requires that government pursue a plan of action aimed at creating opportunities for individuals as compensation for the failure of the marketplace to do so. To a large extent, the modern welfare state does embody this very notion.[20] Chapter 4 examines welfare policy as it was initially intended to create opportunity and yet, ironically, resulted in the opposite. The irony, as I argue, is a function of neutrality. Consequently, this chapter explores the hard issues of dependency in welfare policy and addresses what the objectives of welfare policy ought to be in a liberal society.

Chapter 4 ultimately speaks to the issues of mutuality, obligation, and common purpose. There is a distinction to be drawn between a welfare state that merely distributes assistance because the marketplace has failed to provide sufficient employment opportunities and a welfare state that does provide those opportunities. Mutuality might require a degree of compassion for those who aren't able to succeed, but the liberal tradition also demands that individuals be self-sufficient as a measure of their agency. The exhortation to preserve society and prevent harm to the community would also include the preservation of the community's social and moral fabric. Therefore, a framework aimed at generating opportunities for individuals to succeed would also need to impose obligations if that should prove necessary for the self-sufficiency of its members. Liberalism still requires that individuals be able to think for themselves, and this requires that the integrity of agency be preserved. Mutuality, then, would require that communities help such individuals to help themselves. In the end, if the goal of a reconstructed liberalism is to show how the application of theory to policy could result in a better fit between policy and society's values, there is no avoiding the issue of whether liberalism can ignore questions of personal behavior, even though those questions press against agency. As the trajectory in chapter 3 demonstrates how individual choice may be diminished, the subject is merely broached; chapter 4 addresses it head on.

Chapter 5 examines what are now called public-private partnerships, which are active partnerships between public officials and private business interests aimed at revitalizing sagging economies. Because they represent a *new liberalism*,[21] they warrant attention. But they also warrant attention because in a couple of instances where they have been tried, they have raised issues that only demonstrate the inefficacy of neutrality in a society increasingly requiring stronger linkages between public and private. As with other policies, they represent new and innovative approaches to increasing social complexity, and yet they also underscore most dramatically the impossibility of obtaining neutrality. In the end they speak to why public policy must accord with liberal purposes. They raise the question of how principles are defined and who defines them. If the liberal state has a responsibility to generate opportunities, what are the limits to that responsibility?

Chapter 6 explores the meaning of an inclusive community and just what is entailed in maintaining the social fabric of that community by addressing the distinction between public and private on social issues or what we commonly call the core privacy issues. Because a focus on liberal purposes ultimately requires greater emphasis on communities, the issues involved in privacy matters generally raise the question of just what type of community we are attempting to create. To a large extent, these issues challenge us to refine just where the line between public and private is drawn. In the end, however, the issues raised in this chapter challenge us, in our attempts to reconstruct a liberalism grounded in greater community emphasizing greater civic commitment, to see if and where compromise might be possible on matters such as religion, reproductive freedom, pornography, and homosexuality.

Policy issues in chapters 3 through 6 are specifically chosen because they represent a trajectory of liberal policy making and natural progressions in the positive state. Ultimately, they lead toward chapter 7, which offers a new methodology for analyzing policy—one which takes us away from traditional cost-benefit analysis and moves us closer to one predicated on theoretical presuppositions. On the basis of this new methodology, I argue that we can construct a framework for the analysis of policy through the prism of political theory, so that the positive state is better able to maintain continuity with its philosophic origins. Once this has occurred, the effect will be that we have a reconceived liberalism.

2. *The Lockean Ideal*

LOCKE was perhaps one of the most seminal thinkers of the seventeenth century, and his influence on core American principles has been profound. We are most familiar with his *Second Treatise of Government*, which advises how to construct a government that will be accountable and protective of individual rights. The language of Jefferson's Declaration of Independence, "life, liberty, and the pursuit of happiness," would appear to be very similar to Locke's claim that the chief end of government is the protection of life, liberty, and "the Preservation of their Property."[1] Widely regarded as the philosophic godfather of the American political creed, his ideas are very much part of the American political consciousness, particularly those on natural law and natural rights, the consent of the governed, and the sacredness of private property.[2] Indeed, it is what he has said about property that has led many to conclude that Locke as a political theorist was a theorist of the minimal state. This was a state in which the function of government would be limited to the protection of individual rights and nothing more. It is this view of Locke as an advocate of limited government that represents the traditional conception of Locke. And it is the traditional conception of Locke that has implied that the role of public policy would essentially be a limited one. Policy would never actively be formulated unless it was necessary to protect the rights of individuals. And whatever policy would be sought would be aimed at protecting individuals from the natural tendencies of the state to usurp power for its own aggrandizement.

The purpose of this chapter is to look at this traditional conception of Locke and explain how it has, by and large, been misunderstood. On the contrary, the same tracts in the *Second Treatise* that lead to the belief that government should be limited also seem to suggest that Locke advocates a government that is responsive to the needs of its citizenry. As the needs of society change over time, so too does the role of government. If a set of relatively simple social circumstances dictates a limited government function, a set of relatively complex social circumstances would indeed dictate a broader function and thus a role for positive public policy. But this broader view only emerges within the context of his entire corpus. It should be remembered that Locke's *Two Treatises of Government* isn't a response to Hobbes and his Leviathan but a response to Filmer and his patriarchal government. Moreover, it is crucial to understand just why Filmer has to be repudiated.

Filmer, perhaps the leading royalist of his day and the chief exponent of Tory ideology, was not only out to defend the absolute authority of the monarchy, but the whole concept of the divine right of kings from which the concept of a community in which individuals are subordinated to it is derived. Filmer argued that Adam as the first king derived his authority from God. Adam was the first lord, and by the laws of nature his children fell under his dominion. Similarly, Adam's children had the authority to rule over their own children, "but still with subordination to the first parent over his children's children to all generations, as being the grandfather of his people." Such authority included the power of life and death.[3] Filmer couldn't understand how the children of Adam, or any one else for that matter, could be free from subjection to their parents. This was, after all, a natural condition and, as the author of nature, God was then the ultimate parent. When God gave the Israelites kings, "He reestablished the ancient and prime right of lineal succession to paternal government."[4] Consequently, then, when comparing the natural duties of a father to a king, they are found to be all one, with the only difference being the latitude or extent. From this, Filmer deduced that Adam's family was a commonwealth, and that the king's authority over that commonwealth could therefore be traced back to the ultimate parent, God.

At the time, Filmer's *Patriarcha* was considered to be perhaps the most authoritative statement of Tory ideology[5] and one that Locke, as a political figure and a member of the House of Shaftsbury, was clearly opposed to.[6] This would then suggest that Locke's political philosophy contains an element of political expedience that can easily be lost if it isn't understood that Locke was a political actor himself. Indeed, he was involved in revolutionary activities to overthrow the throne of Charles II and his attempt to secure monarchical absolutism. For Ashcraft, the *Two Treatises* were the manifesto for the Glorious Revolution of 1688. And the *Second Treatise* is particularly a political tract setting out to provide justification for political authority for those who have decided to resist the existing authority on the grounds of self-defense. It was Shaftsbury's attempt to organize a resistance movement among leaders of the Whig Party. Moreover, there was an understood responsibility on the part of radical theorists to develop a declaration of principles for the revolutionary movement. It is Ashcraft's contention, therefore, that the *Second Treatise* represented an outgrowth of the process, as well as the necessity of providing a declaration for the movement.[7] And such a manifesto would be essential, for Filmer's argument in *Patriarcha* legitimized the right of the throne to do what it wanted regardless of the consequences. Therefore, in order to justify resistance to this idea, it would first be necessary to rebut the theoretical underpinnings of the king's divine right to rule, and to show why the king could not possess legitimate authority unless it was derived from the consent of the governed.

Locke, however, is often misunderstood because his *Two Treatises* is often read in isolation from his *An Essay Concerning Human Understanding* and *A Letter Concerning Toleration*, not to mention from his political activities. When read separately, it isn't uncommon to view Locke as an individualist who sees government as having a limited function.

But when the *Two Treatises* are read within the larger context of his entire body of philosophical writing, a very different picture emerges. Nevertheless, the misunderstanding appears to revolve around the following trade-off: If individualism is the primary value, then community must, by definition, be subordinated to it. But as I intend to show later in this chapter, while Locke attempts to protect the rights of individuals to realize their individualism, he does not reject the general concept of community. Rather, he rejects a particular conception of it, the one contained in Filmer's notion of patriarchal government. Still, because of the influence that the traditional reading of Locke has had on American culture generally, and American politics particularly,[8] the role of policy—even positive policy—has been restricted by the need to maintain neutral measures. I thus set out in this chapter a new way to look at Locke, a view that suggests that Locke was more community minded than was commonly supposed. The point of this chapter is to show that reading Locke differently from the more traditional conception has different implications for the shape of public policy. By understanding how Lockean liberalism actually supports a strong and viable community, it becomes possible to understand why policy fashioned and measured against this ideal will ultimately better serve to maintain liberal policy within the confines of community values than would the neutrality measure.

The Traditional Locke

The principal lesson from Lockean liberalism, found in both Locke's *Essay* and the *Two Treatises*, is that all individuals have an equal right to govern their actions as they see fit. This is the quintessential core of liberal political theory. No person has an intrinsic right to govern another.[9] In an ordered society, we know that this principle can never be fully implemented. But in Locke's assumption of individuals living in a state of nature, this principle presumptively existed prior to the formation of civil society. The question is ultimately an epistemological one: How can we know something to be good? Or to put it another way, how can we know that entering into a social contract would necessarily be good? Locke begins from the premise that all our ideas originate from experience, whether it be through the external world—through sensation—or the internal world—through reflection.[10] More fundamental, however, is the notion that individuals born in a state of nature have been endowed by their creator with these particular attributes, and these are the attributes that enable them to develop ideas based on experience.

Locke actually begins with the same premises as Hobbes. Although Hobbes in the *Leviathan* offers an absolutist theory of government, it rests on liberal—or what some suggest are preliberal—assumptions.[11] Beginning with the now famous observation that life in a state of nature is nasty, brutish, and short, Hobbes held out the hope for personal security through voluntary entry into a social contract. By the terms of the contract, individuals would surrender all those liberties they enjoyed in the state of nature to the absolute control of the sovereign and in return would receive protection. As liberalism is ultimately a doctrine rejecting all forms of arbitrary power,[12] critics will rightfully point out that there is nothing liberal in Hobbes's argument. Still, Hobbes's contribution to liberalism cannot be dismissed. Andrzej Rapaczynski holds Hobbes to perhaps be the most important precursor of liberalism. Certainly, he is illiberal in his authoritarian prescription and his call for absolute sovereignty. This absolutism, whether located in one individual or several, is in tension with the individualistic premises of liberal politics. Yet he postulates a "radical priority of individuality over all forms of communal existence."[13]

Hobbes does subscribe to the liberal ideal inasmuch as he assumes individuals to be rational actors capable of thinking for themselves what is in their best interests. And because they are rational, they will come to understand that it is in their best interests to live under a Leviathan. Moreover, their decision to do so is based on their consent to do so. As von Leyden points out, Hobbes rejected the idea of divine sovereignty in political matters and accepted the necessity of secular sovereignty, to which every individual might assent voluntarily. Even though the contract will define political obligation as the surrender of all rights, he is clear in his stipulation that any such transfers of rights must be voluntary. For Hobbes, free choice and assent are essential in all cases of obligation.[14] Although the Leviathan has absolute power, its legitimacy is derived from the consent of its subjects.[15]

But for Locke, individuals born in nature would not submit to a

Leviathan. Rather they are born with natural rights that are inalienable. Locke's view of the law of nature is a declaration of God's will and a standard of right and wrong. It is a law already governing the state of nature. Locke sets out three assumptions: (1) the law of nature is law *governing* the state of nature; (2) civil laws are rights insofar as they are founded on moral laws of nature and designed to regulate and interpret them; and (3) "Since one of the dictates of the law of nature is to preserve human life and liberty, it also follows that, besides natural law itself, the natural rights of life and liberty should set limits to the sovereignty of civil government."[16] Still, just what does it mean to talk about a law of nature? For Locke to talk about a law of nature was by no means anything new. It is, as Gough points out, one of the oldest concepts in the history of political thought. And natural law was essentially the law of reason, a human faculty possessed by no other creature.[17] The important issue for Locke is the definition of legitimate government, and this can only be accomplished through liberal government. Only the liberal state can meet the standards set by natural law, and only the liberal state is compatible with liberal premises,[18] that individuals have an equal capacity to decide how they would like to live their lives and to pursue their interests accordingly. And only a government that respects the rights of individuals to pursue their interests can allow individualism to flourish.

But it is according to this law of nature that each individual's private property is determined. Although God did give the earth for people to use in common, the law sets bounds to what each individual is allowed to appropriate and keep.[19] But if there are limits to what each can appropriate, there must be a mechanism for protecting the rights of individuals, and this mechanism is essentially a contractual arrangement that involves a trade-off between absolute liberty in nature and political freedom to be derived through this contractual arrangement. Individuals will enter into a contractual arrangement in order to protect their property, and it is through the process of consenting to the contract that the government achieves its legitimacy. Government derives its legitimacy from the consent of the governed, and the only means by which this consent can be given is by voluntarily entering into a contractual arrangement. It is specifically its voluntary nature that makes the contract so critical. In the state of nature, individuals possessed full liberty, but they weren't free from an untimely death. This was the Hobbesian position. Therefore, it would be in their best interests to surrender all their liberties to the absolute authority of the sovereign. But for Locke, since all individuals must consent—and indeed have the capacity to consent—they are indeed able to control how much they are going to surrender. While they must be willing to surrender some liberty to form the contract, there are limits to how much. These limits, in large measure, suggest that by the very nature of the contract, government authority is limited by the good will of the public. But at the same time, there would be no government had it not been for the consent of the governed. Government in forming a contract needs to understand its limits in order to obtain the consent of the governed. To achieve freedom, individuals would have to enter into a contract, and this would entail surrendering enough of their liberty so that government would be able to protect them. How much liberty would be surrendered? Only enough for the sovereign to perform its protective function, but not past the point that it might violate individuals' rights generally and their rights to property particularly.

As straightforward as the concept of property may be, the concept is considerably more complex than would be implied. Nevertheless, Locke's position on property has figured prominently into the traditional conception. It is Locke's theory of property and the prominent position it occupies in the forefront of his political system that has been responsible for the common perception of him as primarily an individualist. In fact, his tract on property suggests to many that Locke was in many respects a libertarian who uses property as the ultimate bulwark between individuals and the state. Libertarian conceptions are often derived from his theory of property that merely asserted that one should be able to reap the benefits of one's property because one's labor is what gave it its value. If property contains any value at all, it is a function of one's own industry, as it is one's labor that infuses things with value, thus making it one's own.[20] And we have a right to own that with which we have mixed our labor. As the value of property is derived from human labor, it has to follow that individuals may own and enjoy the benefits of property.[21] In its approach to property, then, the state would have to view it no differently than it would people, for property essentially represents an extension of the individual self. Inasmuch as individuals are assumed to possess natural rights—those rights essentially being nothing more than an ability to think independently and make decisions based on that ability—their property as an extension of themselves also becomes somewhat of a natural right. As a "natural right," it is anterior to the state,[22] which means that limits to government authority are to be placed at the point at which one's rights to property could and would be violated. But as property is seen as an extension of the individual self, infringements upon property are taken to be infringements upon individual liberty.

Locke states clearly that, "The great and *chief end* therefore, of Men uniting into Commonwealths, and putting themselves under Government, *is the Preservation of their Property*. To which in the state of Nature there are many things wanting."[23] On the basis of this, Kramnick has argued that bourgeois radicals in both England and America assumed this to mean that Locke's theory of government meant that individuals had a right to unlimited acquisition of money and wealth. Moreover, this was considered to be a virtue in the establishment of the eighteenth-century liberal agenda of competitive individualism and equal opportunity. And also that he by no means considered unlimited acquisition of money and wealth to be morally wrong. On the contrary, "Locke's Protestant God commands us to work the earth, and in return the hardworking and industrious have the right to what they produce by their work."[24] Among those American patriots trumpeting the new ideology was Thomas Paine, the author of *Common Sense*. For Paine, a nation is "composed of distinct, unconnected individuals, following various trades, employments, and pursuits; continually meeting, crossing, uniting, opposing, and separating from each other, as accident, interest, and circumstances shall direct." It wasn't government's responsibility to promote justice or virtue among clashing individuals and interests. Rather, government was merely to serve as an umpire in a world where the primary value was individualism.[25] Taken to an extreme, however, property can be viewed in purely possessive and proprietary terms. For Macpherson, Locke's conception of property is essentially a theory of possessive individualism. As market exchange required individuals to have possession of what they were going to sell, it was first necessary to establish the principle of absolute individual rights.[26] To Macpherson, "The main significance of Locke's individualism is that it makes the individual the natural proprietor of his own person and capacity owing nothing to society."[27] It is perhaps this view that contributes to the notion of Locke as a defender of atomized individualism. Rather than individuals owing anything to their communities, individuals have rights against them.

What, then, happens if government fails to protect individuals and their property? Locke tells us that once it ceases to perform its function, it invites legitimate resistance:

> The Reason why Men enter into Society, is the preservation of their Property; and the end why they chuse and authorize a Legislative, is, that there may be Laws made, and Rules set as Guards and Fences to the Properties of all the Members of the Society, to limit the Power, and moderate the Dominion of every Part and Member of the Society. For since it can never be supposed to be the Will of the Society, that the Legislative should have a Power to destroy that, which every one designs to secure, by entering into Society, and for which the People submitted themselves to the Legislators of their own making; whenever the *Legislators endeavor to take away, and destroy the Property of the People*, or to reduce them to Slavery under Arbitrary Power, they put themselves into a state of War with the People, who are thereupon absolved from any farther Obedience, and are left to the common Refuge, which God hath provided for all Men, against the Force and Violence.[28]

It is this very idea of resistance that constitutes the core of Lockean political philosophy. Central to this philosophy is when individuals may resist unjust and illegitimate authority.[29] Locke's central concern is when it is appropriate to rebel against existing authority. When is it legitimate to overthrow the monarch? When the sovereign encroaches upon the rights of the individual, it ceases to be legitimate, and individuals are collectively within their rights to rise up in rebellion and overthrow the existing sovereign and replace it with a sovereign that will respect their rights. Of course, it has also been presumed that government would lose its legitimacy when it would cease to protect property. And in fact, the circumstances would indeed be ripe for rebellion once the sovereign encroached upon property. But as I intend to show later, this understanding of property is simply too narrow.

Because the traditional conception of Locke has emphasized the importance of rights generally, and property rights particularly, it has been assumed that Lockean political philosophy is a philosophy of limited government. This follows the distinction between the state and society. And with the distinction between state and society comes a corresponding distinction between public and private. Society is composed of a myriad of private associations—associations with which the state may not interfere unless it is absolutely necessary to protect the public interest. Government—representing the state—should be limited to nothing more than the protection of individual rights. Government's function is essentially that of a night watchman. It only intervenes if the public interest is at stake. This has often meant that government would only intervene in private matters when it would be necessary to prevent harm to others. Not only was the public interest defined in terms of the prevention of harm, but harm was defined in physical terms, largely because this was the most objective means by which harm could be defined. To intervene otherwise is to risk encroachment upon the rights of the public, thereby inviting resistance. A government that intervenes only when it is clear that there is a threat to the public interest is also able to maintain its impartiality. For a government constituted on the equal consent of its members becomes impartial and thereby does not respect the equal standing of its members if it intervenes in such a way that one group's interest is shown favor over another's. Moreover, this is the standard conception of neutrality as understood by modern liberal theorists like Rawls, Dworkin, and Ackerman.[30] The point is that limitations on government's ability to interfere do effectively result in a neutral framework with regard to the pursuit of public policy. The neutrality inherent to this distinction also implies free markets, as they might constitute a framework in which individuals will be able to pursue their own *goods* based on their own abilities to reason what would be good for them.

By maintaining absolute neutrality on issues involving positive public choices, the state doesn't run the risk of offending a group that can call into question the state's legitimacy and thus call for resistance to the state. The problem with this idea is that anybody can make a claim to an interest and assert it as a right against the state. Just where are the limitations on invoking rights against the state? Yet, there has been this perception that each individual, as a defender of his or her own property can, on the basis of that property, claim rights against the state. And it is because of the view that individuals are born with rights that they can claim against the state, under the pain of resistance, that it has become fashionable to view Locke as a defender of atomistic individualism—the notion that we are each born in nature and thus bear no relationship to each other. Locke did believe that we are each born individually and separately from one another, and that we each have the capacity to think for ourselves, but he didn't really believe that it is possible for individuals to live apart from communities.

On the contrary, the reason why we enter into a social contract is the desire to form communities. Moreover, recent trends in Lockean scholarship would appear to suggest that Locke's theory is at root a social theory, rather than one of atomistic individualism. Ashcraft, in particular, maintains that Locke's conception of the state of nature as a natural condition for atomistic individualism in which there is essentially no relationship between one another has been abandoned by contemporary interpreters of his thought. On the contrary, Locke assumed individuals to be members of a natural community, "and that the social relationships within this larger community are evaluated by Locke according to whether or not they further the ends of this 'community of nature.'"[31] Grant, too, has argued that Lockean philosophy strongly supports strong communities and communal institutions.[32] With a different view of Locke, however, it also becomes possible to establish a different framework—a different set of assumptions—for public policy. But the broader conception that I intend to put forth by no means suggests that the concepts we associate with the traditional conception are wrong. Rather they have been interpreted too narrowly. The desire to limit arbitrary government isn't the same as limiting government or demanding that it be passive as opposed to active. And to make government accountable is not to subordinate community to individualism but to make government accountable to the community and to put it in the service of the community.

The Community-Minded Locke

Much of Locke's discussion of the individual's relationship to the community is contained in the *Essay*, and much of this relationship can be illustrated through his tract on language and its development. In the *Essay*, Locke's central moral concern is with what it is possible for individuals to know and with what degree of certainty it is possible for them to know it. It is a work undertaking to define the limits to reason, premised on the assumption that individuals can govern their actions according to reason. But before getting into that discussion, it is first necessary to provide some greater context to understand what exactly Locke is responding to. In the *Two Treatises* Locke is clearly responding to Filmer, but Filmer merely represents the form of a much larger concept. This is the idea that all knowledge is derived from one source, and it is the same source from which all legitimate power and authority are derived. Filmer's theory of patriarchal government is merely part and parcel of what linguists have referred to as Adamicism, or what is called the Adamic language.[33] Today it is simply taken for granted that knowledge is based on experience, but in the seventeenth century this was quite a radical proposition. By demonstrating the relationship between linguistic Adamicism and political Adamicism, I hope to show why it is essential to reject a particular conception of community, without necessarily having to reject the whole concept. This is particularly important because much of the misunderstanding surrounding Locke stems from the view that he is advancing a theory of atomistic individualism, which, if it isn't necessarily anticommunity, at least takes precedence over the community. What his tract on language development shows is just how important the community is. What is often misunderstood is that Locke's rejection of Adamicism is as much a political act as it is an intellectual one. And the implications for policy, as we will see later, are enormous.

The Problem of Adamicism

In language, Adamicism refers to Adam having named the animals in the garden of Eden, and that the only way he could have done so was if God had initially given Adam the tools to do so. Adamicism might also be thought of as the concept of innate ideas. Adamicism, as expressed in terms of innate ideas, is essentially the idea that we are all born with the same understanding of truth—that which has been passed down by God. Locke puts forth this problem at the outset of the *Essay* when he writes:

> It is an established Opinion amongst some Men, That there are in the Understanding certain *innate Principles*; some primary Notions, *Koivai evvoiai*, Characters, as it were, stamped upon the Mind of Man, which the Soul receives in its very first Being; and brings into the World with it.[34]

Adamicism holds that the only language one can speak will be the one that God ordained. Because God created us all, our language is universal. That is, we all possess the same innate principles that have been stamped upon our souls. What it implies—contrary to the core tenets of liberal political philosophy—is that there is a universal good or truth that supersedes all others. Adamicism thus holds the following proposition: Because all knowledge comes from God, we as individuals owe our existence to God, as well as whatever attributes and capacities we possess. If true, whatever capacities we have to reason and understand are not only derived from God, but cannot exceed that which he endowed us with.

Adamicism has political implications as well. The belief that there are innate ideas derived from a singular source lends itself to a whole set of assumptions about what the political structure will be. Politically, we owe our allegiance to the sovereign, whose authority is derived from God. Or so this was the position as advanced by Filmer. Just as Locke puts forth the problem at the outset of the *Essay*, he similarly puts forth the problem at the outset of the *Two Treatises:*

> In this last age a generation of men has sprung up among us, who would flatter princes with an Opinion, that they have a Divine Right to absolute Power, let the Laws by which they are constituted, and are to govern, and the Conditions under which they enter upon their Authority, be what they will, and their Engagements to observe them never so well ratified by solemn Oaths and Promises. To make way for this doctrine they have denied Mankind a Right to natural Freedom, whereby they have not only, as much as in them lies, exposed all Subjects to the utmost Misery of Tyranny and Oppression, but have also unsettled the Titles, and shaken the Thrones of Princes: (For they too, by these Mens systeme, except only one, are all born Slaves, and by Divine Right, are Subjects to *Adam's* right Heir); As if they had design'd to make War upon all Government, and subvert the very Foundations of Human Society, to serve their present turn.[35]

According to the Adamicist theory of Filmer, the king is always above the common individual because his attributes are directly traceable to

Adam, which in turn are traceable to God. Even if there is a community consisting of equal individuals, the king still towers above it. The essence of patriarchal government, then, was that this first man's absolute sovereignty was by definition inalienable and ultimately descended to his successor.[36] Moreover, Filmer's argument insisted that Adam's paternal role as begetter included the power of life and death, and that his dominion over the earth was naturally transmitted through the generations.[37]

More than a theory of authority, Adamicism is a particular conception of community. The idea that Adam named the animals in the Garden of Eden—that he knew what to name them—is the idea that out of Eden came the first language, a single and universal language that represented a universal truth. Despite the fact that we all speak different tongues, philologically speaking their roots could ultimately be traced back to that single language. The common thread holding people together, who otherwise would have different interests based on their own respective cultures, is this universal Adamic language. Adamicism, in other words, meant that between people there was commonality: language. Or to couch it in Filmer's terms, that commonality was the single parent. But then it was from the same parent that both the authority of those who rule over us and the innate ideas implanted upon our souls are derived. Methodologically speaking, the community comes first, and the individual comes second. The community is thus prior to the individual.

Why, then, does Locke need to reject Adamicism at all? Whatever his motivation, Adamicism has to be addressed principally because of its pervasiveness in both intellectual and religious thought, as well as its influence on community structure. In the beginning of the *Essay*, Locke makes it clear that he intends to show that there is no such thing as innate ideas:

> It would be sufficient to convince unprejudiced Readers of the falseness of this Supposition, if I should only shew (as I hope I shall in the following Parts of this Discourse) how Men, barely by the Use of their natural Faculties, may attain to all the Knowledge they have, without the help of any innate Impressions; and may arrive at Certainty, without any such Original Notions or Principles.[38]

The problem is the belief that innate ideas stem from the view that there are certain Truths that may be shared by all. But Locke is nonetheless quick to point out that even if this were to be true, this would not prove the existence of innate ideas. What ideas we do have are based on experience. But the notion that we have innate ideas also stems from the view that because we are God's creatures, we must have had certain ideas imprinted upon our souls at birth. To this Locke responds:

> I grant the existence of God, is so many ways manifest, and the Obedience we owe him, so congruous to the Light of Reason, that a great part of Mankind give Testimony to the Law of Nature: But yet I think it must be allowed, That several Moral Rules, may receive, from Mankind, a very general Approbation, without either knowing, or admitting the true ground of Morality; which can only be the Will and Law of a God, who sees Men in the dark, has in his Hand Rewards and Punishments, and Power enough to call to account the Proudest Offender.[39]

Just as God didn't imprint truth on man's soul, he did not bequeath authority to the single parent. Locke's refutation of Filmer in the *First Treatise* does parallel his rejection of Adamicism in the *Essay*. Just as Locke doesn't deny the existence of God in the *Essay*, he doesn't deny in the *First Treatise* that God gave the world to Adam; rather, he understands biblical Adam to be a metaphor for humanity as opposed to a specific person. As Locke writes:

> Whatever God gave by the words of this Grant . . . it was not to *Adam* in particular, exclusive of all other Men: whatever *Dominion* he had thereby, it was not a *Private Dominion*, but a Dominion in common with the rest of Mankind. That this Donation was not made in particular to *Adam*, appears evidently from the words of the Text, it being made to more than one, for it was spoken in the Plural Number, God blessed *them* and said unto *them*, Have Dominion.[40]

This is also evident from the text because the word *Adam*, when translated directly from the original Hebrew, means man as it refers to humanity. What God gave, he gave to us all on the assumption that we were all born equal in nature. He did not create a line of succession.

Locke rejects the view that God ordained that any one person should ever have absolute dominion over another. To the extent that he acknowledged the legitimacy of Filmer's position with regard to parents having control over their children, Locke maintains that authority to be limited. Children grow up, and ultimately they develop the capacities to reason for themselves. "The Bonds of this Subjection are like the Swadling Cloths they are wrapt up in, and supported by, in the weakness of the Infancy. Age and Reason as they grow up, loosen them till at length they drop quite off, and leave Man at his own free Disposal."[41] Hence Locke makes it clear that parental authority is temporary because all adults are equally capable of rational behavior.[42] God gives individuals born in a state of nature the powers to reason for themselves. God creates individuals so that they are equal. Filmer, of course, maintained that the idea of consent was really a misnomer because the authority of the king in many instances was a product of conquest. But for Locke, this is irrelevant, because a conqueror can only acquire the most limited rights, and they, too, will cease to be valid within a generation.[43]

Nevertheless, students of linguistics hold Locke's rejection of Adamicism to be the crucial moment in intellectual history. Hans Aarsleff has argued that this ultimately paved the way for individualism to come first.[44] If this is true, the logical implication comes down to the following: Insofar as communities arose, they only did so as a function of individuals being able to agree that their formation would best serve to further their individualism. Communities are created by individuals. There would be no need for government if individuals didn't need political societies to live together in peace. This is the end of government and nothing else.[45] The general concept of Adamicism must be rejected in order to justify the rights of the individuals collectively to form a new social order. For, unless this concept can be dealt with, there cannot be anything but the complete submission to the king's authority because that authority is ordained by God. Moreover, whatever hierarchy exists in society is also ordained by God. Therefore, in order to go as far as to develop a theory of an egalitarian community—where there would be no class distinctions—the concept of Adamicism as it has been understood must be rejected, for the community assumed by Adamicism is a hierarchical one.

What the rejection of Adamicism—and its attendant dismissal of Filmer—does is clear the way for the first of Locke's premises. The first being that, since individuals are equal in nature—because no one can claim power over another by right of divine authority—the natural condition of individuals is a "State of perfect Freedom."[46] This premise would appear to be no different from the assumption underlying the rejection of Adamicism: that individuals do exist in a state of perfect freedom to conceive of language as they see fit. Once the premise is established, the second quickly ensues: If individuals in nature are equal, no one has a rightful claim to authority. Authority—political power—can only come about through the consent of every individual. The second premise, in short, comes down to the following: Political power arises from consent. Consequently, the only power the sovereign has is that which has been agreed to. Political power is then conditional and limited ultimately by those who do consent. As such, absolute and arbitrary power cannot arise, or so it cannot be legitimate. Therefore, political power can neither be absolute nor arbitrary.[47] But how can there be a basis for consent if there is no common usage of words that will bind us together?

The connection between linguistic development and politics is critical for understanding the basis upon which a contract can rationally be created. Locke's rejection of linguistic Adamicism does enable individuals to find their own truths, their own goods. And his rejection of political Adamicism does free the individual from the absolute authority of the monarch. The rejection of linguistic Adamicism should be viewed as a critical epistemological foundation for contract theory. Unless political Adamicism is rejected, there can be no basis for individuals to enter into a contract to form their own communities. But unless linguistic Adamicism is rejected, there can be no basis upon which to make the claim that the king, whose authority is derived from God, represents truth. Moreover, if it isn't believed that individuals can come to their own judgments—find truth on their own through experience—on what rational basis would it be possible for them to come to the conclusion that entering into the contract is preferable to the existing authority, or the state of nature for that matter? That authority can only be resisted—and in fact repudiated—once it is clear that that authority is not absolute truth.

The ability to develop one's own language, as Locke suggests in the *Essay*, means that the individual has the capacity to make a rational judgment that entering into a social contract—for whatever reason—is a good thing to do. Unless it is understood that there is no universal truth that would limit individuals' abilities to find their own, there would be no rational basis for determining that the authority which does exist (1) doesn't possess absolute truth and (2) may be corrupt and a transgressor against the natural laws that all humanity is bound to. The rejection of Adamicism, and the attendant recognition it gives for individuals to develop their own thoughts, forms an important epistemological foundation for entering into the contract. So long as individuals accept that God imprints on our souls certain innate ideas, they have no choice but to accept that God also ordained that authority would reside with the divinely chosen. Adamicism, as it was understood prior to Locke's rejection of it, in effect constituted a particular understanding of the laws of nature. What Locke does by rejecting Adamicism, and its attendant assumptions about what the nature of the political structure will be, is attempt to change our understanding of those laws of nature. It is through his discussion of language in the *Essay* that we discover the interdependence between the individual and his or her community.

Language and Community Interdependence

In the *Essay*, we are led to believe that language is essentially the bond that holds us together and the basis upon which we form ideas and communicate them to others. Ideas that people have in their own minds are perceptions based on experience. Because people are different—that is they perceive things differently—ideas will clearly have different meanings. How two people conceive of something can neither be considered true nor can it be considered false because within our natural state, one's perception is just as good as the other's. Locke explains it this way:

> Any *Idea* then which we have in our Minds, whether conformable, or not, to the existence of Things, or to any *Ideas* in the Minds of other Men, cannot properly for this alone be called *false*. For these Representations, if they have nothing in them, but what is really existing in Things without, cannot be thought *false*, being exact Representations of something: nor yet if they have any thing in them, differing from the reality of Things, can they properly be said to be false Representations, or *Ideas* of Things, they do not represent.[48]

The doctrine of Adamicism, by contrast, held that on the basis of a universal language we will come to perceive things in the same way, despite whatever differences in personal background we may have. But such power of interpretation also has to be viewed as a metaphor for the state of nature underpinning the foundations of Locke's political works. The obvious question is if we all have the power to conceive things differently, how, then, are we to communicate our perceptions to others in ways that are comprehensible? If we are to have some semblance of order, we must come to agreement that things—whatever they are—will have the same meaning for person A as they do for person B as they must for person C.

In Locke's political tracts, the solution is clearly contract. Nowhere in the *Essay* does Locke talk about contract, but his explanation for how we develop words does ultimately provide us with the rudiments for one. On one level, Locke makes a distinction between ideas and words. Ideas are those thoughts we have in our own minds and words are the sounds we utter to communicate those ideas to others. Ideas, then, are abstract notions that could be incomprehensible to others, while words form the basis for the concrete expression of those notions in the hope that some measure of comprehensibility will be achieved. But how do we come to attach certain words to certain ideas or things? For instance, how is it that I have come to understand that what I am sitting in is a chair? Why could it not have been called something else? And how is it that everyone else understands without hesitation that what I am sitting in is a chair? With a chair, we are obviously talking about a simple idea. But the words assigned even to simple ideas are by no means random.

Although we are at liberty to conceive of things as we understand them, we are not able to call them as we please without any real thought. As free and capable as we are in thinking whatever we want, we are still restrained in that freedom by the need to communicate with others.[49] Because language is essential to communication, and communication is essential for the ultimate flourishing of ideas, such restrictions on our freedom are in the end essential to the maintenance of language and the initial freedom that gives it its flavor. Are we not then being told that freedom comes not through a state of nature, where no restrictions are in existence, but through a community, and that it is ultimately made possible by the community? If Locke is saying this, he might be considered pre-Hegelian.[50] Steven Smith has argued that Hegel's principal accomplishment was his demonstration that the state and community are not just preconditions for, but dimensions of, freedom. That is, the state is the locus of shared responsibility, not simply an instrument of force and coercion. It is a wide network of shared ethical ideas and beliefs, not simply an instrument for ensuring civil peace. The state is ultimately a meeting of minds because it is contingent on a common cultural history and a sense of civic identity.[51] This shares much with the communitarian notion that individuals are "embodied agents 'in the world' engaged in realizing a certain form of life." Who we are is a function of how we have been socialized, and individuals are shaped by their constitutive communities that provide a background way of being in the world.[52] But to say that Locke believed in the integrity of the community is not to go to the extreme of calling him a communitarian in the contemporary sense of the word. Although he believed in the integrity of the community, he did not believe that individuals should fully submit to the will of the community to the point that they would be fully absorbed. Nevertheless, the nature of this community being formed for the purposes of communication bears much similarity to the actual social contract in the *Two Treatises* that individuals enter into with a sovereign. To put it another way, in that state of nature we may think as we please, and assign words as we please, but once we enter into a contract so that we may be able to communicate those capacities will ultimately be restricted by the need to maintain an ordered and cohesive community.[53]

At the beginning of Book III of the *Essay* we are told that individuals essentially need societies. Locke states:

> God having designed Man for a sociable Creature, made him not only with an inclination, and under a necessity to have fellowship with those of his own kind; but furnished him also with Language, which was to be the great Instrument, and common Tye of Society. *Man* therefore had by Nature his Organs so fashioned, as to be *fit to frame articulate Sounds*, which we call Words.[54]

In the end, we form societies because we are social beings, and we have a need to communicate and interact with one another. Locke certainly makes reference to this in the *Two Treatises* when he says: "God having made Man such a Creature, that, in his own Judgment, it was not good for him to be alone, put him under strong Obligations of Necessity, Convenience, and Inclination to drive him into *Society*, as well as fitted him with Understanding and Language to continue and enjoy it."[55] An ability to communicate in ways comprehensible to others certainly furthers interaction.

The essence of contract theory is that we surrender certain liberties enjoyed in the state of nature in exchange for political freedom ultimately but protection from the state of nature immediately. This, however, presupposes we would naturally gravitate toward associations with others. Through the community we receive protection, and through the community we are able to interact with one another so that those ideas we have in our minds can ultimately be communicated to one another. But if the community is the arena in which we are able to think, it is also that which shapes how we think. It becomes ironic, then, that Locke appears to make the same point that Alasdair MacIntyre has made in his criticism of liberalism: that our search for our good generally occurs within the context of those traditions of which our lives are a part. Insofar as the traditions with which we have grown up shape who we are and how we view the world, pure atomism isn't at all possible.[56] To put it another way, who we are internally is a function of our external interaction with the outside world.

To return to the question of how we know what we know, Locke informs us that things are associated with specific names because of how we have been socialized. Locke asks:

> Why do we say, This is a *Horse*, and that a *Mule*; this is an *Animal*, that an *Herb*? How comes any particular Thing to be of this *Sort*, but because it has that nominal Essence, Or, which is all one, agrees to that abstract *Idea*, that name is annexed to?[57]

Locke answers his question by telling us in effect that by growing up in a community, in which there is social interaction among people, we come to learn these associations because of the common usages made by the community. We learn to speak, after all, from our parents. Their association of words with certain ideas is the association transmitted to us. In effect, all members come to make the same associations so that a sense of order can be achieved.

Locke asserts that the chief end of words is communication and ultimately commerce. But Locke also distinguishes between types of words. There is a double use to the communication of words: *civil* and *philosophical.* By their *civil* use, Locke means "such a communication of Thoughts and *Ideas* by Words, as may serve for the upholding common Conversation and Commerce, about the ordinary Affairs and Conveniences of civil Life, in the Societies of Men, one amongst another." But by the *philosophical* use is meant that which conveys "the precise Notions of things, and to express, in general Propositions, certain and undoubted Truths, which the Mind may rest upon, and be satisfied with, in its search after true Knowledge."[58] But in making this distinction, Locke is suggesting a much larger one: the difference between language and words.

Language would fall within the rubric of *philosophical* use insofar as language can refer to abstract notions and concepts, subject to a multitude of conceptions. Words, however, fall into the category of *civil* use in that they have specific applications to things for the sole purpose of making communication possible and, ultimately, the operations of society. And yet, as endless as the possibilities for the construction of language might be, they are ultimately limited by the need to assign words—the necessary essentials for maintaining community cohesion. Viewed in this context, contract theory has to be viewed as taking a whole new dimension. By entering into the contract we not only surrender certain liberties in exchange for reciprocal protection, but we give up our capacity for raw thought in nature, which can never be fully formed because it is isolated. What we receive in return is the capacity to think in ways shaped by the prevailing standards of the community. And through this effective regulation by the community, our thought will presumably achieve greater coherence. We actually get more from the contract than the mere protection of our lives; we derive the ability to fully develop ourselves as individuals within a community, which will also help us to develop our individuality in such a way that it can be expressive. This is by no means to suggest that the protection of individual rights and interests isn't a primary reason for entering into a contract. But by entering into the contract, the individual will have greater benefits than by simply remaining in nature. Language communication may not be the primary reason for entering into the contract, but it will certainly be enhanced via the contract. And yet, if the need that individuals have to interact and communicate with one another would suggest an informal social contract of sorts based on language, it in many ways parallels the formal one predicated on rights protection. The properties of a contract are effectively the same. Individuals in exchange for an end result—benefits—that will be better, must be willing to sacrifice something.

Words and language are ultimately based on social construction. If words are based on social construction, so too is language because our ability to conceive anything is limited by the words that have already been assigned. Community standards—social norms and mores—are what hold us together. There is room for individualism to be sure, but it is ultimately bounded by the community. One who expresses individualism beyond those boundaries will ultimately be an outcast for speaking a different language.[59] As much as one might be an outcast for this, it isn't quite the same thing as violating community standards. And yet, language is a vehicle for an understanding of those community standards. There would thus appear to be some symmetry between this idea and the one Locke expresses in the *Second Treatise* about the one who chooses to live by different rules from others:

> In transgressing the Law of Nature, the Offender declares himself to live by another Rule, than that of *reason* and common Equity, which is that measure God has set to the actions of Men, for their mutual security; and so he becomes dangerous to Mankind, the tye which is to secure them from injury and violence, being slighted and broken by him. Which being a trespass against the whole Species, and the Peace and Safety of it, provided for by the Law of Nature, every man upon this score, by the Right he hath to preserve Mankind in general, may restrain, or where it is necessary, destroy things noxious to them, and so may bring such evil on any one, who hath transgressed that Law, as may make him repent the doing of it, and thereby deter him, and by his Example others, from doing the like mischief. And in this case, and upon this ground, *every Man hath a Right to punish the Offender, and be Executioner of the Law of Nature*.[60]

Of course, in nature, because there is no governing structure, one can simply come to one's own judgment that an offense has been committed and simply take action unilaterally. But to talk of a law of nature in society is to perhaps suggest that there are social conventions that all individuals understand are incumbent upon them to adhere to.

What this general discourse ought to make clear is that one is free to conceive of things as one desires—to reason for oneself—because one has been released from Adamicism. But at the same time, this freedom is limited by a prototypical social contract—the need for language to hold the fabric of the community together. By viewing the problem within this context, we begin to see how Lockean liberalism places the individual in a social context, as opposed to the more commonly accepted view that Lockean liberalism is really the celebration of atomism, even at the expense of the community. As much as this discourse establishes the concept of human agency within the bounds of community, it also lays a new framework for understanding Locke's political theory as one of community action. Moreover, if this discussion illustrates the interdependence between individuals and their communities, it should become more clear how it is that his political works are really a defense of the community—and even the positive state—as opposed to the more traditional conception of celebrating the individual and the individual's rights against the state.

The Roots of Common Purpose

The concepts of mutuality, common project, and citizen obligation can be traced to Locke's theory of contract in the *Two Treatises*. Whereas the *Essay* establishes the foundations for the social being, his political theory of resistance is more about the binding together of community behind a common project and less about individuals being able to assert their rights against the state. In establishing that there are times when resistance is justified, this theory of community action ends up saying quite a bit about mutuality because mutuality is necessary to maintain the fabric of the community and a common project (that which drives the community as a whole to attain certain ends).

If the central thrust of Locke's *Two Treatises* can be briefly summed up, it is about the rights of the community—comprising individuals who were born equal—to resist authority that has ceased to be legitimate. Under Adamic doctrine, resisting authority was unjustifiable because the monarch's powers were derived from God. Given our discussion in the previous section about the individual's relationship to the community, without ignoring the individual's capacity for independent thought, we might look at Locke's dismissal of political Adamicism, that is, Filmer, as a disingenuous act. Indeed, to justify resistance, the stature of the king had effectively to be diminished, which could only be done if it was understood that no one individual, by any theory of divine right, towered above others; rather, each individual was born equal in nature. What should have become clear from the *Essay* was that, epistemologically speaking, the only way the equality of individuals could be demonstrated was through a demonstration of their equal capacity to reason and think for themselves.

In the *Essay*, Locke has demonstrated this by dismissing the Adamic language. Because there was no universal truth, no one individual could claim to possess that truth that would enable him to rule. But by refuting Filmer, Locke was able to advance the theoretical proclamation of the rights of revolution.[61] By talking about the right of the community to rebel against illegitimate authority, he is talking about a community of equals who must come together and form a consensus that the authority is illegitimate. And yet, Locke is not rejecting the concept of community derived from Adamicism. To reject such a community would merely force the individual to live in a state of nature. The point is this: It isn't the concept of community Locke disagrees with; rather, it is the way it has been organized under the assumptions of Adamicism. As Stephen Holmes notes, if Locke "atomized" human self-understanding at all, it was only for political reasons. The goal was to "attack organic claims of dependence and subordination as well as to undermine dangerous clan and sectarian groupings."[62] The only way individuals could make a legitimate claim to resisting unjust authority was if it had been established they owed no such allegiance to that authority. This would require an understanding that we are each separate. In order for individuals to have the moral basis upon which they can consent to a contractual arrangement, it is first necessary to atomize them. If atomized, each individual is equal. If each individual is equal, no sovereign can lay claim to rightful authority over others. His authority might well have come as a function of conquest, but that the sovereign has authority is not the same as saying that it is legitimate. Atomization becomes a crucial ingredient in establishing the limits to obligation.

Perhaps the view that Locke isn't a strong supporter of community stems from a misunderstanding of rights. The misunderstanding is to believe that if individuals have rights, it is questionable as to whether they have obligations that are equal in importance to those rights. A traditional understanding of contract theory might suggest that the primary function of government is to protect individual rights, and the government can only demand that individuals fulfill certain obligations in cases of emergency. The traditional understanding might similarly misinterpret an emphasis on community to mean that one's obligations take precedence over rights. Locke, however, does not reject the notion that individuals have obligations or must show obedience. The very law of nature imposes obligations on individuals to respect one another, couched in terms of not harming one another, on the grounds that we are each the creation of the Divine Creator.[63] Locke does, however, distinguish between two corresponding levels of obligation by distinguishing between society and government. This can then establish the groundwork for both obedience and resistance.[64] One has an obligation to the community that formed the contract. But one's obligation to the government is limited to the extent to which government serves the community. It is when the government ceases to serve the community that resistance is justified. At the same time, it has to be clear that the dissolution of government is not the same as the dissolution of society. Through resistance, one merely ceases to have any obligation to the government, but one still has an obligation to society. Locke puts it this way:

> He that will with any clearness speak of the *Dissolution of Government*, ought, in the first place to distinguish between the *Dissolution of the Society*, and the *Dissolution of the Government*. That which makes the Community, and brings Men out of the loose State of Nature, into *one Politick Society*, is the Agreement which every one has with the rest to incorporate, and act as one Body, and so be one distinct Commonwealth.[65]

Locke would appear to be saying that the community that brought individuals together to form a contract can never be dissolved, or, for that matter, without the community as a cohesive unit, the government couldn't be dissolved. But then, the dissolution of government is by no means an ideal the community should strive for. Rather, it should strive for the construction of a social contract that will prevent the need for dissolution. Of course, one means by which the society can endure is if there is that common bond that unites us. And one such bond might be language, as it is the vehicle by which we understand a community's culture. To state it differently, what is it that would hold the community together even after it had acted to dissolve its government? A language shared by most, if not all, members of society would serve to create a cultural bond that unites us. It does serve to create a shared sense of community, based on shared values, that will hold us together despite the collapse of a formal governing structure.

It might be easy to read Locke in the same way Hobbes is often read: that man, being born in a state of nature that is nasty, brutish, and short, is driven to form a compact for the sake of receiving protection from an untimely death. But Locke's conception is inherently more positive than Hobbes's. Underlying Locke's social contract theory is the fundamental assumption that individuals, who by their nature are social beings, have a need to form societies so they will be able to interact with one another and perpetuate the freedom of thought that enabled them to enter into the contract to begin with.

The principal point of Locke's natural rights theory is that the first and fundamental natural law is the preservation of society.[66] This first and fundamental natural law, according to Seliger, ties the preservation of the individual to that of society "in accord with the traditional limitations of individual and collective self-preservation by which a proper civil society is distinguished from a happy-go-lucky gang of robbers."[67] It is from this individual right of self-preservation that Locke derives the political guarantee against the defective implementation of natural law: the right of revolt. Does this then mean that individuals can rebel any time and for any reason? Whereas Locke's theoretical argument is that whenever the sovereign usurps its authority, the people on the face of an effectively broken contract can rebel, there is nevertheless the presumption that had the contract been constructed properly to begin with there would be no such need to rebel. For implicit is that, except for those truly exceptional cases, resistance generally is not justified.[68] If this is true, we can begin to see the concept of mutuality emerge. And it is perhaps on this point Locke's position on property has also been misunderstood.

The traditional conception holds that the exceptional cases for which rebellion is justified are when the rights to property have been violated. But just what is meant by property? Property is considerably broader than that which is proprietary. Locke does not make any real distinction between what we commonly call property—that in land and other forms of ownership—and individuals' lives and liberties. He in fact defines property as "Lives, Liberties and Estates."[69] While he maintains the preservation of property to be the chief end of government, it isn't clear such rights are natural in the sense that we are born with those in the same way we are born with the capacity to develop our own ideas. Rather, they are natural in the sense that they are acquired as a result of actions and transactions that people undertake on their own initiative. They are natural in the sense that they are special. Property rights are not rights all can have, but they are rights acquired as a result of the occurrence of certain events. The principal event is the mixing of labor with resources. And yet, the general right to subsistence remains in the background of Locke's theory.[70] For earlier, he states "in Government the Laws regulate the right of property, and the possession of land is determined by positive constitutions."[71] If government is ultimately to preserve society, we can only infer that he is talking about a balance that must be struck between the interests of individuals on the one hand and those of the community on the other.

By using the language of positive constitutions, Locke is leaving room to regulate for community interests, and thereby denies the absoluteness of property. On the contrary, while government action might be constrained by the special rights to private property, those property rights themselves are constrained by what Jeremy Waldron refers to as "a deeper and, in the last resort, more powerful *general* right which each man has to the material necessities for his survival." This then forms the basis for what Waldron calls the "entitlements of charity in Locke's system." For Locke, the raison d'être of property is sustenance. Property rights, therefore, must never stand in the way of sustenance.[72] Or as Ashcraft points out, Locke believes that God has a wider purpose than simply providing for the individual's self-preservation. Rather, individual labor is seen as contributing to the improvement and benefit of life in the collective sense. He isn't so much concerned with individual motivation for property development as he is with the moral and social concerns to which property can be put.[73]

This isn't to say that Locke believed that property could be regulated at any time in the name of the community interest, but that if a serious dispute arose, the community must ultimately take precedence. As Gough points out, Locke was able to believe that property in a strict sense did exist in nature independently of government because the state of nature was considered to be social, with the law of nature being a genuine law. True enough, Locke's theory of labor as an origin of the right of property does lead to the labor theory of value. Nevertheless, Locke was not an advocate of laissez-faire, nor did he believe that economic relationships would automatically balance and adjust themselves. He was a mercantilist and thus believed in the regulation of trade.[74]

It isn't clear that Locke believed in unlimited acquisition at all. On the contrary, there would appear to be certain limitations to the amount of property one may possess. One may possess "as much as any one can make use of to any advantage of life before it spoils." But Locke also makes it clear that one is not entitled to more than one's share, what one needs. Rather, "Whatever is beyond this, is more than his share, and belongs to others."[75] This would seem to suggest that as much as one has a right to property, one's right is not absolute if the effect should be that the community is deprived. Moreover, Locke, according to Christman, does not regard the right to one's labor as justifying anything more than the right to use and manage that property that was labored on. The point is that contractual rights are always subject to limitations, revisions, and the like necessary for the securing and the promotion of the common good.[76]

Thomas Pangle argues that Locke's concern was always the public interest, but that Locke was conceiving it in terms of a commercial republic for which free trade would be essential. In short, the emphasis on property, as well as limited government to ensure its protection, was necessary for the creation of such a commercial republic in which the public interest would best be served. What was in the public interest was a market economy that would be free from the constraints of old-fashioned institutions and customs.[77]

Still, barring the importance of markets during Locke's lifetime, property still achieves a functional position if it is seen as being parallel to American constitutional interpretations of the Fifth Amendment's just compensation clause. If property is considered sufficiently valuable that it must be compensated every time it is taken, the effect is to erect a tangible barrier between the individual and the state. If government must always compensate owners of property at fair market value, it will be loathe to seize it unless there is a compelling public interest to do so. Instead of being an end unto itself, property becomes a practical barrier to arbitrary government action. This point is in part borne out by the fact that Locke's theory of property is an essential part of his polemic against Filmer.[78] Tarcov points out that the reader of the *Two Treatises* who finds that property is joined to liberty in opposition to absolute and arbitrary power will be surprised to learn that in *Some Thoughts Concerning Education* Locke joins the desire for property with the desire "for the submission of others to one's will as an expression of love of dominion." Moreover, they are the "two Roots of almost all the Injustice and Contention, that so disturb Human Life."

It might be that what Locke opposes is not necessarily the desire for property as such, but the desire for property as power over others. What Locke opposes in the *Two Treatises* is the arbitrary authority of government and the ability of government to then use property as a means of exercising power over another. In his *Thoughts*, however, Locke wants to stress the power that property gives the individual and a right to dispose of things as one pleases.[79] This also accords with Waldron's view that Locke's view of property is wide enough to encompass the concept of security.[80] But this means that property does achieve a functional purpose. It stands as a barrier between the individual and the state. More important, if property is conceived as a positive grant of power, individuals are being affirmed in their rights to pursue their interests without interference from the state. On the one hand, there is the question of deriving benefit from one's work. On the other hand, there is the question of the right to work and to use one's labor. And it is this idea that is encompassed in Locke's idea of property. Still, this isn't the same as saying the community cannot seize one's property if the public interest should be at stake. Rather, a set of fair procedures must be in place that will not only protect individuals from arbitrary authority but also protect their rights to make choices.

If Filmer's thesis could be said to epitomize the privilege of absolute sovereignty—arbitrary authority—it isn't merely enough to deny the sovereign absolutism, rather an effective barrier must be constructed between the sovereign and the sovereign's subjects. The important point is that Locke never considered property rights to be absolute; they were rights that were justified on the basis of the common good. Even acquisition is justified on the basis of the common good.[81] Property in effect becomes a tool in the state's guarantee of due process. Locke's view of property isn't necessarily one of ends but of means. What Locke, above all, wants to maintain is human agency as much as that might be possible. But by exhorting government to protect property, he wasn't attempting to pit the individual against government.

Locke didn't even think that government was bad. On the contrary, according to Aaron, Locke viewed government as an instrument for the positive good. Locke was a mercantilist and believed there was a need for government to be in control of trade. And yet, if it did intervene, it did so to better the prospects of the greater number of individuals. What is important to stress is that for Locke government is an instrument to be used for the good of the individual. The state is in fact made for the individual and not the other way around. It is in this sense that Locke is a champion of individualism. Locke's view of individualism is that the individual has a right to make claims against the community, but the community, through the instrument of government, should promote the individual's good. The civil society—which is the community—doesn't exist for any other purpose than that of the public good. In this vein, Locke's individualism is a question of emphasis. He stresses the rights of the individual, which shouldn't be sacrificed unless it is an extreme case in which one's freedom would need to be curtailed in order to give freedom to others.[82]

Because Locke dedicates the *Two Treatises* to William of Orange, hoping that what he has written will be "sufficient to establish the throne of our Great Restorer,"[83] there has been a tendency perhaps to view them as no more than a rationalization of the Glorious Revolution. But, as Laslett argues, the *Two Treatises* is more than a rationalization; it is a treatise about the revolution to come. If it were merely a rationalization, its import would be limited to a particular conception. But if there is a general revolution to come, it is implied that the theory contains general concepts that become generally applicable to changing conceptions. Locke isn't merely legitimating the new rule of William of Orange but is sending a clear warning to him that there is no turning back. That which can justify his assent to power can also justify his removal. Locke, through this manifesto, is ultimately arming the public with a rational basis upon which the king's power can be maintained under some semblance of contractual control. The use of property as a barrier between individuals and government is clearly one way. He is also making it clear that the ultimate source of power and authority is the community. The government, whether in the form of monarchy or polyarchy, is nothing more than a receivership. The community that had the first word will also have the last. The message is quite clear: Government, if it isn't responsive, will inevitably be rebelled against. This is only natural. Through his refutation of Filmer and his political Adamicism, this natural act is thus transformed into a right. Because there is no such thing as divine right of kings, and because legitimate government is derived from the collective consent of the community, government has an obligation to be responsive to the collective needs and will of the community. Ultimately, it is a celebration of the liberal community in which equality, mutuality, and common purpose are the norms. Consequently, in its constant need to be responsive to the community, the liberal state can never avoid policy but must always be prepared to employ it.

Locke's contract theory, whether it be interpreted as a blueprint for legitimate government or a doctrine of resistance, assumes both the importance and essential necessity of community. The whole discourse in the *Essay* on the development of words through socialization is an effective statement on the development of norms for the behavior of individuals within their communities. It is somewhat superficial to think that government can be limited to no more than the protection of our interests because ultimately we all desire such and do not need government. Rather, if we do not need government it is only because of an underlying assumption that individuals' behavior will be shaped and ultimately controlled by forces outside of government—general norms of the community, private, civic, and religious institutions, and the family.[84] Simply put, our allegiance to those rules that are propagated isn't commanded but is derived from the fact that they reflect, if not codify, the prevailing norms of society.[85]

When we get right down to it, what preserves mankind is the society, and what preserves society is the ability of individuals to structure their social arrangements in accordance with natural law. And yet, resistance isn't justified so long as legal channels for the resolution of disputes still exist.[86] Resistance, then, is a final resort after communal institutions have failed to achieve peaceful resolution. But in order to have resistance, there must be a community that has concluded through some process accounting for the equal standing of its members that resistance is in fact appropriate. One person surely cannot decide when conditions are ripe for resistance; rather, there must be a general consensus among a majority of individuals—who presumably came to this conclusion by their own capacity to reason—that conditions are ripe for resistance. This requires no less than mutuality and cooperation and some type of structure that will institutionalize them.

If Locke's theory is essentially one of resistance, it follows that there must be a presumption of a community of sorts that ultimately is being violated by the sovereign. If the community comes to the conclusion that the regime is tyrannical, now justifying resistance, a common project can be said to exist, albeit forged out of a set of adverse circumstances. But the converse also has to be true. If the government is in fact responsive to the people—to the community—those individuals who constitute the community have obligations. They have obligations in large measure because of the contract they theoretically entered into.[87] The issue for the sovereign is how to ensure that the public will not feel the need to resist. But if the government does serve the public, does it not have a right to expect some obligations on the part of its citizenry?

Mutuality

This emphasis on community and the communal bounds of agency lead to the principle of mutuality, even if for no other reason than preservation of the framework. But as resistance is viewed as a final result, the ultimate conclusion is for a community founded on democratic institutions. A society comprising equal individuals requires a community structure and institutions that will hold it together. Legal channels for the resolution of conflict would presuppose the need for an institutional mechanism reflective of the initial equal consent necessary to give it its legitimacy. Such a mechanism ultimately assumes community. But such a mechanism also relies on mutuality—the give-and-take between individuals that allows for open discussion of issues. Locke never really talked of democracy as such an institution, but his emphasis on the equal consent of those entering into the contract might well be said to presuppose that democracy will ultimately become the institution for the resolution of disputes. Moreover, contained in Locke's very rejection of paternal authority—the notion that governing authority is limited by the willingness of each generation to accept it—there would appear to be a presumption in favor of democratic institutions. Even though Locke doesn't mean for every generation to formally renew the contract, he assumes that the basic contract will continue to have legitimacy through tacit consent.

Although obedience is one means of demonstrating acceptance, it cannot logically follow from Locke's epistemology. The only logical conclusion is for some institutional framework in which individuals can affirm their consent in a positive fashion and ultimately as a community. But if mutuality would require institutions designed to enable equal individuals to participate in fair give-and-take, it also requires reciprocal arrangements between individual citizens and their communities. Just as individuals expect their communities to protect them and their right to pursue their self-interests—their own conceptions of good—they do have a corresponding obligation to their communities to maintain the social fabric of their communities. Another way to talk about mutuality is to talk about the common project.

If mutuality involves such an institutional structure, it also requires that individuals participate in the common project. The common project would require the participation of the community's members in the affairs of the community. Participation, then, has to be viewed within the broader context of socialization and the collective desire of people to work toward a common project. Locke takes the view that one's obligations to others isn't simply the abstinence from activity that will be harmful to others, but the positive duty to preserve humanity, as much as this would be possible.[88] And it is this preservation of humanity that Locke takes to constitute "the two principles to regulate our religion, politics, and morality by."[89] This injunction would appear to have much connection to modern liberal political theory, as expressed by Rawls, as he maintains that society must offer assistance to the least advantaged by helping to make them better off.[90]

To a large extent, this understanding has to be viewed no differently from the essence of Locke's contract theory. With the freedom that individuals derive from entering into a contract—a community—ultimately come corresponding obligations. It is the obligations we all subscribe to that ultimately form the essence of community. By entering into the contract through our consent, we agreed to take on certain obligations, those being essential to maintain whatever order we contracted to create.[91] The individual, by "consenting with others to make one Body Politick under one Government, puts himself under an obligation to every one of that Society, to submit to the determination of the *majority*, and to be concluded by it; or else this *original Compact*, whereby he with others incorporates into *one Society*, would signifie nothing, and be no compact, if he be left free, and under no other ties, than he was in before in the State of Nature."[92] Those obligations being to respect the rights and interests of others as we would expect others to respect ours. We also assume an obligation to defer to the legitimate authority—whose legitimacy was obtained through our consent—on those matters that will be essential for preserving community interests. Without obligations, the community falls apart.

Even if we were to concede the traditional conception that the function of the state is no more than the protection of rights, those rights cannot be protected without communities to do so. Rights, after all, are socially defined. What is a right if it is not some interest that is enjoyed by an individual and worthy of protection? A right is no more than a trump[93]—an institutionally defined claim that I may use against others and the state. Rights aren't ends unto themselves, but are functional—they serve to protect areas of freedom and control against incursions by others.[94] They offer "insulation to the exercise of individual liberties from governmental intervention."[95] Within the liberal framework, I am attempting to protect those interests that are derived from those choices I have made regarding what I consider to be the good life. Only by defining my interests as rights, can my capacity to make choices be assured by both other groups and by government. This becomes a powerful reason for defining rights in terms of property.

But to talk of rights is to talk about obligations. For a particular interest or liberty to be called a right, it generally has to be agreed by the community that it is worthy of protection. Moreover, the community has to be willing to respect it as such. As rights are highly contingent on the community for both definition and protection, it then follows that their scope cannot exceed the bounds of community acceptance. Critics of rights-based liberalism often talk of a doctrine that posits the rights of the individual against the state at the expense of the community.[96] Logically, however, this does not completely follow. The community isn't likely to respect those interests and liberties that aren't worthy of respect.

Tolerance

Mutuality that involves the common project and a sense of obligation does in the end obligate members of the community to work for the community's preservation. A community based on mutuality must in the end create an air of tolerance. All these principles do lead to a society tolerant of diversity, which in simple terms requires that harm to others, especially those who are different, be prevented. An inclusive community is built on tolerance for those who are different. This requires that the state respect minority rights. It requires that individuals be permitted to make choices for themselves in private that will have no discernable impact on others. Also individuals must respect the choices others have made. It requires that the political system be open and accessible to all and that all government actions be justified in accordance with a conception of pubic reasonableness. But it also requires that it be intolerant of those forces that have the potential to fracture and divide. It must be intolerant of those activities, whether intentional or not, that cause harm to others. The reciprocity inherent in the concept of mutuality requires a balance between individual interests and community interests. The principle often invoked to strike the appropriate balance is J. S. Mill's harm principle. Though it has a parallel to the Lockean exhortation for government to preserve society, it is also more specific in terms of what government is supposed to do.

Assuming, as Locke did before him, that individuals derive their greatest happiness from their liberty—their ability to make choices and act upon them—Mill asks what the appropriate limitation is. What then is liberty? For Mill, liberty is the limitation on the power a ruler can exercise over the community. But he doesn't restrict his conception of liberty to the potential tyranny of the magistrate; he broadens it to include the passions of the majority as well. Individuals must not only be protected against tyrannical and despotic rulers, but against irrational majoritarian impulses too. To illustrate his point, Mill talks about prevailing public opinion. And yet, his discussion has echoes of Locke's *Letter Concerning Toleration*. For at the heart of liberal toleration is the right to express ideas that are either unpopular or downright offensive. To put it another way, the essence of liberal toleration is being able to believe what you will and to practice accordingly on the basis of your own ability to do so and not to be coerced into it. Expressing this idea in terms of religion, Locke asserted that "The care of souls cannot belong to the civil magistrate, because his power consists only in outward force, but true and saving religion consists in the inward persuasion of the mind, without which nothing can be acceptable to God."[97] But one cannot be coerced into religious belief because a church is a voluntary association. One presumably joins for reasons very similar to those for entering into a contract. It is a question of choice, and therefore different choices have to be respected.[98] Respect for others' choices leads to mutuality.

This principle was tested with the Supreme Court's ruling in *Texas v. Johnson* on the issue of flag burning, and it is precisely because of this embodiment of liberal tolerance that many Americans perceive liberalism to have lost its connection with mainstream thought and opinion. The Court ruled that as offensive as it might be to burn the American flag, the expression of political protest that it represents must be permitted and cannot be stifled simply because a majority finds it offensive. Speaking for the Court, Justice Brennan asserted: "If there is a bedrock principle underlying the First Amendment, it is that the Government may not prohibit the expression of an idea simply because society finds the idea itself offensive or disagreeable."[99] Underlying this is the assumption that as offensive as it might be, it by no means harms anyone. The object, as it might have been expressed by Mill a century earlier, is to protect "against the tendency of society to impose by other means than civil penalties, its own ideas and practices as rules of conduct on those who dissent from them."[100] Echoes of this can clearly be found in *Texas v. Johnson* when Brennan asserts, with reference to an earlier case: "Nor may the government, we have held, compel conduct that would evince respect for the flag. 'To sustain the compulsory flag salute we are required to say that a Bill of Rights which guards the individual's right to speak his own mind, left it open to public authorities to compel him to utter what is not in his mind.'"[101] Or as Locke had made clear in his *Letter*, religious faith could not be imposed upon anybody because a church is nothing more than "a voluntary society of men, joining themselves together of their own accord, in order to the public worshipping of God, in such a manner as they judge acceptable to him, and effectual to the salvation of their souls."[102] This would certainly suggest the need for institutional arrangements designed to protect individual liberties from democratic majorities.

As a utilitarian, however, Mill is by no means prepared to assert that individual liberty means having a well-defined right that can be invoked against the state. Rather, Mill is out to find the balance. The concern is "how to make the fitting adjustment between individual independence and social control."[103] One is presumed to have liberty to pursue one's interests, but not past the point at which the pursuit of those interests would cause harm to either himself or the general community. Mill explains it this way:

> The object of this essay is to assert one very simple principle, as entitles to govern absolutely the dealings of society with the individual in the way of compulsion and control, whether the means used be physical force in the form of legal penalties or the moral coercion of public opinion. The principle is that the sole end for which mankind are warranted individually or collectively, in interfering with the liberty of action or any of their number is self protection. That the only purpose for which power can be rightfully exercised over any member of a civilized community, against his will, is to prevent harm to others.[104]

The real question, however, and one that ultimately divides conceptions of liberalism, is just what constitutes harm? Why can't my speech be harmful to another? For those who fought and risked death in defense of their country, is the burning of the flag not a source of great emotional pain? In his dissent, Chief Justice Rehnquist expressed such sentiments:

> The American flag, then, throughout more than 200 years of our history, has come to be the visible symbol embodying our Nation. It does not represent the views of any particular political party, and it does not represent any particular political philosophy. The flag is not simply another "idea" or "point of view" competing for recognition in the marketplace of ideas. Millions and millions of Americans regard it with an almost mystical reverence regardless of what sort of social, political, or philosophical beliefs they may have.[105]

And yet, Rehnquist's dissent is also indicative of the problem. For if the basis of harm can revolve around any type of emotional feeling or sacred symbolism, what checks are there on arbitrary exercises of authority thinly disguised as checks on harm? If harm is defined too broadly, is there not the danger that any matter, which individuals think is a matter requiring government action, can be defined as harmful? And once this happens, how will we know what is truly harmful and what is not? This is the principal reason for neutrality; to prevent the possibility for arbitrary exercises of power, even if they should find expression in democratic majorities. On the other hand, if harm is defined so narrowly as to include only those matters affecting one's physical body, can government truly respond during times of crisis? The task of any reconstructed liberalism is to attempt a definition of what matters will fall within the rubric of harm and what matters will not. It is to establish clear criteria for public intervention into the realm of the private. And within the tradition of Locke and Mill, this book seeks to find the balance through policy, while also accounting for the increased complexity of American society.

The task is by no means an easy one. Liberalism's injunction to be tolerant of diversity would require allowing any form of speech no matter how offensive it might be as an expression of individualism. But at what point does one's legitimate expression of individualism press against the social fabric of the community? If the flag in its symbolism can be said to embody the very fabric that Americans have historically made their common project, and have demonstrated their citizenship through military service, is liberty not pressing the limits of public tolerance?

What is important about Locke's *Letter* is that not only is it about the importance of tolerance for the purposes of building an inclusive community, but also it is about the limits that must be placed on that tolerance so the community can be preserved. Whereas Locke tells us that government isn't to interfere in people's private faith because the care of individuals' souls is not the appropriate responsibility of the magistrate, he does assert the responsibility of the magistrate to uphold the public good. Locke defines this public good as "life, liberty, health, and indolence of body; and the possession of outward things, such as money, land, houses, furniture, and the like." The magistrate's responsibility is to secure this "civil interest," and only if it is threatened can the magistrate have license to intervene.[106] The line, then, is to be drawn at the point in which one's belief threatens the public good. It is perhaps worth noting that Locke's toleration did not necessarily extend to Catholics who owed their allegiance to a foreign potentate "who pretended that Kings forfeited their crowns if he excommunicated them."[107] To put it bluntly, if Locke's position on tolerance represents a defense of neutrality, it also represents the subordination of neutrality to the community interest.

On the contrary, should neutrality inevitably lead to licentiousness, it cannot serve the purpose of preserving the community. It has to be stressed that Locke's commitment to human agency requires the maintenance of the community structure, for without it agency will effectively be meaningless. The consequence of community collapse is a state of nature in which individuals are enslaved to the passions of others through the sheer force of raw power.

Locke's Relevance for Contemporary Policy

How, then, does this reinterpretation of Locke affect public policy? At a minimum, it makes the values constituting the Lockean ideal such that they ought to be the basis upon which public policy is framed. Although there is an element of neutrality in Locke insofar as government is supposed to be impartial in its approach to people as a means of respecting them as equals, neutrality is only part of the Lockean formula. There is considerably more. If neutrality were the sole essence of Lockean political philosophy, there would be no role for government except for the protection of individual rights, as they have been defined in terms of property. But this would make government ineffective in the face of contemporary problems. How would a government be able to maintain its legitimacy if it could not respond to the changing needs of society?

A government that must continually be accountable and responsive to the public as a means of maintaining the tacit consent necessary to keep the contract alive is a government that must pursue policy aimed at serving the changing needs of the community. If the government is to serve the individual, it must ensure a framework in which individuals have opportunities to flourish. And to some extent, this would require that certain forms of government largess be defined in terms of property so the rights of individuals to choose is maintained.[108] But as much as the government is to be responsive to the needs of the community in a positive sense, it doesn't follow that individuals owe nothing to their communities. To invoke a Lockean ideal in both the formulation and evaluation of contemporary policy is not to say that individuals may have license. Rather, it is to say that there needs to be a balance between the rights of the individual on the one hand and the community on the other. Contrary to what communitarian critics of liberalism suggest, Locke did not imagine "the state to be an artificially fabricated combination of naturally separate individuals; he did not champion the individual against the community, and barely considered the possibility of conflict between them."[109]

To some extent, the Lockean ideal involves Dewey's vision of liberalism as a blueprint for social action. This was the notion that government should take "affirmative action" to see that the public interest was served. It represented the view that a public philosophy would have to adapt yet further to an even more changing environment so that the basic principles core to the underpinning political philosophy would achieve relevance.[110] For liberal values to be revitalized and to become the basis of a democratic society, liberals would have to become alert to the historical circumstances in which their philosophy had developed. The key liberal value was individuality: liberty and freedom of "intelligence." Dewey was most eager to reconstruct the liberal value of liberty. Liberty was more than just an abstract principle; it was power to do specific things. Questions about liberty were essentially questions about the distribution of power. As Dewey understood it, liberalism was committed to an end that was both enduring and flexible: the liberation of individuals so that they may be able to realize their capacities, and the creation of a social organization that will enable individuals, if not empower them, to achieve effective liberty and opportunity for personal growth.[111] Ultimately, this means that one feeds the other.

For these principles to be applicable to the contemporary world, they cannot be limited by the conceptions by which they were framed. Though the particulars of history may be helpful in understanding the origins of these concepts and their significance for addressing specific circumstances in time, history isn't static. Liberalism did not become a blueprint for social action during the 1930s; rather, it became a blueprint for social action when Locke formulated the theory of resistance against a corrupt government. But a government isn't merely corrupt when it usurps power; it is corrupt when it ceases to maintain the confidence of the public. The issue is responsiveness and accountability.

It was social action in the seventeenth century to resist illegitimate authority and to construct a community made up of equals. And certainly the theory of resistance was appealed to in order to justify America's separation from the English crown. But social action isn't simply a matter of resisting when the need arises; it is a matter of creating an accountable governing structure that will be able to maintain its legitimacy through actions that prevent the need to resist. This, of course, cuts two ways. Government must respond to the needs of the community by meeting its needs, whether it be through regulatory activity or positive public policy. This is one means by which the government theoretically forestalls revolution. Many will argue that much of the New Deal revolution of the 1930s was in part inspired by the need to prevent the type of revolutions that were taking place on the European continent. But a government also responds to the needs of the community by preserving its moral fabric. One way to preserve its moral fabric is to ensure that its actions are consistent with its values and cultural traditions. This, then, becomes yet another means by which it theoretically forestalls revolution. Both types of response constitute the Lockean ideal, which means that when applied to public policy the Lockean ideal is about achieving balance. The Lockean ideal supports the positive state insofar as it furthers the ends of the community. But in order for policy to be consistent with the Lockean ideal, it must rely less on neutrality and more on the values already enunciated.

The principles that I have laid out, and have derived from the tradition, would imply the following for policy in terms of its parameters: At a minimum, there must be a framework conducive to the pursuit of individual choices. Within the political realm, democratic institutions must allow individuals to make choices, to present their own conceptions of good on a more or less equal footing. Within the private realm, a market economy is still the most open framework to make their choices in the form of economic self-interests. But the key here is that the framework must remain open, and it can only do so when the public sector is prepared to intervene as necessary to ensure its openness and its ability to generate further opportunities for individuals to make choices. On the negative side of policy this means regulation to prevent harm, not only in terms of physical harm, but the types of private economic decisions that could effectively restrict opportunities for others. This has traditionally referred to the creation of monopolies in restraint of free trade. And yet, such decisions that might effectively restrict the opportunities—choices—of others could include location decisions that often result in plant closure. When it comes to social issues, government must do what it can to maintain an inclusive community in which everybody feels welcome and is tolerated. Although individuals do have rights that need to be protected—because this will (1) help to maintain an open framework and (2) maintain the inclusiveness of the community comprising diverse points of view—the community has a right to expect that individuals will meet their obligations to their communities because this helps to further the common project. As we will see in the chapters to follow, it is when policy strives to maintain neutrality that it actually loses sight of the Lockean ideal. The issue in the chapters that follow is whether American public policy has in any way coincided with these values.

3. *Economic Stabilization*

STABILIZATION policies fall into two broad categories: regulation and economic management. Regulation is essentially a set of negative measures designed to constrain actors in the marketplace in conformity with Mill's harm principle. Economic management includes a broad array of policy designed to maintain a competitive economy in which employment levels are maintained at a reasonably high level and prices are stable. Price stabilization, which can include wage rates as they are defined as prices paid for labor, means prices not subject to runaway inflation. In this chapter I explore four specific types of policies: regulation, monetarism, plant-closing policy, and corporatism because they reflect in part the evolution of the positive state and, hence, liberalism's evolution from its classical form to its modern one.

Regulation and monetarism are, by and large, maintenance policies and, to some extent, parallel neutrality. Plant-closing policy and corporatism, however, assuming that American political institutions are predicated on liberal tradition (generally and particularly its neutral elements), may appear to require serious changes in organizing ideology and institutions. Specifically, they demonstrate how the nature of complexity requiring these specific responses results in an abandonment of neutrality; indeed, there is no way they can be predicated on neutrality at all if they are to seriously accomplish their objectives. When the four policies are arrayed on a trajectory, neutrality is diminished as we progress along it. The trajectory is thus intended to illustrate the following dilemma: As more "state"-oriented policies may be needed to maintain economic stability, these policies must find their justification in those principles essential to maintaining the community if they are to be considered liberal. The ends, after all, are to preserve society. The problem with state-oriented policies is that they effectively constrain individual freedom, something that neutrality has been instrumental in protecting. And yet, the dilemma may be more apparent than real, for an examination of these policies also reveals that the degree of neutrality in these policies has not been as much as commonly supposed. But perhaps what becomes most clear is that, whereas the trajectory would appear to press against the limits of the Lockean liberalism as it has been traditionally understood—especially as it is often assumed to be epitomized by neutrality—these policies actually do find justification in the Lockean ideal when considered within the context of the other principles.

Regulation

Regulation, as already alluded to, can be justified either in terms of Locke's exhortation to preserve society or Mill's to prevent harm. Regulation can represent the means by which the community attempts to restrain individual actions or choices for the sake of community interests, or to merely further mutuality. In American constitutional law it is the essence of the state police power and is justified on the grounds that (1) its aim is the prevention of undue harm to others and (2) it ultimately preserves society, there is in fact a compelling state interest. Regulation involves external controls on what economic actors may and may not do, and it constitutes an effective abridgment of some of their liberties. Consequently, regulation in a market economy entails the imposition of restrictions on property owners' rights to freely and fully dispose of their property as they would see fit. In this vein it involves a narrowing of the framework in which some individuals may choose their respective goods, ostensibly so that others may realize theirs. To put it in the language of tolerance, a broadly inclusive community built on principles of tolerance must to a degree be intolerant of those forces that could in any way fracture and result in the effective exclusion of others.

In the history of liberal evolution from the night-watchman state—characteristic of classical liberalism—to what is now referred to as the positive state—characteristic of modern liberalism—regulation is principally derived from a phase known as corporate liberalism. This was a period in which economic interests were conceived less in individual terms and more in corporate or more collectivized ones. The objective was to preserve the ideas of human dignity and personal independence at a time when the nature of the economy was changing. In addition to being a time of waves of immigrants, it was also a period of urbanization, with more people living in cities and working in factories. Fewer people were going to achieve independence by being farmers. To an extent, the meaning of independence—if it meant not being dependent on others—was to have a job. But if having a job in a factory was to be a basis for independence, new ground rules were being established so as to preserve the human dignity that would naturally be a prerequisite for independence of mind and thought.

During an earlier period, when the base of the economy was agriculture, there had been little need for government to interfere with private economic interests. These new circumstances, however, were dictating an even greater linkage between the public and private sectors or, in Lockean language, between society and the state. At issue was how those traditional values, which appeared to be slipping away, could be restored. At the same time, how could business confidence and economic stability be maintained while not stifling individual initiative? The answer, of course, was regulation. The state would be called upon to regulate, not so individualism could be hindered but so conditions conducive to it would be restored. At the heart of corporate liberalism, then, was the positive state predicated on the concept of administration. Its legitimacy was recognized as being necessary for the regulation of the corporation in particular and the preservation of the public interest in general. But, in substance, there were still similarities to its classical ancestor in which the public and private realms were theoretically distinct. And yet, writers such as Sklar, Lustig, and Weinstein argue that insofar as corporate liberalism represented the institutional and legal adaptation of American society to this economic transformation, it was repudiating any classical notions of neutrality and limited government grounded in Locke.[1] It is an interpretation arising out of the more traditional reading of Locke. And yet, corporate liberalism actually maintains continuity with liberalism predicated on neutrality.

Corporate liberalism rejected statism—the notion that government should direct the market and that corporations would be treated as public utilities and agents of public policy. It rejected the concept of state control, which in essence was a rebuke of calls for a political economic arrangement along the lines of command. Instead, it opted for a halfway house in which private corporations might find themselves subject to the regulations of independent regulatory commissions.[2] But in proportion to society's increasing complexity, government would still remain limited. By no means was government becoming all too intrusive; rather, in a world where "individual units" were increasingly being constituted by collectivities, a more positive government would be needed to preserve the old traditional values associated with individualism. In an ever changing and more complex society where new impersonal forces would strip people of their individuality, government action or intervention would serve to preserve a semblance of individualism by protecting individuals' rights to human dignity.

The view of Locke as the defender of individual rights and liberties is also the view that he is an opponent of regulation. Hence, to embrace regulation is to reject Lockean liberalism. But as I have already suggested in the last chapter, this doesn't follow. Regulation can end up maintaining a broadly inclusive community if it successfully achieves a balance between the needs of individuals to maintain their agency and the needs of the community to preserve itself. Locke's theory is one of affording dignity to individuals and of preserving the community. In part, the whole discourse on resistance, while it creates a safety valve for the public, does presuppose that government, if it is truly upholding the contract—even tacitly—will have institutional channels in place to avoid the resort to rebellion. Resistance theory speaks less to the rights of individuals than it does to the obligations of government. It is no less than an exhortation for government to be responsive to its citizens in order to maintain their confidence. Should a change of objective circumstances then require positive actions, those actions must then be seen as being in full accord with the spirit of the Lockean ideal. In this vein, corporate liberalism is not a repudiation but a reaffirmation of the essence of Locke. And yet, as corporate liberalism represented an attempt to join the tradition of the past with the changing reality that was to mark the future, it effectively became an exercise in neutrality, as reflected in the antistatist tradition.

Difficulties in Regulation

As ambiguous a term as harm is, and subject to a multitude of perspectives, within the economic sphere it could be conceived of in the following ways: On the one hand, harm could be defined as those negative externalities arising from the capitalist economy running its course. Such externalities might include all types of environmental pollution. On the other hand, harm could be regarded as the negative impact corporate or other business decisions might have on others, whether made out of miscalculation, shortsightedness, negligence, or greed. While harm may be clearer in the first instance, it is less so in the second. The negative impact arising out of a corporate decision to form a massive trust in restraint of trade doesn't necessarily cause physical harm to anybody, but it might be the source of economic harm to the larger society. The harm inflicted may merely be an assault on the social value of free market competition.

Harm may clearly be visible when there are identifiable and tangible consequences, but what about the intangible effects of private activity on, say, political values such as the meaning of democracy? Michael Reagan has referred to this traditional regulatory paradigm as essentially a "halfway house" between the extremes of pure laissez-faire capitalism and pure socialism.[3] As such, it might also be argued that the maintenance of economic stability serves to preserve the basic outlines of the capitalist system. The means of regulation thus serve the dual ends of economic stability and the preservation of markets, neither of which are mutually exclusive. But the ultimate ends of regulation are the prevention of undue harm to others.

Regulation, then, derives its legitimacy from its service to the public good. But if legitimate for the common good, it must also be clear that the community as a whole is served, and not just a specific element that would wrap itself in the language of the common good. The question that has to be asked then is what is it about regulation that makes it neutral? Then to be asked is whether regulation is in fact neutral. Only if this distinction is preserved might we then go as far as saying that regulation would clear the neutrality principle in liberalism. The question we need to address then is what set of criteria would regulatory policy have to satisfy in order to satisfy the requirements of the neutrality principle?

To be in conformity with neutrality, the social benefits of regulation would have to surpass the immediate costs to those bearing the burdens of regulation. The problem with this is that although the tangible costs can be measured, the benefits aren't easily measured. We regulated trusts at the beginning of the century in order to preserve the values of competition and smallness. Not only was centralized economic power considered to be monopoly power threatening independence, but also it was a threat to the competitive spirit of the market economy built on principles of individualism. At the same time, it was also believed that if nothing was done, the situation would be ripe for a political uprising. Hence regulation would not only preserve American values but also neutralize union militancy.[4] To this end, benefits weren't necessarily intangible but were clearly evident in whatever diminution of tension that may have resulted. The regulatory measures adopted, and the subsequent regulatory apparatus that was established, were part of an effort to reaffirm in concrete terms those values core to the American creed.[5]

But is government being neutral, or is it effectively making a serious effort to determine which values will have greater priority? If the primary value of liberalism had been capitalist competition, the case could be made that regulation should not have been legitimate because it was effectively interfering with that process. It certainly was not neutral in terms of impact. Some were clearly being asked to bear costs so that others would derive benefit. On the contrary, regulation was aimed at reaffirming core values, for the effect was for there to have been a substantive ranking of values. In this case, the affirmation of "first principles" was viewed to be of a higher order than free, unfettered capitalist competition. It would be a very difficult case to make that no conception of the good was being embraced. Because regulatory policy has been employed for the purposes of maintaining general economic stability and otherwise preserving social foundations, its general purpose, it might be argued, exceeds whatever detriment might befall those parties subject to regulation.

Regulation has two objectives: to ensure that a framework is preserved in which individuals can continue to make choices for themselves as to how they will live their lives, and to give substantive meaning to the basic principle of equality in the face of those forces that would undermine it. If these are the objectives, and they can be justified in public debate, then regulation neither violates the neutrality principle nor defies liberalism's principle of a limited government, or at least one that is relatively limited. Nor does it disagree with the idea that the ultimate ends of public policy in the liberal state should be the maintenance of an inclusive community, which certainly includes mutuality and restraint on arbitrary authority. But the corollary also holds regulation to only accomplish these ends when it has been clear that a demonstrable harm has arisen from private actions.

The question of who benefits, however, is not to be dismissed lightly. *Who* and *how many* are questions cutting to the very core of regulatory legitimacy. Regulation derives its primary legitimacy if viewed as no more and no less than an attempt to balance the rights of individuals to pursue their self-interests with the rights and interests of society.[6] To make this case, however, entails a very narrow conception of neutrality, one confined to matters of procedure. Substantively speaking, there can be no neutrality if a goal is being embraced, even if it be a commitment to procedure.

While regulation abridges the liberties of some, it protects the rights of others. If regulation is pursued specifically for this purpose and it is clear that such measures are indeed necessary, the case can plausibly be made that it doesn't violate the neutrality principle. It isn't violative only because regulation wasn't pursued as a means by which one group received preferential treatment over another, but also because it was needed to protect the group from undue harm. Though this demonstration of necessity may clear the policy of the neutrality principle, it doesn't dismiss the issue entirely. For by what criteria do we define harm, and who defines it? Stalemate on definition could put us into a position of inaction. Theoretically, harm is defined through the democratic process in which each group is able to present its claims. But some in the political process have more voice than others. And yet, one of the legacies of corporate liberalism was the independent regulatory commission so that such decisions could be removed and further isolated from popular pressure. As such, regulations may simply be promulgated by bureaucratic elites who pay no real attention to the public. Ironically, however, the nature of this type of implementation was probably more neutral than other forms of government intervention.

Monetarism

Monetary policy essentially entails control of the money supply or the flow of money within the economy. Through control of the money supply, the federal government attempts to macromanage the economy. The object is to maintain a stable economy through stable, sound money. The money supply is usually affected by either money aggregates (an aggregate amount of money required to be kept in reserve) or interest rates, as these rates in turn are affected by the rediscount rate charged by the Federal Reserve Board (the Fed) to its member banks. By increasing the amount of money a member bank must pay to borrow from the Fed, the Fed can effectively drive up interest rates, thereby making it more costly to borrow. An effective tool to this end has simply been to increase money aggregates, which has had the effect of reducing the amount of money and capital in the economy.[7] The effect of either is to contract the money supply, thereby inducing a recession for controlling inflation.

Conversely, by reducing money aggregates or lowering rediscount rates, the Fed is able to pump more money into the economy, aimed at stimulating production. By allowing greater amounts of money to flow during times of recession, the government hopes to stimulate new investment, which will yield greater growth and prosperity. It increases the supply of capital for economic expansion by devaluing the dollar, printing up more money, or lowering the interest rates. If successful, the economy expands, guaranteeing lucrative returns to investors and new jobs for the otherwise unemployed. Supposedly, then, a legitimate argument can be made in favor of monetarism because of its distributive benefits. Though not everyone benefits equally, such policies are often couched in terms of what best preserves the public interest, that is, the maintenance of economic growth and prosperity.[8]

Monetary policy, while its intellectual foundations are found in the work of Milton Friedman and the Chicago school of economics, has institutional grounding in the Federal Reserve System and derives ultimate authority from the Employment Act of 1946. Its liberal foundations actually sit on the fence between corporate liberalism and the New Deal era, which became the mantra for activism. The Federal Reserve was established during the early part of the century to give commerce and industry security from the vicissitudes of the marketplace by providing financial institutions with a reservoir of emergency funds.[9] The same vicissitudes that necessitated the adoption of regulatory measures in the first place also necessitated the creation of a central bank. As the institution was established, it was then well poised to serve the objectives of the Employment Act. The Employment Act created the Council of Economic Advisors (CEA) in the White House, whose job it was to monitor the economy. Moreover, it established that it would be "the continuing policy and responsibility of the Federal Government to use all practicable means . . . to promote maximum employment, production, and purchasing power."[10] Monetary policy, then, could be a means by which government would use "practicable means" to fulfill a general maintenance function in the positive state, the principal maintenance function being to control for both recession and inflation. As the Employment Act established that government would have a role to play in the overall management of the economy, and monetary policy is clearly implied, the case can be made that society believed there would be a demonstrable public benefit. Moreover, as Reagan points out, since the Federal Reserve Act of 1913 didn't establish a mandate for policy stabilization, which the Fed currently engages in, it is only from the Employment Act that any real contemporary purpose can be inferred.[11]

If the objective of monetary policy is the maintenance of economic stability, it would appear to aspire to the Lockean criterion in that its justification at all is the preservation of society. But is it enough to just look at the objective, or do we need to also examine the effects as well? Although the objective may be the preservation of society within a Lockean framework, what if, in the process, harm is the effect experienced by members of the community? If we return to the premise that the initial basis for government intervention at all is the prevention of harm to others, it must then follow that the intervention can only be justified if it does not in the process cause any more harm. It would have to be clear that regulation designed to ensure the well-being of a specific subgroup—to protect it from harm—would not end up jeopardizing the well-being of the larger community in the process. In American constitutional jurisprudence, there is precedence for this, dating back to *Loan Association v. Topeka* in 1875. Here the Court ruled that it was not a valid exercise of state tax power to levy a tax on an entire community for the immediate subsidy of a particular economic class without any discernible "public" purpose.[12] Ultimately, then, there was a concept of a "larger community," which would have to be a factor in the balancing act government engages in when it seeks to resolve conflict. What, then, does it mean to talk about preserving society in the Lockean sense? Whose society?

Monetarism might just challenge this principle. Most economists would regard both inflation and recession as long-term threats to economic stability, and yet the strategy designed to resolve one problem invariably results in the further exacerbation of the other. The greatest difficulty in the use of monetary controls is striking the appropriate balance between recession and inflation. On the one hand, a tightening of the money supply in efforts to curb inflation means that economic growth and expansion will be slowed, which will most likely result in new layoffs, only contributing to the problem of unemployment. On the other hand, loosening the money supply in efforts to raise the economy out of the depths of recession means that as the economy is expanding and more people have more money to spend, prices are bound to go up, thus contributing to the problem of inflation.

Peripherally, monetarism would thus appear to be an example of zero-sum policy. Though some will benefit from monetarism to be sure, others will invariably lose. On one level, monetarism is justified by the need to serve the public interest, to preserve society. On another level, however, it would appear to violate liberalism's own neutrality. But does it really? Although the policy will have its adverse effects, it is probably the most impersonal and impartial zero-sum policy we are bound to see. What monetarism effectively suggests is that there is a public problem that needs to be addressed for which certain tools will be employed. Rather than targeting a group in particular to shoulder the losses for the greater "collective" good, it simply applies these tools to the economy with the expectation that the chips that do fall, will in fact fall where they may. The impact, it might be argued, is neutral because those forced to suffer the adverse effects are only doing so coincidentally and not because they were deliberately intended to.

This somehow begs the question of neutrality. Let's accept for the moment that it is neutral. Monetarism might conceivably be viewed as an example of a faceless mechanism implementing a policy under a Rawlsian-style veil of ignorance—a state in which we are ignorant of each one's resources and attributes.[13] But is it? One could argue that any policy that effectively gives one benefit at the expense of another is anything but neutral. Broadly speaking, however, it might be, because its victims aren't clearly identifiable. The effects, then, fall into Lowi's category of distributive politics, in which government will distribute benefits to a variety of different groups but effectively pass the costs on to others who are neither visible nor clearly identifiable.[14] But are these groups really invisible and unidentifiable? Do we not know that certain groups might be bound to suffer more than others? Those most likely to lose their jobs during recessions will be low-wage workers.[15] Also, members of the underclass may suffer disproportionately.[16]

Ackerman attempts to square egalitarian democracy with liberal neutrality by positing a dialogue as a procedural mechanism that could effectively extricate the state from the inherent stalemate to neutrality. As the effects of any decision in the end cannot be neutral, the decision nonetheless can be legitimate if made through a dialogue in which everyone has had access to present a claim as to what would constitute good. Conflicts are adjudicated and public decisions are made through the process of dialogue, in which everyone who makes a claim must also justify that claim relative to the public interest. Democracy is ultimately a procedural tool for sorting through conceptions of good because all members must be allowed to participate. In fact, they must participate.[17] Although the effects of monetary policy are anything but neutral, the case might be made that they are neutral, at least within either Dworkin's or Ackerman's construction of neutrality. For it isn't clear that monetarism is an example of a policy that gives A preferential treatment over B. Rather, groups A and B are both exposed to the effects of the policy, in which case each will experience them to different degrees. The only problem with this is that while monetarism may not violate this version of the neutrality principle, its falsification rests on the premise that the justification for monetarism in the first place is in fact neutral. But is it? The case could just as easily be made that a policy designed to either control inflation or recession is just as much a conception of what constitutes goodness as any other. Why is it preferable for government to deal with either of these problems as opposed to simply allowing the economy to run its course and to resolve itself? Or, once we have decided that the issue of stability is an appropriate topic of public policy, why is it preferable to deal with inflation at the risk of incurring recession or vice versa? Rather, the decision over how and when to deploy monetary tools is only too fraught with politics.[18] Even if it conforms to Dworkin's neutrality, does it still conform to Ackerman's?

At this point, we are talking about community objectives. We are also talking about the ability of the community to determine its own destiny by the very principles at the root of Lockean liberalism. As true as it may be that inflation does harm the general community, and that it ultimately threatens that community's economic stability, there is nonetheless a conflict of purposes if its cure results in others suffering the pangs of unemployment. Are we not, then, running into problems with Mill's harm principle? For instance, in William Grieder's study of the Fed, when the Fed attempted to achieve its stated money aggregate in the early 1980s in an attempt to once and for all reign in inflation, the price paid was a severe recession. Though the banks benefited from this policy, industrial manufacturers and those in their employ were the big losers. It is easy to look at numbers and apply economic formulas to the nation's economic problems, but the dispassionate application doesn't dismiss the real pain and suffering felt by millions of Americans.[19]

Monetary policy, as it is administered by the Fed, is still perhaps an interesting case because it does not easily fit into Lowi's classification of "interest-group liberalism." We are not really talking about a bureaucratic capture in which there is an iron triangle between members of Congress, members of the Fed, and members of the banking industry. At the same time, we do not have the type of institutional accountability—responsiveness—that should forestall the type of resistance theory that Locke had invoked as the means by which governing institutions would ultimately be held accountable. Resistance, after all, was a final recourse assuming that legal channels existed for the resolution of conflict. But as the Fed operates in isolation from public access, there are no legal channels for adversely affected individuals to press their claims in a direct fashion. Their only recourse is to voice their complaints before Congress, which, short of writing new legislation to assert authority, has abdicated all power on this issue to the Fed.

We clearly have precedent from corporate liberalism in that the Fed functions like an independent regulatory commission. And yet, as it was structured, it was specifically designed to serve the interests of—to be responsive to—one particular group: banks. Given that, can it really conform to Ackerman's precondition of a dialogue in which everyone must in fact participate? It also needs to be made clear that even if neutrality shouldn't be the ultimate goal of the liberal state, some measure of it must be maintained before the state can legitimately ask that its members fulfill their civic obligations as citizens by participating in the common project. In order for there to be mutuality from society's members, there must first be public justification from the state. In this vein, Ackerman's scheme becomes quite informative.

If we could couch this in terms of one of Ackerman's contrived debates, but in much simplified form, the result might be as follows: Group A, arguing for a tight money supply, argues that the economy will be better served if the problem of inflation is in fact resolved. Group B, however, argues just the opposite, that the economy will be better served if the problem of recession is in fact resolved. By suggesting that the economy will be well served either by tightening or loosening the money supply, both groups are effectively advancing their respective conceptions of what constitutes the good society. But which group is more likely to argue for tighter money? Banks and other financial institutions? Conversely, which groups would argue for looser money? Industries that are sensitive to interest rates, like housing and autos? Hence good, in the name of general economic stability, is still conceived of in terms of respective self-interest. Government can either tighten or loosen; it cannot do both. Therefore, it effectively favors one over the other. In making the choice, then, government ultimately violates the neutrality principle, although it does so only if both sides weren't equal in their rights to present their claims. The fact that the policy's impact may be neutral doesn't dismiss the partiality of the policy's justification.

But to claim that there was debate in accord with Ackerman's dialogue is to miss the fact that monetary policy is an instrument of the Fed, whose principal constituency, as provided by statutory mandate, is the banking industry. Because the central bank intended to maintain stability in the nation's financial markets, the Fed is therefore likely to view the issue of economic stability through this constituency's lenses. Both sides in the debate are not really equal then; rather, there is an institutional prejudice—predisposition—in favor of one. Given current institutional arrangements, it seems doubtful that monetarism can even approximate Ackerman's neutrality. Because an elite constructs the policy, only the elite understands the issues.[20] On the other hand, the Fed could always argue that its actions are neutral simply by relying on the natural rate theory of unemployment. According to this theory, there is a natural rate of unemployment, and when unemployment drops below that rate, it triggers inflationary pressures. Hence the basis for when to modify interest rates is the unemployment rate in relation to its natural rate.[21] In other words, the natural rate constitutes an objective set of measures by which to make a determination.

Then again, as most groups in society have come to expect that government will in fact address economic problems, the issue of the policy's justification with respect to so-called neutral principles becomes a moot point. While the policy might at one level violate the neutrality principle, that criterion, in and of itself, does not suffice to disqualify the use of the policy entirely. For what is still at issue is whether the policy fulfills the objectives of the liberal state, those objectives being a fair framework in which individuals are free to choose. But will it also work to preserve the framework by immediately preventing the financial collapse of the system and, ultimately, generating more opportunities? That is, is there a demonstrable public benefit to be derived from monetarism? Once this leap is made, it becomes a misnomer to talk of policy based on neutrality.

There is, however, a problem with this argument. Only the public—as an extension of the initial consent theory—can determine just what those objectives are. If the public cannot decide because it lacks the training and technical expertise to fully comprehend the issues, it cannot fully live up to the liberal ideal. The public has to make an initial determination as to what its objectives are in any given economic policy and periodically reevaluate them. To an extent, this happens during elections when we either maintain those in power or install others based on their positions. At the same time, however, it does not really happen if our elected representatives—agents of democratic expression and ultimately the embodiment of our reaffirmation of initial contractual consent—do not ultimately maintain substantive authority. If truly in the service of liberal objectives, not only do institutional arrangements have to be changed so that the Fed becomes accountable to all the people, but the effects of its policies must be measured against the objectives of the general economic policies the community as a whole supposedly agreed upon. Ultimately, then, the natural-rate theory cannot be viewed as neutral because it serves a particular end result in the service of a particular constituency.

In monetarism, the public has a vested interest in ensuring economic stability. If it should be clear that stability will only be maintained through the pursuit of one of these policies, the case could then be made that the overall benefit to the public will in fact supersede any concerns a particular subgroup may have. But there is yet one other criterion by which this policy must be measured, at least within the context of the American constitutional tradition. That is, does this policy have the effect of depriving citizens of their rights either in terms of their property or their pursuit of self-interest? Or the question is, does the benefit to society justify the encroachment of individual rights or interests?

Although the typical observer might conclude there to be no obvious violation of rights, Ackerman suggests that a distinction be drawn between "ordinary observing" and "scientific policy making." While the ordinary observer would not conclude there to be any visible or direct deprivation of rights, the scientific policy maker would suggest that, because tight money resulted in a loss of business so that the value of the firm is less, property may have been taken without just compensation.[22] That if it could be established that monetarism was the sole cause of this firm's misfortune, this would only be true. Can we really be sure that this firm wouldn't have lost business in the absence of the policy? Even Dworkin would concede that unless it is beyond a doubt clear that a policy violates rights, public policy may be pursued on the basis that it furthers some socially optimal goal.[23] And Rawls himself would use the criterion of making everyone better off.[24] But then, what about the argument that if government is truly neutral, it will do nothing and allow the market to run its own course? For if government does anything, it is violating the principle of limited government. Of course, the argument for doing nothing is no more neutral than the argument for doing something. Government doesn't necessarily adhere to the neutrality principle simply by doing nothing; rather, it only shirks its responsibility to resolve a serious problem.

On another level, monetary policy may raise questions about the limits to legislative experimentation. With the demise of what has often been referred to as the *Lochner* era—the epitome of judicial activism where the Court used its power to invalidate legislative attempts to regulate the marketplace—there were serious questions as to whether legislative bodies were to be given a blank check to do as they pleased, unconstrained by any courts.[25] And yet, as late as 1978, in *Penn Central Transportation Co. v. New York City*, the Court did make it clear that there were limitations. Although this is essentially a case challenging the limits to regulation, the parallels to implementation of monetary policy are striking because they ultimately speak to the issue of arbitrariness.

As early as 1922, Justice Oliver Wendell Holmes stated in *Pennsylvania Coal Co. v. Mahon* that "while property may be regulated to a certain extent, if regulation goes too far it will be recognized as a 'taking.'"[26] Regulation would be considered a perfectly legitimate police power so long as it would not impinge on the basic integrity of property rights. What was not clear, however, was just what rights would impinge on this basic integrity. Couldn't the antitrust laws adopted during the period of corporate liberalism have been regarded as an abridgment of property rights? And yet, they were justified on the grounds that they preserved the competitiveness of the economy. The breakup of monopolies was considered to be a matter of the public interest—an abridgment of property rights perhaps, but one probably to be sanctioned by Locke on the grounds that it was viewed as being essential to the preservation of society. Even though they were an abridgment of property rights, were they of the nature to justify an invocation of resistance theory? Antitrust laws only restricted what one could invest in, not whether one could dispose of one's property. They certainly did not prevent one from pursuing a lucrative business opportunity.

But the *Penn Central* case involved a law that effectively did prevent one from pursuing a business opportunity. Under New York City's Landmark Preservation Law, Grand Central Terminal, owned and operated by Penn Central Transportation, was designated a landmark and the block it occupied a landmark site. In pursuit of a business opportunity, Penn Central entered into a lease agreement with a third party to build a multistory office building over the terminal. The city's Landmark Preservation Commission rejected plans for the building as being destructive of the terminal's historic and aesthetic features. At issue was whether the application of the law was tantamount to a taking. Also at issue was whether the company was not also being denied control over its property.[27] While Holmes in *Pennsylvania Coal* had been ambiguous as to what would be considered going too far, was this not going too far? As far as the Court was concerned, the law was not a regulation going too far because Penn Central was not only allowed to profit from the terminal but could still obtain a reasonable return on its investment.[28]

On the basis of this case, Laurence Tribe has constructed the following calculus for determining the limits to regulation. The Court would be unlikely to consider a measure a taking if it "(1) advances some public interest, but (2) falls short of destroying any classically recognized element of the bundle of property rights, (3) leaves much of the commercial value of the property untouched, and (4) includes at least some reciprocity of benefit."[29] The Court seemed to be making it rather clear that there were limits to legislative experimentation, even if they did not necessarily apply in this case. In *Penn Central,* the Court found the zoning ordinance to advance the public interest with no negative affect on either commercial value or the traditional bundle of property rights. Moreover, it assumed there to be reciprocity of benefit insofar as Penn Central was deriving tax advantages and whatever other advantages were associated with the designation.

But there was more to it. *Penn Central* really was not a case involving a value judgment to be made, that is, a substantive choice between interests of individuals and those of the community. That really was not a matter for the Court to say. The Court did not even presume to define the public interest; rather, it only assumed that determination to have been made, as evidenced by passage of the law in the first place. The case really turned on technical questions—issues of procedure—as to whether the appropriate channels existed for Penn Central to contest the designation and to have a fair hearing. From the Court's perspective, Penn Central had exhausted its normal channels, and therefore, the decision by the Landmark Preservation Commission could in no way be said to have been arbitrary. What is telling about this case is the implicit suggestion that had none of the above conditions been met, the Landmark Preservation Law might well have been considered to be a law exceeding its boundaries. In essence, then, the law as it was applied to Penn Central was ultimately concluded to be in accord with those procedures of liberal dialogue. This, of course, raises the question as to whether monetarism could be said to meet similar conditions.

The mechanics of monetary policy and regulatory policy, however, do differ. One is adopted through the democratic process—liberalism's procedural tool for sorting—whereas the other is not. Although the specifics and mechanics of regulation are formulated by specific independent regulatory agencies, the framework for regulation is provided by Congress, often following heated debate in which all sides have been allowed to present their views and press their claims. Simply put, decisions to regulate, as well as the form which the regulation shall take, are made by Congress. Congress, however, does not formulate monetary policy. Rather, monetary policy is established by the Fed, which is independent of both Congress and the president. Although presidents attempt to influence the Fed's policy through the appointments they make to the board, decisions over when to tighten or loosen money are ultimately made by the board. Though Congress can curb the power of the Fed through legislation,[30] a congressional response will only be a reaction to an action that has already been taken. Hence competing claims aren't pressed before the board prior to policy implementation; rather, policy is implemented on the basis of elitist views of what is in the best interests of society and often in accord with the theoretical model of the natural rate. Should competing claims then be presented to Congress because of resultant adversity, the dialogue is only post hoc. As the Fed is independent and doesn't include public debate in its own policy deliberations, there is very much an undemocratic aspect to monetarism.[31]

Therefore, it might not easily be said to clear the neutrality principle because the dialogue that would have paved the way for legitimacy hasn't really taken place. On the other hand, it may secure legitimacy from an unwillingness to radically defy the mainstream of public opinion on what economic issues are important especially as they are articulated by the president and Congress. For as Woolley reminds us, Congress possesses considerable authority and power to affect the Fed's conduct of monetary policy, and the Fed always operates under the fear that Congress just might use its authority.[32] Still, one wonders whether this is actually true. Deferring to the Fed seems to serve the same purpose as deferring to any bureaucracy immune from popular pressure. It absolves Congress of responsibility. The Fed becomes another whipping boy for Congress in its effort to show the public that it cares. But when it comes time for substantive action, Congress is not at all prepared to act because it would then have to make the hard choices it has felt comfortable delegating to others. As much as one might argue that monetary policy is formulated within the parameters of public acceptance so as not to risk incurring the type of wrath that would strip it of its independence, the record of Fed performance during Paul Volker's tenure as chairman calls this argument into question. Ultimately what an examination of monetarism shows, especially as it was used during the 1980s, is that if there wasn't a complete absence of neutrality, there was a further erosion of it. It is on the trajectory between regulation and monetarism that we can begin to see the erosion.

Plant-Closing Policy

Whereas regulation and monetarism illustrate policies framed with liberalism's neutrality in mind, plant-closing policy illustrates the limits to that neutrality. At the same time, plant-closing policy is a prime example of how liberal society may find it difficult to clarify its objectives. On one level, plant closure could be conceived of as a matter that should fit into a traditional paradigm of regulation. As plants close, a simple regulatory framework calls for some restrictions on the part of corporate managers for the benefit of the larger community. It perhaps ought to be viewed no differently than the establishment of ground rules for the disinvestment of capital. As such, it would be no different than the ground rules we commonly impose on business when it comes to maintaining the larger public interest, especially in areas of environmentalism, consumer product safety, and fair labor legislation. On another level, however, plant-closing policy, especially depending on how it is constructed, is not really like other forms of regulation and therefore may sit outside the philosophical bounds of liberalism.[33]

Plant closure actually presents the liberal policy maker with an interesting dilemma. On the one hand, closure is part and parcel of a dynamic capitalist economy running its course. It could be viewed as the concrete manifestation of Joseph Schumpeter's abstract model of "creative destruction," whereby the destruction of the old and obsolete is supposed to make way for the new and technologically more advanced.[34] Plant closure, therefore, is a neutral by-product of a healthy and dynamic capitalist economy. Instead of termination being an ending, it is actually the beginning of something new and wholly different. It is essentially part and parcel of a natural life cycle in which entities have beginnings and ends. Ultimately, it is indispensable to positive change because positive change requires the replacement of the old and obsolete with the new and technologically more advanced. If this is true, closure must be allowed to happen because in the long run it will be essential to the maintenance of stability.

On the other hand, the price of that long-term stability may well be short-term instability. The consequences for those falling victim to closure are quite severe. Inasmuch as closure reflects the nation's economic transformation from an industrial manufacturing-based economy to a postindustrial service sector-based economy, it is a crisis speaking to the consequences of economic transformation no differently from various past crises that called upon government to act as a means of maintaining stability. In terms of the consequences alone, closure causes massive dislocation and does perhaps threaten the core of the American middle class. More than simply a question of recessionary layoffs, where workers may be called back during better times, closure is the permanent elimination of those jobs, and the consequence is permanent labor displacement—where workers will most likely never be called back at all.[35] For example, the Bureau of Labor Statistics (BLS) estimated that close to eleven million people lost their jobs between 1981 and 1986 as a function of closure.[36] Or for the years 1983 to 1988, total displacement was estimated to be 4.7 million, with 551,600 per year due to closure.[37] The BLS further estimates that, from January 1991 to December 1993, an additional 4.5 million workers were displaced from jobs they held for three years or more.[38]

Market theorists will clearly argue that these workers can be reabsorbed into the economy as they have been in the past.[39] But to focus solely on those who are displaced overlooks a plant closure's wide-ranging impact on the larger community. The closure of one plant often results in the loss of contracts to supplier plants, which in turn are forced to reduce their workforces as well. These are the ripple effects. But there are tertiary effects as well, as closure adversely affects a community's fiscal base. The community's revenue base is effectively reduced when it loses tax revenues on personal income, corporate income, and property. At the same time, communities need to offer more services to the displaced. They need to spend more, but they have less to spend. In all likelihood, they will not compensate for their fiscal losses by raising taxes for fear it will create the image of an unfavorable business climate and subsequently deter investors from creating new jobs. By the theory of creative destruction, these consequences, as painful as they may be, ought to be temporary, and, ultimately, workers will be reabsorbed. Contrary to theory, however, the displaced, if they are reabsorbed at all, are often reabsorbed into a lower paying retail economy paying 20 percent to 30 percent less than before.[40]

At issue in closure is whether it might not also threaten society in the Lockean sense of the word. When discussing regulation, is there an issue of preserving society? But what is there about closure that is a threat, and if there is one, can we agree that it exists, let alone just what it might be? Bluestone and Harrison argue that closure typifies the deindustrialization of America and is an example of "runaway capital," ultimately threatening the economic infrastructure of the country, as well as the existence of a middle class.[41] And yet, not everyone agrees that this is a serious enough problem to warrant action. They do not see this as evidence of industrial decline.[42]

Nevertheless, as the consequences are the product of a marketplace that is neutral, closure is neutral too. But are they? The effects appear to be experienced disproportionately by the industrial middle class. Still, this isn't all there is to it. Closing decisions are private decisions, a legitimate matter of managerial discretion in a private-market economy predicated on individualism and private-property rights, but the effects are profoundly public. Given the effects, a central question is whether arguments of economic dynamism and private-market economies serve as sufficient justification to make private closing decisions without any real accountability to the public at large. There are two key issues here: (1) who is empowered to make investment and disinvestment decisions that ultimately affect us all and are not simply a matter of private-market actors pursuing their conceptions of good?[43] and (2) can true democracy be achieved if decisions affecting us all in such wide-ranging ways can be made without being subject to our ultimate control?[44]

Those arguing from the position of neutrality might appeal to a literal reading of Locke's resistance theory on the grounds that government through restrictive legislation would be usurping the rights of citizens. The broader reading of this theory demands that government do something about the problem because government can cease to be legitimate if it fails to respond to those forces that effectively strip individuals of their human dignity. Government must always be responsive to the needs of its citizens. In as much as closure may create a problem, Lockean philosophy can just as easily be invoked as a justification for regulating the activities of private actors, especially if the crisis is deemed great enough that action is essential for the preservation of society.

During the summer of 1988, Congress, over the objections of President Ronald Reagan, passed the Worker Adjustment and Retraining Notification Act (WARN). Because it was an election year, and the Democratic opposition was preparing to make an issue out of plant closings, Reagan simply allowed the bill to become law by letting it sit on his desk while Congress was still in session. WARN, which took effect in early 1989, provides sixty days' notice for those plants employing over 100 workers. It fails to provide for any enforcement mechanism other than the tenacity of workers to take to court those employers who fail to give notice. In short, the policy amounts to voluntary compliance. As this was the nation's first plant-closing policy, it could be hailed as a great step in easing the transition for those workers who have to suffer the adverse consequences. But given the vast number of loopholes, it is doubtful that many workers will benefit from this legislation.[45] And yet, this legislation pales in comparison to previous bills introduced before Congress, which in some cases envisaged as much as two years' notification, severance payments to workers, and community assistance payments as reimbursement for declining revenue bases. In general, though, plant-closing legislation generally was unable to gain much support in Congress, largely because the business community was so successful in fighting it as an infringement of management prerogatives.[46]

The Challenge

In order to comprehend the challenge of plant-closing policy, we have to ask whether WARN can be considered effective legislation. If not, what would effective legislation look like? Is our objective to assume that closure is simply a fact of life we must live with and hence to adopt policies that aid the transition? Or is our objective to prevent closure as a means of maintaining our industrial base? If the former, WARN may well be a good first step if it both affords workers some time to plan for the closure and affords communities time to perhaps offer managers a plan designed to enable them to keep their plants open. If the latter, WARN is by no means effective, and we need to consider just what effective legislation would look like. Proponents of restrictive legislation often conceive of it as containing several elements: notification, severance, and community assistance. Although such legislation has never been passed, and most likely never will be, it would be useful to look at the hypothetical possibility. For only by looking at a hypothetical model can it become clear just what the challenging issues are.

Notification requires that employers provide their employees with advance notice of intent to close down a plant. While the intent may appear to mandate socially responsible behavior on the part of employers, the ostensible purpose is to achieve greater efficiency. Provided with advance notice, workers may be able to plan for the closure and possibly arrange for new employment.[47] There is also evidence to suggest that, in those few cases where notification has been given, the percentage of displaced workers finding new jobs has been slightly higher than when notification has not been given.[48] Discounting considerations of efficiency, however, notification does effectively make employers accountable to both workers and communities irrespective of questions concerning human decency.

A severance policy requires employers to compensate their employees for the time they have invested in the company. The amount of severance is often commensurate with length of service. Peripherally, the purpose of severance is to provide workers with some monetary protection upon closure. Implicit, however, is the notion that a worker's physical labor is tantamount to a shareholder's liquid investment. Just as the shareholder is entitled to a return on an initial investment in the form of dividends, the worker is entitled to a return on an initial investment of labor or time in the form of severance. Severance, with what it implies, ultimately equates human capital with monetary capital and suggests that through their investment of human labor workers acquire a stake or vested interest in the company.

Community assistance, on the other hand, would require a firm to reimburse a community for lost revenues as a consequence of closure. Ostensibly, the purpose is to provide assistance to communities experiencing strain on their diminished fiscal capacities. But, as with the other policies, there is an implicit message here as well, for community assistance effectively raises the specter of an implied social contract whereby firms are obligated to provide more to communities than merely the payment of taxes and the provision of jobs while they are there. Or it raises the specter of a new social contract in which the efforts of the community are viewed as investments for which compensation is required.[49] On the contrary, firms do in fact owe more to their communities, and if their actions are going to inflict harm on these communities, they are going to be made to bear the consequences.

The three of these policies together may effectively create financial barriers to the liberty and mobility of capital. By attempting to raise the costs of closure, they serve to create disincentives, if not financial penalties for capital mobility. Not only do these policies attempt to restrict capital mobility, they also attempt to make capital more accountable to workers and communities, and in the process they raise the specter of democratic control over the liberty of capital. But more than this specter of economic democracy, they raise the specter of a new conception of the just society predicated on the rights of workers and communities to possess a degree of control over their own destinies. This becomes clear if we just examine the issues in notification. Once the threatening nature of notification is revealed, one can only imagine what the addition of the other two accomplishes.

Although notification currently doesn't require any more than the simple provision of notice, it does restrict managers' ability to make quick and hasty decisions. Managers often protest that a notification provision limits their options, and although it may not be the same as the physical seizure of property, the limitations placed on flexibility and discretion may have the effect of diminishing the value of their property. If property is understood as a bundle of rights—legal relations between persons governing the use or control of things—notification might just affect the nature of the controlling relationship of corporate property. Does notification not effectively limit the control a manager may exercise in that the manager cannot make a disinvestment decision without first having planned for it? In effect, notification may involve a transfer of control from management to workers. The obligations imposed on employers are no less than effective rights transfers from employers to their workers. This right to accountability that notification grants to workers does give workers some indirect control in that it effectively results in the diminution of absolute control over how quickly a manager may opt to disinvest in one venture and ultimately reinvest in another. Should this constraint inevitably result in a diminution of company value (as measured in terms of profit), this by some standards might constitute a taking. If we return to Ackerman's distinction between ordinary observing and scientific policy making, we can see some similarity between the effects of notification and severe controls on the money supply under monetarism.

If notification could be viewed as a taking, and as the language of *Pennsylvania Coal* makes clear its scope would ultimately determine if it was, the obligation it imposes on employers effectively transfers rights from employers to their workers. The transfer alone could serve as the basis upon which a property right to a job might ultimately be defined. At a minimum, it could be viewed as presaging one.[50] Therefore, if notification forms the basis for a socially defined right to a job, severance, when coupled with notification, only takes the concept one step further. The two together would appear to imply that workers do in fact possess job rights that not only are going to be considered but also are going to be compensated for upon closure.

By mandating these policies, the provision of these protections is no longer a function of the employer's altruism but is an obligation to which the worker is now entitled. Even though the property right might be limited, the precedent essentially exists for the definition of a far more encompassing one. But inasmuch as a worker may acquire a property right to a job, the worker also acquires a degree of control over the use of the plant that would have an impact on this job. If so, the employer, then, also loses some control. And it is this notion in particular that liberalism, as it has evolved in America, has some conceptual difficulties with. Herein lies the dilemma, for even if there is some social benefit to be derived from giving workers a greater measure of control, should such benefits come at the expense of what are already perceived to be the rights of managers?

Values of Society

If closing policy has a basis at all in liberalism, it certainly cannot be on the face of neutrality. Closure and the issues it raises may also speak to our fundamental values. To a degree, discussions of closing policies call into question the viability of a capitalist system in which the essence is free trade. To impose the types of controls on capital suggested by our hypothetical model is to ask just what constitutes the public interest? Has the nature of society become so complex, especially given the interrelationship between our national economy and the larger global economy, that the arrangements that governed us during a time of relative U.S. economic hegemony no longer serve the national interest? Ultimately, plant-closing policy, especially if it is designed to prevent closure, may come close to suggesting that the values of openness and free competitive markets associated with traditional conceptions of liberalism are no longer viable. Rather, there is a need to return to some form of mercantilism. If plant-closing policy is to find justification within the parameters of liberalism, it does raise the question of how the liberal society will define justice, which really speaks to the larger issue of perhaps two competing conceptions of liberalism—neutral versus community.[51]

If justice in liberalism is characterized by the priority of the right over the good, it then follows that in the liberal state there will be a procedural form of justice rather than a substantive one. As there is no objective and substantive definition of goodness, liberalism must embrace procedures—means over ends.[52] The former holds outcomes to be just when guiding principles, such as the protection of individuals' rights to equal respect and treatment, have been completely adhered to. But at the very least, if the outcome is to be truly just, the guiding principles must be uniform, constant, and known by all. Or as Unger would argue, "rules must be impersonal in the sense that neither their making nor their application is determined by individuals and subjective rules."[53] The latter, and one that plant-closing policy in part aspires to, holds outcomes to be just when the community as a whole considers them as such. This would be an obvious implication flowing from neutrality. A substantive conception of justice arising from plant-closing policy suggests that the needs and concerns of the community ought to be placed above the individual pursuit of personal profit—there is in fact a moral absolute that should take priority over individualist goals. This may aspire more to community interests, to citizen obligations and mutuality.

Neutrality requires a demonstration of necessity as essential to striking the balance between responsiveness to the community on the one hand and individual interests on the other. Although advocates of restrictive legislation could point to the social good to be derived from public policy that takes into account concerns of workers and their communities, they would have to make the case that their social goals are so overwhelming that the rights of managers to freely make investment decisions could legitimately be abridged. Or that their rights to a job are more in the interests of society. For if we are to adhere faithfully to the principle of rights, there can be no justification for constraining liberty, no matter how well the general interest may be served.[54] As Sumner reminds us, Mill identified the realm of justice with the realm of perfect obligation, hence rights. For "justice implies something which it is not only right to do, and wrong not to do, but which some individual person can claim from us as his moral right."[55] If liberal society is that in which each is entitled to equal respect and treatment, then liberal society is in fact just when individuals can press their claims for equal respect and treatment as though they were in fact moral rights. If a right, it cannot be denied by the will of the demos on the basis of utility, but on the basis of necessity; that it in fact caused harm, that is, it encroached upon others' rights. So far we have not really deviated from the Lockean ideal.

Equal treatment in plant closings should at the very least mean that those affected by the decision to close enjoy an equal opportunity to be heard. They enjoy the same right to be heard as do those who own and manage capital. For their preferences to prevail is to presuppose that they are worthy of more concern. But to do nothing might be said to allow the preferences of capital to prevail. Dworkin, however, might respond in the following way: Government, if it does nothing, is remaining neutral and hence abides by the principles of the liberal conception of equality, even though there may be an appearance of favorable treatment. Although it might be argued that such a position isn't neutral because it effectively gives preferential treatment to business, the appearance as such wouldn't necessarily suffice to claim that the neutrality principle had been violated. Rather, it would have to be clear that the intent was to favor business, not simply that it had that effect.

If it has been established that a policy of doing nothing wouldn't violate the neutrality principle, the result must be as follows: If those affected by the decision to close are dissatisfied by the outcome of a neutral stance in the face of what they perceive to be a threat, they must respect the rights and liberties of capitalists just as they would want and expect capitalists to respect their rights and liberties. If these are the principles by which we in a liberal society have agreed to live, then it is incumbent upon us to accept them and respect them. But does this not assume too much? Can we really be expected to respect those principles even if they no longer support current reality? Objective circumstances do change. We did not agree to live by principles of neutrality; rather, we consented to have government serve society. While plant closings may result in inequalities in wealth and income, they don't violate liberal neutrality as might, say, restrictive legislation. At issue, then, is whether restrictive legislation effectively gives preferential treatment to a group of workers at the expense of others. If so, not only is it at the expense of managers' rights, but also it might be at the expense of the larger community if the case can plausibly be made that restrictive legislation would amount to nothing more than restrictions on plant openings.[56] What if, in the course of affording protection to the workers of plant A in community B, the health of regional economy D, of which B is only a part, suffers?

Dworkin makes a distinction between law and policy—the difference between that which people are necessarily entitled to and that which it is desirable for them to have. By distinguishing between the two, policy can find justification on the grounds that it is of benefit to society subject to a constraint that it not impinge on people's basic and fundamental rights. The distinction thus serves as a foundation for a positive state. It isn't entirely clear where Dworkin would fall in this debate, but there is an argument to be made in favor of—as much as there may perhaps be one against—closing restrictions in Dworkinian terms. The case might be made that equal respect and equal treatment entitle those who are to experience the brunt of the closing decision to some form of notification. That to close a plant without the minimal provision of notification is to deny a segment of the population equal treatment and concern. The capitalist, however, would argue, and indeed Dworkin himself might argue, that to close without notification is a violation of equal treatment only if workers have been led to believe that their jobs are permanent and that there was in fact some understanding that jobs would not be terminated unless proper notice was in fact given.

The real question, then, is what would fall within the rubric of basic and fundamental rights? We thus have to ask whether people have a right to their jobs? Can the closure of a plant be said to constitute a deprivation of that which workers are entitled to? To a certain extent, plant-closing policy might be said to be confusing a concern for what is good for workers and communities with what workers and communities have a right to. Although it might be desirable from a public-policy position to adopt measures to slow down the movement of capital if that would put a halt to shutdowns, it doesn't mean that workers and their communities have a right to expect government to adopt such measures. While liberalism does sanction regulation for the protection of the public's health and welfare, is there necessarily a case to be made that this standard is seriously threatened when displaced workers are forced to accept new jobs at lower wage rates? Do workers necessarily have a right to be protected against those forces which would lower their standards of living?

Individuals living in a liberal society, especially one embracing freedom of markets, are assumed to be rational actors. As rational actors they understand the costs and benefits of all their actions. This implies that they understand the meaning of risk; that when they take a job they also understand that there are never any guarantees. At any time, they can lose their jobs and when they do, it is incumbent upon them to find others. So long as people accept these principles, the closing cannot be taken to be a violation of any liberal conception of equality. Consequently, it is not to be taken as the fault of the manager that the displaced found reemployment but at a considerably lower income level. The question again is whether workers can be said to enjoy rights to those specific jobs that they have been displaced from over other jobs that might be available upon reentering the job market. If workers can be said to be entitled specifically to those jobs they have, is the effect not to coerce employers to remain in business against their will? Simply put, what now happens to the framework in which individuals would be free to pursue their own conceptions of good? It is true that regulation in the past effectively limited one's pursuit of good for the sake of the community's larger good. But is there not a substantive difference between restricting what one can do so as to prevent harm and coercing one to do what one would simply prefer not to on the basis of some community conception of entitlement?

The history of liberal evolution is the history of restricting the rights of private actors in the marketplace for the larger community. Some people even see the trend as part of a general erosion of property rights.[57] Moreover, given a general rights revolution that had the effect of immunizing individuals from risk, it is understandable that workers would come to view protection of their jobs as an entitlement.[58] Nevertheless, a democratic society whose sovereignty is based on all the people must in fact represent all the people. Advocates of effective policy are effectively requesting a more evenhanded distribution of decision-making power. According to Michael Walzer, the political community should be the setting for the distribution of goods. This would at the very least be the appropriate arena for the distribution of goods in a democratic society. But once democratic society undertakes to provide some needed good, "it must provide it to all the members who need it in proportion to their needs. The actual distribution will be limited by the available resources; but all other criteria, beyond need itself, are experienced as distortions and not as limitations of the distributive process." A community according to these principles may not allow its members to starve if food is available to feed them. "No government can stand passively by at such a time—not if it claims to be a government of or by or for the community."[59]

Application of this formulation to plant closings should then result in the following postulate: A government claiming to be democratic, predicated on principles of popular sovereignty, cannot allow its citizens to suffer the hardships and economic dislocations of plant closings, especially if it has the wherewithal to mitigate and ameliorate those hardships. To stand by and do nothing is to abandon the principles of community. More to the point, however, Walzer's formulation just might be an appropriate statement on the evolutionary nature of liberalism. Which is to say that if liberal society has allowed itself and has found justification for government intervention (the provision of needed goods) in the past, it would not be justified to stop here. The evolution of liberalism from its classical conception to its contemporary interventionist version presupposes certain obligations by government to the public. By intervening in the past, the expectations it has generated among the public may ultimately be tantamount to obligations on the part of government to meet them. Government has an obligation to deal effectively with the plant-closing issue. Though this isn't to say that government has an obligation to pursue a specific set of policies, it would be shirking its responsibility by simply doing nothing. The important point is that an obligation of liberal society should not be confused with a specific policy course. It can hardly be said to be meeting its obligations if its policies end up being at cross-purposes with the underpinning ideal. And this is perhaps the ultimate dilemma that the hypothetical model of closing policy may present to liberal public policy predicated on neutrality.

The issue that plant closings present us with is whether it is possible to preserve the liberal promise while at the same time enabling democratic government to meet its obligations to its citizenry. Is it possible to reconcile the liberal conception of equality with community notions of justice as they would be determined by the community to fit the needs of the community? Liberalism as it has evolved in America has held the protection of rights to be a matter of principle and the formulation of policy to be a matter of social desire. But can the community arrive at a new conception of justice that is also based on principle? Just as social goods and justice are relative concepts, so too are social principles. Plant-closing policy might be justified in Dworkinian terms if it can be shown to be in fact necessary for the protection of the public's health and welfare and not something that simply makes workers better off. But in demonstrating the necessity of such policy, it must also be clear that it wouldn't have an adverse impact on the public at large. This would require some proof that regulation that might restrict the rights of property owners' investment decisions would not have a destabilizing impact on the economy, either because plant-closing restrictions might potentially mean fewer new openings or because the tone it sets is such that it jeopardizes investor confidence. Though it isn't entirely clear that plant-closing policy would have this effect, in part because it hasn't adequately been tested, the burden of proof ought, from a moral stance, to be on those seeking the policy. Within the context of Ackerman's dialogue, they must justify why their position is not just simply a question of a particular good that might be better, but why their position is in fact necessary for furthering the public interest. Or to satisfy Rawls's criteria, it must make everybody in society better off.[60] But more than making everybody better off, it must be shown why they will be better off.

For those seeking a plant-closing policy, the premise of neutrality-centered liberalism may simply be wrong. For the one closed out of one's job, *right* is then defined as the protection of social and communal welfare. Perhaps the real challenge is that liberal theory predicated on neutrality asks that workers imagine themselves as though they were under Rawls's contrived veil of ignorance where, in the absence of knowledge about their resources and each other's, they would choose those principles that would protect their rights. They would automatically choose the traditional liberal conception of procedural justice because the neutrality inherent to that concept would protect their rights and, by so doing, preserve their claims to equal respect and treatment. But this presupposes that there is such a thing as *principle* transcendent of individual conceptions of it derived from visions of *goodness*.

On the contrary, as Sandel and others would argue, one's identity can never be divorced from the circumstances in which one lives. To suggest otherwise only negates the reality that we are as such creatures of our environment. We are members of a community, and we can't simply separate ourselves from social circumstances and imagine ourselves under Rawls's contrived veil of ignorance. Who we are is shaped by our own personal experiences, and it is these experiences that give us a sense of what constitutes principle.[61] And yet, as we have seen earlier, this is the essence of Locke's theory of socialization. Consequently, concepts of right and good are nothing more than relative. They are in fact socially defined. Hence if liberalism is indeed a doctrine of openness—a rejection of absolutes—there can be no such theory as inviolable rights. Rather, rights are designed to protect claims to certain guiding principles: "first principles." Hence, they could just as easily be defined to protect substantive equality. Rights, then, are not natural, they are utilitarian. The implication being that it ought to be possible to arrive at a more community-oriented conception of justice while still remaining within the confines of liberalism.

What is particularly critical about the preceding discussion to the issue of plant closings is that, simply put, they don't occur under a veil of ignorance; rather, they occur in the bright sunlight of understanding. Whereas Rawls's principles would serve to protect the rights of capitalists against the encroachments of restrictive legislation, it doesn't aid those who might feel that once these liberal principles of justice have been accepted, what is to prevent those who are protected by those principles from abusing them? Both Rawls and Dworkin would hold that once rights have been seriously dealt with, it's then government's responsibility to deal with the questions of the general good. But as Sandel points out, there can be no concept of the general good that is separate and distinct from conceptions of individual good. What the problem of plant closings suggests is that, given the inherent substantive inequalities in liberalism, there is a need for a conception of justice that takes into account considerations of community. But our problem with this is the need to reconcile community predicated on the good with rights. Plant closings in effect require that we reconstruct our social values. Or that we at least be willing to redefine the nature of property rights.

By shifting the focus from the individual to the security of the community, issues in plant-closing policy do underscore the problem of basing policy on neutrality. To return to a point made earlier, policies, like plant closings, do force us to define in clear terms just what the objectives of the community are and what set of circumstances represent a crisis that directly threatens that community's very survival. In the end, if according to neutral criteria individuals cannot be prevented from disinvesting and the costs to the community are such that it is effectively wiped out, what happened to the value of mutuality? On what basis is an inclusive community revolving around a common project built? Or, for that matter, on what basis is any community built?

Corporatism

If there is a progression at all from regulation characteristic of the Progressive Era through monetarism to plant-closing policy in its hypothetical form, it is this: The role of government is transformed from one of simple mediation to active management to ultimate control. By government assuming the type of control that effective plant-closing legislation would impose, if it could be enacted, there is an effective joining of the public and private realms that neutrality, by contrast, had required be separate. Full democracy is effectively achieved if the public as a whole is able to exercise final control over private investment decisions and to subordinate private concerns to the larger public interest.[62]

Through this progression, the neutrality principle has effectively been abandoned.

The history of plant-closing legislation in this country shows that the hypothetical model is by no means likely, not only because it presses against our reigning ideology, but also because closure has never been considered a serious enough problem that it could gain support. WARN, as we have seen, is the result. But this alone does not signify victory for neutrality. The question underlying WARN still is, to what end? While the objective is to ease the transition for workers, it is also to ease the transition for communities. It was also intended to give communities an opportunity to present managers possible options for keeping the plant open. But what options?

Given the nature of today's global economy, the implications would appear to be clear: national survival or the preservation of American society perhaps requires policies whose goals of maintaining economic stability assume a strong connection between society and state. If such policies are to be framed within the parameters of those liberal principles core to the civic tradition, then ultimately the measure of policies has to be whether they further liberal objectives of maintaining the social fabric of the community, and not whether they are framed according to a Rawlsian or Dworkinian formula of neutrality. Among those policies aimed at stabilizing economies these days, especially in Europe, is corporatism. The hypothetical model of plant-closing policy may or may not go beyond corporatism, depending on how one views it. The hypothetical model of plant-closing policy certainly does raise the specter of economic democracy in which private investment and disinvestment decisions would be subject to democratic control. The interests of the community are placed above capital, and stability is assumed to be achieved through preservation of community. While policy advocates, especially in the time-honored tradition of incrementalism,[63] view WARN to be a good first step, it could well pave the way toward corporatism. One way to view the hypothetical model, then, is as a final recourse if corporatism fails. Nevertheless, there are those who might view corporatism as even more controlling, because it might not be considered to be as democratic as the economic democracy that the hypothetical model of plant-closing policy might achieve.

More common in Europe than in the United States, corporatism entails a cooperative relationship between government, business, and labor. The objective is to reach an agreement on wage levels so as to maintain economic stability, presumably in the larger public interest. In part, corporatism rests on the assumption that wage inflation, a product and factor of general inflation, ultimately results in unemployment. As Kerry Schott explains: "In modern conceptions of corporatism, organized labour, an organized employer group, and a social democratic form of government together articulate their concerns at a tripartite level and decide their actions. These three groups, it is argued, are the important and powerful actors in society."[64] It is essentially a system of regulating conflict between interests groups in society. Though it in part rests on the assumption that the community's economic growth does rely on greater cooperation between the major economic interests, it also assumes instability to be a function of conflict between these groups. Corporatism, as Leo Panitch explains, finds its "modern roots in those versions of nineteenth-century social and political thought which reacted against the individualism and competition which characterized the emerging dominance of the capitalist mode of production, and against the industrial and political conflict between classes which was the ineluctable product of this development."[65]

Corporatism, then, is nothing short of planning. What, then, is the ultimate purpose of notification laws if not to provide communities a basis upon which they can plan? The concept of corporatism, best summed up by Philippe Schmitter, is that "societal corporatism can be traced to the imperative necessity for a stable, bourgeois-dominant regime . . . to associate or incorporate subordinate classes and status groups more closely within the political process."[66] It is a political structure that "integrates organized socioeconomic producer groups through a system of representation and cooperative mutual interaction at the leadership level and of mobilization and social control at the mass level."[67] But Gerhard Lehmbruch takes the concept a little further by suggesting that more than simply a pattern of articulating interests, "it is an institutionalized pattern of policy formation in which large interest organizations cooperate with each other and with public authorities not only in the articulation (or even 'intermediation') of interests, but—in its developed forms—in the authoritative allocation of values and in the implementation of such policies."[68] Ultimately, though, corporatism is a model of social control.[69]

Although it is questionable as to who benefits the most from a corporatist arrangement, it is often seen as a subordination of labor interests to those of capital with the aid and blessing of government. As David Cameron puts it: "Corporatism can be seen as a system of institutionalized wage restraint in which labour, acting 'responsibly,' voluntarily participates in and legitimizes the transfer of income from labour to capital."[70] Because capital holds the upper hand in this arrangement, we can see a parallel with the traditional liberal society that cannot force individuals to do anything but can only offer incentives for them to do so.[71] As Charles Lindblom has made clear, investment and prosperity in the market economy predicated on liberal foundations is induction as opposed to command.[72] And yet, there is the assumption that the functional representation of trade unions and business organizations is equal in power and influence in economic decision making.[73] Such an assumption may not say much however. Although labor is represented in the equation, is it going to be taken as seriously as business?

Corporatism in this country is regarded as a form of fascism, in large measure because of the liberal tradition out of which we view it. As Lehmbruch points out, with neocorporatism, the classical liberal distinction between the state and society is being blurred. Also, as individuals succumb to social pressures to join large interest groups, much of the voluntary character, which is supposed to distinguish it from an authoritarian system, will be eroded.[74] It is considered to be an example of centralized planning in a society with a long tradition of either decentralized planning or no planning at all.[75] By establishing wage rates at the government level, workers are denied the freedom of contract. This runs contrary to the essence of freedom as Americans have traditionally understood it. But does it really? Should the National Labor Relations Act (NLRA), which for all intents and purposes institutionalized such a framework, not be viewed as a precursor to corporatism? The NLRA was premised on the belief that stability could be assured if management and labor could be forced to the bargaining table, even under the threat of a strike if necessary.[76] True enough, it isn't the type of economic democracy that Peter Bachrach and Aryeh Botwinick talk about,[77] but it does presuppose the partnership of labor, albeit at the junior level. Or by protecting workers' rights to strike, labor is able to achieve some equality in the bargaining process.

Whereas corporatism is often described as a top-down approach in which labor's interests are often subordinated to those of capital, corporatism may still be an example of economic stabilization policy allowing for some worker participation, unlike the others already discussed. As we have already seen, labor has not participated in traditional forms of regulation, nor has it participated in monetarism. In fact, the challenge these policies pose to liberalism is that they are not necessarily responsive to the public at large. Plant-closing policy, especially if it was framed according to our hypothetical model, is inevitably the response of the public to what are often regarded as the irresponsible business decisions of private economic actors. Could not some element of democracy be considered to be contained in corporatism insofar as it does allow for some participation on the part of labor? Also, if some version of corporatism could be achieved in this country, would it not also be on the basis of some contract similar to that which created and still continues to sustain legitimate government? The problem is that corporatism isn't the same as pluralism. Whereas pluralism assumes voluntary association, corporatism requires compulsory association.[78]

Corporatism is a response to the same pressures that managers often claim compel them to close up shop. Hence it could be the next step in a pattern of public responses following the type of minimalism displayed in WARN. Even though it does not go quite as far as, say, the model of economic democracy embodied in the hypothetical model of plant-closing policy, the important point is that it is a potential policy aimed at achieving stability. But it is also one that would clearly defy neutrality, largely because it is premised on centralized state activity. Whether we choose to recognize corporatism as part of the American arsenal of stabilization policies, we can see any number of traces of what Schott refers to as weak corporatism. By weak corporatism, she means little cooperation between employers and trade unions, with frequent lockouts and strikes.[79] This is clearly assumed by the NLRA, as it was assumed that economic stability would be achieved if labor was empowered to bargain for reasonable wage and labor conditions. Underpinning the theory was the assumption that the right of labor to strike would give labor a potent weapon to force management into negotiations. After all, neither side would want to suffer the hardships of either a labor dispute or disruption in the production process. It was legislated into law on the further assumption that the public had a vested interest in ensuring tranquil labor-management relations. But corporatism also presses against liberalism because of its compulsory nature.

Hence the question of what happened to neutrality. If it violates neutrality, corporatism cannot be liberal. But is this really so? Corporatism may well rest on authoritarian assumptions. The question, however, is whether it is arbitrary and coercive. Clearly, corporatism shares something with the other policies insofar as it seeks to preserve the larger community. It does presume a degree of contract and assumes some mutual benefit. In the typical exchange relationships in Europe especially, employers get considerable support from the state. Labor achieves organizational stability and incremental change, and all it really has to give is its commitment to social order. The state gains influence over economic management in a capitalist economy, and the price it pays is that it allows for the participation of organized producer interests.[80] But is it placing the burden fairly? Is it not assuming that much of the cause of economic instability is ultimately the demand of labor for higher wages? This may not be a fair assumption—any number of studies on plant closure hold closure to be a function of managers' insatiable greed in some cases and their inefficiency and ineptitude in others.[81] Just what sacrifices are the community and business interests to make? Is neutrality not violated if one group is effectively being singled out to make primary concessions? Government's role is primarily that of coordination. But why shouldn't business be expected to give more?

Dilemma

The ultimate question is, just what is in the national interest? Politically speaking, government cannot antagonize capital for fear that it might engage in a capital strike.[82] Constitutionally speaking, insofar as the constitution represents our central faith as a nation,[83] government cannot seize private property and effectively run the business itself. The

Court made this abundantly clear in *Youngstown Sheet & Tube v. Sawyer* when it held the Truman administration's seizure of the steel mills during the Korean War, in an attempt to prevent interruption in steel production, to be an unconstitutional abridgment of private property. It violated the due process clause of the Fifth Amendment, not only because government had no intention of compensating the owners for their property, but also because Congress, through the Taft-Hartley Act, had provided for a procedural mechanism to maintain production precisely during a national emergency.[84] The Taft-Hartley Act specifically provided for a cooling-off period during a labor dispute. This, then, is the point. Seizure of property doesn't violate the public interest; rather, the issue is the arbitrariness by which it may be seized. This is really the issue in Locke's tract on property.

Because all the policies discussed so far raise some important questions about relying on liberalism's neutrality measure, we are forced to ask whether neutrality can really serve as a measure for determining whether policy framed in the name of liberalism can be said to achieve the ultimate objectives of a liberal society. What becomes clear from this trajectory is that as government must find ways to respond to greater complexity in the economy, the discord between the type of neutrality at the root of earlier liberal responses and these is even greater. And yet, they are often pursued in the name of achieving a greater sense of community. These policies, in short, are justified in the name of liberalism.

It would appear that if neutrality is the measure by which we determine whether these policies are liberal, we have moved from liberal to nonliberal as we have progressed through the trajectory. If the liberal state wants to employ such policies—as greater social complexity may require—and still call itself liberal, it must then make the case that other principles exist by which they can be measured. This isn't to dismiss neutrality altogether but to move beyond it.

4. *Welfare Policy*

WELFARE in the liberal state may ultimately present liberalism with some of the most serious challenges because the whole concept raises questions about the self-sufficiency of individuals. On the one hand, respect for personal autonomy requires that government not interfere in people's personal lives so they are free to make those choices that best reflect their conceptions of good. That some people are poor in society is assumed to be a function of the choices they have made. Theoretically, if individuals required government to stand by and allow them to make their choices, they have no right to ask government to pick up the pieces when those choices go awry. They must bear the consequences of those choices government was obligated to allow them to make. Welfare thus challenges liberalism because it raises questions about the actual freedom we have to make choices. It may well be a critical reminder that the choices we do make are not completely of our own volition but are affected by, and often are the product of, circumstances and forces beyond our control.

Welfare presents liberalism, especially that which is neutrality based, with a serious dilemma. As Donald Moon notes, certain tensions exist at the heart of the liberal theory of the welfare state. On the one hand, liberalism seeks to limit the sphere of political authority by creating as much room as possible for individuals to organize their social lives through voluntary interaction and exchange. Welfare provision is suspect because its compulsory character limits the scope of individual liberty, and also because it poses the danger of paternalism. On the other hand, contemporary liberalism has sought an expansion of the scope of social provision so that individuals can secure those welfare rights necessary to maintain moral agency.[1] Welfare is, and has been, resorted to as compensation for the marketplace to allocate resources.[2] It thus bears similarity to other forms of government intervention, most notably regulation. What perhaps distinguishes it from regulation is that it is more positive because it is an attempt to assist people.

And yet, welfare seems to engender greater enmity than other interventions. Responses often tend to be more visceral. Although there is considerable acrimony over regulation and other forms of intervention, opposition to welfare tends to be more emotional. In the 1980 presidential election, Ronald Reagan capitalized on certain abuses in the welfare system. By charging fraud and talking about the "welfare queen," he was able to exploit widespread resentment among blue-collar workers, particularly in the southern states. Much of the emotion stems from the redistributive nature of the policy. Those who receive must be supported by those who work and pay taxes. But some of the dissension may also stem from ambiguity over the very meaning of welfare and how it is best achieved. Hugh Heclo observes that Americans are perhaps caught between two conflicting traditions of welfare. On the one hand, there is the tradition of "welfare as self-sufficiency," a conception supremely individualistic, and very much in accordance with classical conceptions of liberalism grounded in narrow constructions of neutrality. On the other hand, there is a tradition of "welfare as mutual dependence," a conception dealing with social or group-oriented rationality.[3] It is this second tradition that accords more with community and tends to support arguments about the moral imperative of social provision. Whereas the first reflects the atomism of individuals, the second reflects the interconnectedness among persons in a community.

At the same time, the dichotomy would also appear to be well reflected in popular conceptions of social policy generally. Americans have no principled objection to national government action on the poor's behalf, but they aren't necessarily supportive of specific programs on their behalf. As Americans still believe in capitalist markets and many of the underlying tenets of laissez-faire,[4] a premium is still placed on the value of independence. Though Americans are willing to help those who cannot help themselves, the poor are still expected to make good-faith efforts to help themselves.[5] Such a dichotomy clearly raises questions as to what ought to be the objective of welfare. Should welfare policy merely be for the amelioration of poverty? As much as this may be an immediate goal, insofar as it strives to provide the poor with some minimum level of subsistence, welfare policy perhaps ought to extend beyond this. Might independence not be another goal? That is, if individuals are poor because they lack the necessary skills and competence to hold down a job and effectively make it on their own, shouldn't the objective of a welfare policy be to enable individuals to become self-sufficient by providing them with the necessary skills and competence? The ambivalence of the public might appear to support the contention that social policy ought to be geared toward enhancing personal independence while simultaneously ameliorating poverty conditions.

Arguing from a philosophical position, Robert Goodin suggests that the task of the welfare state is the promotion of people's welfare—to do what is good for them. But how do we determine what is doing good for people and by what criteria? Moreover, who decides? To even talk about doing what is good for people is to construct a paternalistic relationship between those who are doing good and those for whom good is being done. The purpose of the welfare state isn't so much to satisfy people's desires as it is to simply meet their needs. By meeting people's needs, the welfare state fulfills the ultimate purpose of contributing to personal autonomy.[6] But just how has it sought to do this? The injunction to meet people's needs still begs the question of just what needs must be met and whether they can be met in such a way that the objectives of society are furthered. The latter question may actually be more important because the validity of those needs may speak more to whether the means can really be justified.

Criticism against welfare policy in the United States has come in two varieties. The first, as exemplified by Murray and Banfield, is what could be regarded as the rational activist critique. It argues that as individuals add up their benefits from public assistance and weigh them against the benefits of working at unskilled minimum wage jobs, along with the costs of working—the loss of some forms of in-kind assistance—they will find no incentive to work and plenty of incentive to stay on welfare. For Murray, in particular, the result of U.S. social policy, especially since the 1960s expansion, has been that the poor have been hurt. In essence, there were no incentives to get off welfare, but plenty to stay on.[7] Or as Banfield suggests, some simply would rather go on welfare than accept low-paying, even minimum-wage, jobs. The existence of "informal minimum" wages predicated on middle-class notions of reasonable compensation generally above the official minimum makes it socially acceptable for the poor to accept handouts instead of working. It would, after all, be "unreasonable" to accept less than what middle-class opinion considers to be "fair."[8] But such studies show that recipients do take a "commonsense" approach to work when weighing the overall benefits against the costs.[9] The welfare system was not designed to encourage people to work; rather, it was designed to allow women—mostly widows—to stay home with their children.[10] The welfare system as it was structured simply contains no work incentives.[11]

The second model, best exemplified by Mead and to a lesser extent Mickey Kaus, can be regarded as the social breakdown critique. According to this model, welfare doesn't accomplish its goals, not because the incentives are wrong, but because recipients have not been socialized into norms of appropriate behavior.[12] Mead specifically tells us that the poor do not work because of some "mysterious" reasons.[13] Though to a certain extent this model is willing to concede welfare realities, the issue boils down to so what? What is at stake is the work ethic. Mead's principal quibble with the welfare state, especially as it expanded during the 1960s, is its permissiveness. Welfare policies have been too permissive because they failed to demand anything from recipients in return. Because no expectations were made of them, the poor as a result have been hurt by welfare policy.[14]

There is still a third variety of criticism, and that is the purely libertarian critique. Best represented by philosopher Robert Nozick and constitutional theorist Richard Epstein, this critique is important because it cuts to the essence of neutrality-based liberalism. And, to a considerable degree, it fuels Murray's own philosophical assault on American social policy. For as much as Murray falls into the rational activist model, he nonetheless touches on some philosophical issues cutting to the core of liberal theory. Murray asks: "If social policy may be construed . . . as transfers from the haves to the have-nots, the proper first question is, 'What is the Justification for any transfers at all?' Why should one person give anything to a stranger whose only claim to his help is a common citizenship?"[15] Earlier, Nozick suggested that to give welfare to those who do not work is to effectively force others to work on their behalf. As expenditures for social programs for the benefit of the poor require the imposition of taxes on those who work, the system entails nothing less than forced labor. To take taxes from one's labor to give to others is no different from forcing one to work additional hours for another's purposes. Such transfers, then, simply constitute a form of compulsory charity. But a system of taxation effectively obscures this effect, largely because people do not stop to calculate their withholdings in terms of additional hours worked.[16] These transfers, then, constitute in Epstein's words, "coercive actions whereby the government assumes the role of Robin Hood, taking from the rich and giving to the poor." Though the ends might be noble, the means are bad, just as Robin Hood was a "bad man with good motives."[17]

Critics often tend to brush these concerns off as unduly selfish, with claims about our moral obligation to feed the poor on the basis of "just" principles.[18] Yet, to simply ignore these questions may raise questions of legitimacy. Ironically, perhaps, these criticisms, while no less an assault on modern liberalism, are actually the language of civic liberalism. Murray has a simple solution: Just eliminate welfare policies so that the poor will have incentive to go out and work. This may be too simplistic. Aside from the obvious political difficulty that would arise from attempts to dismantle the whole welfare-state bureaucracy,[19] it assumes poverty to be a personal problem. It fails to account for many of the structural sources of poverty; that (1) there may be more unemployed persons than jobs, and (2) many of the poor simply lack the education, resources, and training necessary to obtain employment, or to obtain employment that will pay livable wages.[20] One can hardly argue that those forces requiring regulation of business for the prevention of undue harm may bear absolutely no responsibility for individuals' personal poverty. Also some of the data would suggest that Murray's claim about the failure of social policy is just plain wrong. Some data suggest that when factoring in-kind assistance in with AFDC (Aid to Families with Dependent Children), the number of persons living below the poverty level decreased. In 1960, the number living below the poverty line was 18 percent, but by the mid- to late 1970s that percentage decreased to between 4 percent and 8 percent.[21] Moreover, the claim that social policy has further eroded the family may rest more on coincidence than solid cause-and-effect analysis. It is less likely that AFDC has been the source of marital breakup, than that AFDC has provided women with alternatives to marriage, especially fragile ones. At a time when a number of marriages were breaking up generally, it doesn't follow that it was the existence of AFDC and other programs that caused them to dissolve.[22]

Still, to simply focus on the data also misses the point. Murray's critique really hinges on theoretical presuppositions of what constitutes the good society. Insofar as he has a moral case to make, the successes and failures of the War on Poverty become totally irrelevant. The issue isn't so much whether current programs have been relieving poverty, but whether past efforts have worked to foster greater self-sufficiency and, in a larger sense, whether policy has served to further the interests of society. The challenge Murray presents to liberalism is whether welfare policy in the form of gifts or transfer payments can be said to further the philosophical tenets of liberalism. Can liberals who championed such policies honestly say that it accords with their own philosophical precepts? It is a challenge that only becomes more compelling when joined by Nozick and Epstein.

Still, underlying all three varieties of criticism is the unstated challenge that welfare policy, whatever it is intended to accomplish, is going to be problematic if framed in accordance with liberalism's underlying premise of neutrality. To an extent, the underlying assumption has been that if government would simply provide the opportunities and the tools for the poor to make it on their own, they would naturally know what to do with them. As rational individuals who could think for themselves, they would have the capacity to discern what was in their best interests. Neither would government have to coerce, nor would it have to be in the business of making choices for people. It would simply tinker with the framework and leave the choices up to individuals. In line with neutrality, the incentive system could be modified. In accordance with incentives, it was always assumed that welfare would be nothing more than temporary. Welfare, it was assumed, would never be as attractive as work. Moreover, the provision of assistance wasn't really the objective of the War on Poverty programs.

Rather, the objectives were to generate opportunities so that more Americans would be able to realize the core ideals of independence. Inaugurated during the Kennedy administration under the influence of writers such as Galbraith and Harrington, they were a response to the poverty personally observed by Kennedy on the campaign trail in Appalachia. It was at Howard University during a commencement address in June 1965 that President Johnson unveiled his Great Society program. Echoing a long-embedded ideal of liberalism in America, the president spoke of equality of opportunity. What individuals needed were not handouts, but opportunities to work—jobs—so that individuals would be able to realize for themselves the ideals of the American dream. But more than opportunities, they needed the skills that would enable them to take advantage of opportunity. Coming on the heels of passage of major legislation in civil rights, Johnson proceeded to declare the next stage in the battle for civil rights. This was to comprise a set of programs designed to create opportunity and to provide the skills and competence necessary for blacks to be able to achieve economic equality as well.[23] But in talking about equality of opportunity, Johnson was clearly evoking a traditional liberal image of independence and self-reliance. This was no different from the language of the eighteenth-century bourgeois radicals who shaped America's classical liberal public philosophy[24] and those who assumed that the Lockean ideal was about opportunity to acquire unlimited wealth.

The War on Poverty saw the introduction of such in-kind assistance programs as medicaid, food stamps, and public housing and rent supplement programs. Model Cities programs also targeted depressed areas for revitalization, and residents of those areas were to be provided with training and other resources necessary to achieve economic empowerment. On one level, these programs would appear to be nothing more than public charity. And yet, altruism has rarely been a precipitous policy unless attached to some crisis. The expansion, constitutive of the Great Society, would appear to also have been influenced by those political pressures unleashed by the civil rights movement.[25] The Howard University speech had been preceded by the Moynihan report on the black family, a report initially drafted as a working paper for the purpose of carrying civil rights into its next stage: equality as economic empowerment. Moynihan's report, as well as the politics surrounding it, would also influence the expansion of AFDC and other entitlements.[26] During the 1960s, eligibility had been broadened to include certain unemployed parents in two-parent families as a response to charges during the 1950s that AFDC was in fact encouraging families to disintegrate.[27] But, increasingly, more and more single mothers were receiving assistance under AFDC. Moynihan attributed the increase to the deterioration of the family, a function of the cycle of unemployment, despair, and subsequent marital breakup. This cycle only tended to reinforce patterns of matriarchal domination, clearly evident in increasing numbers of female-headed households.[28]

The 1960s generally was perceived to be a period of crisis. It was a period of intense protest, ranging from the civil rights movement—as a movement for political equality—to the violence of radical groups demanding social justice and other redress for past injustices. It was also a period of assassinations and rioting, as well as antiwar protests. In the minds of many, it may have represented the ultimate in social failure, for which a government response would be needed. To adopt programs so that individuals would be able to ultimately stand on their own two feet could be viewed as preserving society within the context of the Lockean ideal. At the same time, part of the Great Society included the hiring of attorneys who would sue the welfare bureaucracy on behalf of the poor, thereby leading to an even greater explosion. Welfare came to be viewed as a right, and all those on welfare were considered to be equally deserving of a helping hand. Among those welfare rights fought for were rights not to be raided in the middle of the night. During the 1950s and 1960s, welfare officials would typically stage midnight raids into the homes of recipients to enforce the "man-in-the-house rule." Moreover, as many of these raids were directed against blacks, the removal of barriers to the receipt of benefits became yet another cause of the civil rights movement.[29]

Nevertheless, in responses to claims in the 1970s that welfare was encouraging dependency by removing incentive to work, Congress did attempt to reform the system by allowing recipients to keep a portion of the benefits in addition to whatever wages they would earn. Recipients who did work would typically suffer a reduction of benefits on a dollar-for-dollar basis. But there was a problem with incentives, which Nathan Glazer illustrates well when he describes the issues involved in the Family Assistance Plan (FAP) introduced by the Nixon administration. The idea was to create a minimum-income floor. Families would receive this supplement regardless of whether the husband or father was there. To preserve the work incentive a negative income tax would be imposed, whereby FAP would be reduced by a certain percentage as earned income increased. The favored rate was 50 percent, which produced the following dilemma: A dollar-for-dollar reduction meant that there was no incentive. The question, then, was how much of an incentive would exist if the negative tax was set at 50 percent? If the FAP grant was set at $4,000, household heads would receive FAP money until they earned $8,000, after which they would receive nothing. But if the negative tax was set at 25 percent, recipients would be eligible for FAP money until they earned $16,000. Moreover, all those families of four earning less than $16,000 would be eligible for FAP money. "In practice, either total costs ballooned to the point where conservatives (and not only conservatives) were frightened, or the FAP allowance was so reduced, and the tax rate so increased, that liberals rebelled."[30] On the other end, there was the issue of work incentives. To provide a minimum-income floor was to lessen the incentive to work, and for many this was sufficient to mobilize public opinion against it.[31] While this reveals a political limitation to adoption of what some might deem an effective social policy, it still begs the question: Even at a 50 percent negative tax rate, wouldn't most rational people find it more lucrative to work? One clearly receives more money than the allowance itself. That incentives do not result in people behaving according to the rational activist assumptions in liberalism should only suggest that there are other behavioral patterns that liberalism has either been ill-equipped to deal with or has simply failed to address.

Nevertheless, the nature of criticisms raises serious issues in welfare policy. First and foremost is the question about objectives. What should the objectives of the liberal state be when it comes to the formulation of welfare policy? If welfare policies derive their justification from liberalism, have they been successful in furthering liberal objectives? By offering assistance, is the liberal state ultimately undermining its own very foundations? Second is the question of behavior. If it is determined that there is a problem of an underclass whose values and behavior are considered deviant by the general population, is there a set of adoptable policies that can be aimed at forcing compliance with middle-class norms but will not compromise human dignity in the process? Can the liberal state demand something in return for benefits? Again, as with the other policies discussed so far, if such policies can be justified on the basis that they further liberal purposes, they may not be able to rely on neutrality for any real justification.

Perhaps as a starting point, we ought to be clear as to what criteria welfare policy, whatever its form might be, has to satisfy if it is to aspire to liberal idealism. At a minimum, it would be agreed that with as much latitude as there may be regarding policy specifics, they must conform to criteria in accord with the goals of personal autonomy and integrity. Goodin suggests the obvious criteria of exploitation and arbitrariness, neither of which is mutually exclusive. But they do flow from neutrality. A policy in conformity with these principles may be neither exploitive nor arbitrary. As the objective of the welfare state is the protection of the vulnerable, and it is based on a moral responsibility to meet our duties to dependent others, it can hardly meet its obligation if it exploits. For Goodin, "exploitation" consists of a certain type of behavior in a certain type of situation, which would essentially boil down to taking advantage.[32] And yet, the means of taking advantage may not be as obvious as they appear. Insofar as the prevention of exploitation and arbitrariness does work to ensure a framework conducive to human agency, they are in keeping with liberal objectives. But the other criterion which clearly must be considered is whether the policy in question works to preserve the moral fabric of society—that which binds the community together or effectively undermines it.

Is Welfare Policy Exploitive?

The proper first question to consider is whether welfare policy has been exploitive. However, not only should the question be addressed from the vantage point of the poor but also from the vantage point of the nonpoor. When talking about programs that take advantage of people, it is important to consider that there are two sides to the equation. If exploitation is going to be a criterion, at issue is whether policies can be formulated that strike an equitable balance between both sides.

The Poor

Questions of exploitation regarding the poor generally turn on the application of administrative procedure and the fairness of the requirements that recipients must satisfy. All federal assistance is means-tested. To qualify for assistance under AFDC, mothers must demonstrate that they have no substantial savings, no earned income, and no spouse (or significant other) who would offer support.[33] If there is no spouse, mothers are still required to furnish information regarding the whereabouts of the father.[34] Many will undoubtedly show little sympathy for fathers failing to support their children, but the argument might be made that the administrative requirements do occasion the possibility of arbitrariness, especially if failure to cooperate should result in nonreceipt of benefits. By offering benefits—but subject to a host of administrative constraints—are we not putting those whom we are charged to protect in a situation whereby they are likely to be exploited?[35] If so, are we then affording these individuals the equal respect and treatment not only assumed by neutrality but to which they are rightfully entitled as citizens of a liberal democracy? They, too, are entitled to mutuality.

At issue for welfare agencies has been whether those on assistance would be free from legal constraint, free from arbitrary administrative procedure. Speaking to this concern during the early 1960s, Charles Reich suggested that when government gets into the business of providing largess, the administrative requirements necessary to the provision of that largess, especially in the absence of well-defined rights to it, occasions the possibility for arbitrary exercises of state power.[36] Two possible implications could be drawn from this: (1) that welfare should either be defined as a right analogous to other rights we enjoy and protected by the same laws of due process, or (2) that those who receive benefits do so in accordance with clear and explicit procedures, including a right of appeal. While the two may ultimately accomplish the same objectives, the second is less absolute than the first. Instead of defining a right to welfare as such, the second simply states that those who qualify for benefits will be treated equally and according to the same rules of fairness. Yet, the rights and freedoms of those putting money and resources into the public welfare system have perhaps been protected at the expense of those taking money out. The freedom of recipients is effectively limited by procedures designed to protect the interests of taxpayers or the "public at large." The loss of freedom for the former, then, is viewed as compensation to the latter for its sacrifice.[37] To do nothing, as some critics of the welfare state might prefer, would be equally exploitive.[38] But doesn't the issue of exploitation cut both ways? Though there is the issue of exploitation of recipients, who by no means surrender their rights as citizens, there is also the question of exploitation of nonrecipients, those who may view their tax dollars that support the welfare state to be a form of compulsory charity.

The Nonpoor

The issue of exploitation of the nonpoor, as we have already seen, finds good expression in the conservative critique articulated by Murray, Nozick, and Epstein. Consider, then, the Nozick-Epstein claim that transfer payments are essentially a form of compulsory charity. Even those who do not necessarily agree with the position will concede the welfare state to be an institutionalization of charitable giving whereby those who give do not possess direct control over the gifts they give. The welfare state is, in crude terms, a form of "government-directed charity."[39] Jeremy Waldron, for instance, attempts to address this claim by distinguishing between active intervention and passive forbearance. Within the context of active intervention, refusal to be charitable is simply an omission—passive refusal to intervene. But in passive forbearance, refusal to be charitable entails the withholding of forbearance. The uncharitable act becomes one of positive intervention—to prevent one from partaking of that which one needs. In the former, enforcement of charity is simply coercion—forcing one to do what one otherwise would not do. In the latter, enforced charity becomes a response to coercion involved in the refusal to be charitable. For the enforcement of charity in this case "involves preventing someone from stopping someone else from doing something." Thus, if liberals subscribe to the second model, the enforcement of charity "will always be a response to coercion or the threat of coercion, it is never, on any account of the causes of social deprivation, to be taken as an illegitimate first use of force." As the withholding of charity is already coercive, enforcement of charity can always be viewed as a liberal response to that coercion. Though passive forbearance may dismiss the Nozickian charge of forced labor, holding it to instead be "enforced idleness,"[40] it still begs the issue of exploitation. At issue still is just what the community is willing to forbear.

Even if passive forbearance is not to be regarded as coercive, the question still remains as to whether the liberal community can rightfully attach conditions to the receipt of benefits. Also at issue is whether through these conditions recipients are exploited insofar as their freedom may be limited. Insofar as tensions in constitutional jurisprudence reflect tensions in liberalism,[41] we can obtain some guidance from a series of Supreme Court rulings that support the view that conditions can be attached to the receipt of benefits without intruding on individuals' fundamental rights.[42]

In *Dandridge v. Williams*, for instance, the Court ruled that Maryland's imposition of a ceiling on monthly AFDC benefits, regardless of family size or actual need, was neither in contravention of the 1935 Social Security Act nor the Fourteenth Amendment's equal protection clause. Plaintiffs argued that limiting benefits without regard to family size would effectively discriminate against those children who perhaps had the misfortune of being born into larger families, thereby creating invidious distinctions. But the Court held that in the area of economic and social welfare, a state does not violate the equal protection clause merely because classifications ensuing from its laws are imperfect. On the contrary, it asserted the public interest in a state's policy aimed at offering incentive to seek gainful employment. It is important to note that recipients could work without a reduction in grants.[43] What is most important about this case, however, is the attempt by the Court to appeal to people's basic sense of fairness. Equality was to be viewed more broadly than simply a condition between recipients. Rather, equality involved the comparative relationship between the welfare poor and the employed poor. As the Court asserted: "And by keeping the maximum family AFDC grants to the minimum wage a steadily employed head of a household receives, the state maintains some semblance of an equitable balance between families on welfare and those supported by an employed breadwinner."[44]

Three years later, the Court in *New York State Department of Social Services v. Dublino* held that New York State's work rules, which required the cooperation of employable individuals as a precondition to continued receipt of benefits, were not preempted by the federal government's Work Incentive (WIN) program, which was presumably less demanding. The work rules presumed that certain recipients were in fact employable, and hence certain expectations could be made of them: They would have to (1) file every two weeks a certificate stating that no suitable employment opportunities were available, (2) report for requested employment interviews, (3) report to officials the result of a referral for employment, and (4) willingly report for work when available. The Court concluded that these rules represented a legitimate state interest in encouraging work among those who want it. WIN would not preempt New York's work rules because it was regarded as a partial program and thus a minimum set of standards, but there was absolutely no prohibition against states building upon them. On the contrary, the Court asserted the legitimacy of a state to promote "self-reliance and civic responsibility, to assure that limited state welfare funds be spent on behalf of those genuinely incapacitated."[45]

The Court only reinforced the position that conditions could be attached to the receipt of benefits in *Lavine v. Milne*.[46] Here, the Court held there to be no constitutional violation by a statute that would disqualify from the receipt of benefits for seventy-five days anyone who voluntarily terminated employment just to qualify for benefits. The Court made it clear that there was absolutely nothing in the Constitution that would entitle one to benefits prior to a determination of an applicant's qualifications. Or, for that matter, there is absolutely no entitlement to benefits at all. What becomes clear is that the reasoning in these cases parallels the second possible implication of Reich's argument, not the first.

Nevertheless, the argument might still be made that the very fact that recipients are able to bring suit, as they did, presupposes a right to welfare provision. The point that might be lost, however, is that these cases simply revolve around policy implementation, for which no one is entitled to anything. Rather, at issue is when government has agreed to implement a program—to, in fact, provide something—whether that implementation in any way violates the equal protection clause. Even then, there would appear to be implicit in these rulings the notion that invocation of the equal protection clause isn't entirely legitimate. As the equal protection clause seeks to prevent either discrimination or unfair treatment of individuals regarding that to which they clearly have rights, it can hardly be invoked on those matters for which they have no rights. Further justification for this position can be found in the traditions surrounding interpretation of the Fourteenth Amendment's privileges and immunities, due process, and equal protection clauses, which have roots in the *Slaughter-House Cases*.[47]

The language of these cases would clearly point toward the conclusion that welfare is nothing more than policy predicated on the altruism of the community. If the community offers it as part of its desire to achieve certain goals, it may do so on its terms. Similarly, if the community desires to achieve a basis for fairness as its goal by attaching conditions, it may do so. The Court made it abundantly clear that the language of rights had no place in welfare. The Court was not prepared to say that welfare recipients could be shielded from responsibility simply because they were in a vulnerable position. Rights talk, as Glendon argues, effectively shields us from responsibility to others and effectively misses the fact that our ability to pursue our individual goals and ideals is intimately connected to the setting in which that pursuit takes place. On the contrary, the experience of other liberal democracies only demonstrates that forceful rights talk can occur and not to the exclusion of a well-developed language of responsibility. This is the notion that "rights need not be formulated in absolute terms to be effective and strong; and that the rights-bearer can be imagined as both social and self-determinant."[48]

But is the Court saying that traditional neutrality is irrelevant, or simply that there is another dimension that must be considered? In the meantime, however, if we take it as a given, as modern liberalism has in recent years, that individual freedom isn't a real possibility without some minimum standard of equality—itself entailing a degree of economic security—it must obviously follow that through some institutional mechanism the state has a responsibility to ensure it. And while the welfare state is clearly a supplement to the market mechanism for ensuring some minimum level of equality, there is nonetheless the question of how we balance the claims of those receiving benefits against those being asked to provide them. Can we strike a balance between the rights of recipients and those of nonrecipients?

The welfare system in the United States has attempted to strike this balance through the establishment of administrative rules and regulations designed to ensure, if nothing else, that public money is being spent responsibly. Though the rules and regulations have added to the stigma of poverty, they have also perhaps been necessary, at least for political purposes, to find the middle ground between the two welfare traditions of which Heclo speaks. As authorities in the United States expect applicants for assistance to prove need, there is a presumption that they will have exhausted all their personal resources and effectively impoverished themselves first. This assumption of welfare as a last resort actually parallels a fundamental assumption in neutrality that government intervention is the last resort in the mediation of conflict. But might we not be able to achieve a balance, more common ground, through another policy approach? What about work? The point about these Court rulings is they concern the imposition of administrative procedures. Insofar as procedures also serve to diminish discretion—hence the arbitrary power of bureaucracy—the Court may well have been speaking to the other side of neutrality. The most neutral policy would be to simply give people money and allow them to do as they please. But that does not satisfy the public's need for accountability—to know that public money is being used responsibly. Moreover, it might be sending precisely the wrong message. By simply giving away money without any corresponding demands, are we not picking the easy way out? Are we not expressing little faith in the poor's ability to function like the rest of us?

Welfare and Work

If society does have a responsibility to feed its poor, and we should take it as a given that a just society does, is it necessarily obliged to offer assistance in the form of transfers or can it rightfully require them to work? As liberalism has been a social theory relying heavily on agency, wouldn't a work-oriented policy aimed at fostering independence be more in keeping with the liberal tradition? As an alternative to simple transfers, and somewhat of a throwback to the work programs of the 1930s, is the concept of work for benefits, or what has come to be known as workfare. In its simplest form, workfare calls for those receiving public assistance to work off the value of their benefits. It is often argued that tying welfare benefits to work teaches recipients the lessons of social obligation without making them feel as though they are parasites on the rest of society.[49]

Those who argue the value of work couch their argument in terms of obligation, citizenship, and public benefit. They talk about the need to administer the welfare state according to juridical principles. Mead, for instance, suggests: "Programs imply a certain balance of benefits and obligations seem critical for the success of the program." Welfare recipients might function more appropriately when society makes expectations of them abundantly clear.[50] Kaus views it as essential to the revitalization of liberalism because it appeals to the lost civic tradition. The ideal of civic liberalism is to achieve social equality as opposed to income equality. Yet, social equality is threatened by the existence of an underclass—a group or subculture that does not share the same values of the majority of citizens. The goal of civic liberalism, then, is to achieve social equality by stressing our equal obligations as citizens, and this can only be achieved through the common project of work. As Kaus explains, the goal is to break the culture of poverty by providing jobs for ghetto men and women with little work history and few work habits. This in the long term should result in the welfare culture being absorbed into the working, taxpaying culture. Not only will this result in a budgetary payoff, but one for social equality as well.[51]

In this vein, critics like Mead depart from market purists like Murray. On the contrary, Mead recognizes the need to support the needy, but insists that they should also be expected to work if able-bodied. That is, they shouldn't be treated differently from anybody else. To be treated the same as everyone else is the very meaning of equality, one of the leading values of American life. But equality entails common obligations, which would appear to specify certain social duties alongside political ones. The clearest social obligation is work for the employable, an obligation no less in conformity with America's traditional work ethic. Equality "demands that they take back the duties to work. . . . For, given the even-handed nature of citizenship, only those who bear obligations can truly appropriate their rights."[52] In the name of equality, then, demands must be placed on the poor; that if they are to receive public assistance, they must offer society something in return. Or as Fullinwider explains: "The reason for tying work requirements to welfare is to prevent welfare aid from undermining the capacity of recipients to fulfill the responsibility of self-sufficiency."[53]

Arguments for work are not just about self-sufficiency and citizenship but are also about simple fairness. Many might find it to be both inequitable and unjust if government were to create public-sector jobs and recipients could legitimately choose between those and not working at all but still receive benefits. This just might "effect an erosion of the will to work among those who now have it." Moreover, work requirements would not only enable the poor to fulfill their obligation to society and become more independent, but also through the public-sector jobs they would create, they would help to improve the appearance of our cities.[54] Would a welfare policy predicated on work requirements be more in keeping with traditional liberal precepts? Mead argues in theoretical terms that those who seek benefits should be forced to work. Kaus, however, gets more specific by advocating that the type of welfare we currently have should be completely eliminated and replaced with a Works Progress Administration (WPA)-style program in which everyone would be guaranteed a job at a rate of pay slightly below minimum wage. Those who need assistance would simply have to report to job sites and perform service in exchange for benefits.[55] Under Kaus's plan anybody could show up and get paid, even affluent individuals, but because the rate of pay would be less than minimum wage, there wouldn't be any incentive for them to do so.

Workfare

Workfare was first legislated at the federal level in the Omnibus Budget Reconciliation Act of 1981, which permitted states to establish Community Work Experience Programs (CWEPs) in conjunction with existing AFDC. States participating in CWEPs would then require participants to "earn" their welfare benefits by working a specified number of hours in projects serving a useful public purpose. The specific number of hours would be determined by dividing the value of a household's benefits by the prevailing minimum wage. Initially, state participation was voluntary, but the Reagan administration later expanded its scope by making participation mandatory. Still, the reach was limited.

Liberals have generally considered workfare to be coercive because of the requirements that recipients work. They are often critical because its implementation raises the specter of authority. Also underlying it is the assumption that the poor are responsible for their own poverty. From the Left, critics of workfare, like M. E. Hawkesworth, hold workfare to be punishment specifically for being poor. More than imposing authority, it seeks to manage and control the poor, thereby denying them their rights to be themselves in resistance to the conformity of the majority. It incorporates many hallmarks of discipline because it conceives of the individual psyche as an object to be managed and controlled. Ultimately, then, it embraces punitive sanctions for nonconformatory type of work.[56] In essence, then, the authoritarian nature of the program effectively denies recipients their personal freedom. Yet, Auletta's study of the Manpower Demonstration Research Corporation (MDRC) in New York shows that the goals were as much to socialize recipients.[57]

This particular emphasis on individuality actually distorts liberalism. The notion that government should be respectful of individuality holds that government ought to establish a framework in which individuals are free to make choices for themselves regarding what is good and how best to live their lives. It is not a concept embracing the view that individuals should behave in ways contrary to community standards. Locke makes this abundantly clear in his tract on the development of language and socialization.

Perhaps the real challenge of workfare is the assumption behind the so-called coercive element. By mandating requirements, there is the presumption that individuals are not behaving according to the rational activist principles assumed by liberalism's virtue of individualism. Rather, behavior on the part of the poor is not in conformity with general social norms, and therefore these norms must be addressed before the problems of the inner city can be seriously addressed.[58] The presumption is that individuals must be resocialized. In other words, the traditional approach, which relies on neutrality, of throwing money at a problem simply does not work. At issue for liberalism is whether by engaging in serious discussions of individuals' behavior, there is then a presumption that certain types of individuals are not capable of making choices that are agreeable to society unless instructed on how to do so. Is this not then another way of appealing to a distinction with deep roots in classical liberalism between the "worthy" and "unworthy" poor? The "deserving" poor, including widows, orphans, the disabled, and the elderly—those who were poor through no fault of their own—were to be treated with sympathy and charity. The "undeserving" poor, those who were simply lazy and otherwise lacked "moral character," were to be treated harshly. And the underlying assumption of AFDC, that those in need would principally be widows with young children, only tended to reflect this distinction. The assumption that households with fathers would not need support was also reflected in AFDC's initial title of ADC, Aid to Dependent Children. The newly defined "unworthy" poor lack not only the skills and resources essential for acquiring employment but also the moral character to be considered worthy of participation in the community. Could this not be viewed as a basis for discrimination on the basis of invidious classification?[59]

Given the efforts liberals have made over the years to tear down the walls of discrimination, this can be problematic. Neutrality, after all, does require that if we are to treat people equally and not to discriminate, we cannot make exceptions to general rules unless we have good cause. The real question is whether there is a problem of underclass that rises to the level of a crisis. Even by Mead's own admission, only a small proportion of the poor can be said to fall into the underclass. Depending on how it is defined, the number of people falling into the underclass is only two million to eight million people, or .9 to 3.5 percent.[60]

Returning to the idea of a framework for a moment, a framework is just that: a zone of freedom in which there is a presumption in favor of individuals, but not necessarily one of unrestricted freedom. Moreover, the very existence of such a framework presupposes the existence of obligations. On one level, government is obligated to respect the interests of its citizens. On another level, if equality is to prevail, citizens are then obligated to respect the interests of each other. Liberals often talk of their interests in terms of rights, but rights always carry with them corresponding obligations. Obligations are, after all, the corollary to rights, as rights can never be secure unless someone, some group, or some institution feels a moral duty to respect them. Moreover, if obligations are defined by the polity in a democratic society, the minority—those who do not necessarily believe that the obligations ought to apply to them—do have a moral responsibility to abide by them. They have an obligation to obey laws "because of the benefits that are necessarily accepted along with residence, in part because of the expectations aroused among one's fellow residents, and finally because of the universality of obligation in a democracy, from which no resident can easily exclude himself." Individuals have obligations to submit to even those laws that they do not like so long as there are available channels for "open disagreement and political struggle."[61] Essentially, the obligations we have are derived from the same consent that formed the Lockean contract, which formed the basis for the definition of rights in the first place.

Though many might concede workfare in its simplest form to be exploitive, the Hawkesworth claim that workfare attempts to legislate a type of conformity does pose some conceptual difficulties. Implicit is perhaps the notion that nonwork is a legitimate expression of individuality. Is this not the type of claim that the conservative-libertarian critiques of Murray, Nozick, and Epstein capitalize on? Certainly, we all enjoy the right to opt for unemployment, but if we freely choose unemployment, can we legitimately ask society to subsidize our decisions? Accepting for a moment Waldron's claim that forbearance may not be coercive, if the public is being asked to forbear what it does not consider to be reasonable, does it not then have a right to set forth expectations in accordance with what most rational individuals would consider to be reasonable? If people are on welfare because of choice, most would consider the limits of public forbearance to be pressed, in which case the public would have the right to expect those existing outside the norms to conform. Such programs may not be coercive, but they are exploitive in that they are taking advantage of the altruism of those who work. In a truly democratic order, the public has the right to define the terms of its existence and whatever norms are essential for its existence. Is this not then pressing the limits of neutrality?

Of course, this presupposes that individuals freely choose to be on welfare. Conservatives often miss this point. There is a difference between actively choosing to be unemployed and being forced into unemployment because of circumstances beyond one's control. Part of the argument made by conservatives relies on the assumption that any number of unskilled jobs go unfilled because many of the poor consider such jobs to be beneath them. What if people are on welfare either because there are insufficient jobs or because they lack appropriate job skills? Is workfare not then exploitive if its only purpose is to keep people busy, but the experience isn't transferable to the job market? If workfare fails to prepare individuals for permanent employment in the private sector, is it not then exploitive in that it fails to foster self-sufficiency? As with its welfare counterpart, workfare of this variety may still leave the poor dependent on the welfare bureaucracy administering the work program. Instead of providing recipients with good, solid, transferable skills, it may effectively punish them for lacking those skills. If this is so, workfare does rest on fallacious assumptions about the nature of poverty.

People aren't always poor because they lack drive and determination but because they lack opportunities and the necessary resources to seize upon them when they arise. Work requirements without the necessary support programs to make work viable do not enable the poor to work off the value of their benefits.[62] Moreover, states trying this approach have failed. Massachusetts, for instance, tried mandatory workfare for fathers on AFDC, but two-thirds of those who were placed in jobs left them within thirty days.[63] This statistic would only lend support to the argument that many of the poor do not share the same work ethic, or that the poor may have different values and attitudes from mainstream norms. This point would only appear to be confirmed by Auletta's study of the MDRC, which was not completely effective in reforming deviant behavior on the part of the poor. MDRC was essentially aimed at the hardest to reach of the poor—those considered to be the core of the underclass—and it effectively guaranteed a job for a year. Although such job guarantees did reduce crime slightly, they did not reduce drug use. Moreover, an attitude problem was discovered among many recipients, especially those who failed, in which they perceived the world as being against them. This perception alone served to justify behavior not in accordance with general social norms.[64]

On a practical level, though, workfare has been criticized for failing to foster self-sufficiency because its goals are simply to keep people busy and because the busy work they are given doesn't provide them with any skills transferable to the job market. Instead of providing recipients with good, solid, transferable skills, it effectively punishes the poor for lacking them. Work requirements without the necessary support programs to make work viable do not enable the poor to work off the value of their benefits.[65]

Liberals, however, might well be missing the point here. The objective is not to enable the poor to satisfy a reciprocal relationship with society—quid quo pro—but to teach them about their obligations to the community so that they can become responsible citizens. Success is then measured in terms of understanding what is expected of them and then being able to act accordingly. Consider Mead's comparison study of WIN offices in New York State, where he found that those offices that were clear in conveying work expectations and obligations to recipients were the most successful in getting them to actually participate in training and search for work.[66] The objective, then, isn't punishment but socialization.

The rejection of work requirements, or other conditions, really has no solid grounding in liberal philosophy. On the contrary, the emphasis on individualism, and the corresponding requirement that government be limited, implies that individuals are capable of being self-sufficient and that government must afford them the necessary room to be. From a policy stance, a state that attaches a premium to individualism will do what it can to ensure that individuals achieve as much self-sufficiency as they can. Conceived in this way, it then follows that the liberal promise will be upheld when government, in prizing the self-sufficiency of its citizens, affords them the room to be self-sufficient. Therefore, liberalism should reject all government interference—even welfare provision—on the grounds that it effectively intrudes on the ability of individuals to live independent lives and may ultimately affect their ability to make choices.

Mead suggests that liberals in many respects have come far afield, that there has almost been a reversal. Liberals have abandoned the "competence assumption." They have essentially become pessimistic about the poor's ability to make it, and hence they have attributed to them a more vulnerable identity. Conservatives differ in that they assume the poor are competent enough to work and to meet their obligations. Although cognizant that the poor may not be competent enough to take advantage of incentives, conservatives demand work from them because they are more optimistic about the abilities of the poor.[67] If this is true, liberals have betrayed their own underlying philosophy. Freedom of choice, after all, does assume that one has the competence to make choices. If they aren't competent, then why should they be assumed to be able to reason for themselves what is good? But if they aren't assumed to be competent, and that as vulnerable people they need to be protected in a paternalistic way, why would liberals assume that simple modifications in the incentive system would suffice to reform the system and motivate the poor to work?

Liberals have assumed that if the state attaches conditions to the receipt of welfare benefits, it is being coercive. But if this is true, liberals would have to reject the welfare system as it exists now on the same grounds. If the procedures currently in existence (that is, eligibility requirements) might be said to be coercive, why is this any less coercive than requiring people to work? Are liberals assuming that the former enables autonomy while the latter does not? As Stephen Holmes notes, liberals have always accepted some degree of paternalism "so long as it was autonomy-enabling—somehow a reinforcement of individual freedom as well as an expression of collective self-rule."[68] If so, work requirements, because they would effectively socialize people into responsible work habits, are ultimately autonomy enabling.[69] By instilling within recipients the values, as well as the skills, necessary to confidently enter and remain in the active workforce, individuals are then able to rely on their own abilities for subsistence and not on public assistance programs. By requiring recipients to work, they will in time acquire the competence necessary to rely on their wits in the labor market.

Liberalism's Dilemma

The principal argument against attaching conditions to welfare benefits is that it is coercive. It is coercive in that one who is forced to work due to a condition beyond one's own control is effectively being punished. It is analogous to servitude: it restricts the freedom of the recipient. To force one to do something in exchange for basic subsistence lacks compassion. It is the imposition of authority over these people's lives. This can be considered nothing less than cruel. Liberalism is a doctrine traditionally rejecting authority and coercion. Its origins lie in the rejection of the authoritarian structures of the feudalistic order in Europe and the coercive tendencies and effects of that order through the imposition of moral absolutes. To respect human dignity, as liberalism requires, means we have to tolerate all individuals regardless of their status, and we have to be willing to help those who are less fortunate. But there is more to this. To couch the issue in terms of citizenship really strikes a raw nerve.

Judith Sklar has made an interesting argument about the importance of the American work ethic to the concept of citizenship. Seventy-five percent of the American public believes that something is wrong with not wanting to work. The problem, as she points out, is that when recipients are told that they must work in exchange for their benefits, or that they must work at whatever job is available, they see the specter of slavery. "And the persistence of racism makes that fear plausible. To those who want to see workfare made compulsory, the idle poor are no longer citizens. They have forfeited their claims to civic equality and are well on their way to behaving like unemployed slaves, kept consumers who do not produce."[70]

To those who viewed the civil rights movement as a quest for inclusion—the attainment of full citizenship—calls for workfare must seem like a regression. The language of workfare, after all, isn't really punishment, but the meaning of citizenship. And yet, herein may lie the problem: The civil rights movement was about who were citizens and who would so become. Are those who talk about obligations not suggesting that they really are not or should not be so considered? Such arguments may come close to implying that for those who struggled to obtain citizenship, it would be permissible to now revoke it because many of the same people aren't conforming to the new demands of the majority. But why focus only on the work ethic as the basis of citizenship? Why not deny citizenship to those who choose not to vote? The problem may in part be the messenger. Because conservatives have generally been opposed to both civil rights legislation and welfare, there has been a perception that those seeking to attach conditions to welfare are simply looking for yet another reason to deny citizenship. The liberal response naturally has to be that if we are all equal before the law, citizenship is a basic right and that it cannot be made conditional.

Still, the question remains, how do we help those who are less fortunate without being too paternalistic in the process? Mead's discussion of the competence assumption is particularly interesting because, by abandoning it, liberals are effectively placing less faith in the ability of the poor to work than in those who assert their need to do so. Liberals are effectively assuming them to lack the ability to function appropriately, so let us just take care of them. This effectively trivializes them and thereby reduces their moral worth. Maybe this serves a political purpose of diverting attention and effectively ignoring the issue. But this clearly does not square with liberal philosophy. By emphasizing the capacity to make choices liberal theory assumes individuals to have moral worth worthy of respect. If liberals truly respected the poor, they too would assume that the poor do have the capacity to meet obligations and would expect them to do so. On the other hand, it isn't clear that Mead as a conservative has any greater faith in their competence than do the liberals he criticizes. To talk about teaching them how to behave is to make the same assumption that there are individuals in society who are incapable of distinguishing between right and wrong unless government comes in and instructs them.

But as much as liberalism opposes authoritarianism and coercion, it isn't clear that workfare, or policies like it, reach the level of coercion characteristic of the moral absolutism imposed by the ecclesiastical orders of sixteenth-century Europe. The argument that attaching conditions to the receipt of welfare is coercive suffers on the following grounds: selectivity, amnesia, and a distorted obsession with authority. Although a case can be made that state efforts to affect behavior—at least in dictating how people ought to behave—defy the moral neutrality that Rawls, Dworkin, and Ackerman attribute to the liberal ideal, it would nonetheless be a difficult case to make that attaching conditions to the receipt of benefits does so as well. This is all the more true if it is done in accordance with some procedural ground rules. Moreover, talk of neutrality here would appear to be either contradictory or plain hypocritical. One cannot invoke neutrality as a means of affording each equal respect and treatment while at the same time assuming these same people, to whom we are to afford equal respect and treatment, to be incompetent and therefore in need of protection. Dealing with complex problems does require that we make hard choices and, in fact, resort to an ordering of values, not that we do what is easy because we think it is the most neutral.

Selectivity

Liberals can hardly justify unrestricted provision for fear of coercion but at the same time justify general regulation, such as protection of the environment. Is a regulation—what may well be referred to as a cost of doing business—not the same as attaching conditions to one's pursuit of private interest in a market economy? Consider the case of physicians who rely on largess in the form of licensure to practice their profession. Conditions are regularly attached, and, as with welfare, they vary from state to state. Is this not then coercive? Granted, the conditions for medical licensure, and even conditions for doing business—general regulation—are in the larger public interest. Or, as liberals might argue, the positions of physicians and welfare recipients are unequal because the poor are vulnerable. Both arguments, however, fail. If one of the arguments that liberals want to use against conservatives is that the language of poverty is essentially the vocabulary of invidious distinction,[71] they must then recognize that, at least on an abstract level, the conditions for one group may be equally as coercive as the conditions for another. Failure to recognize this fact only perpetuates invidious distinction.

Even if liberals, in their attempt to impose a certain type of behavior, wanted to argue that conditions for welfare are different, the argument still runs into some trouble. Regulation, generally speaking, is a state effort through the force of law to force people to behave in certain ways. Are environmental and consumer product-safety regulations not predicated on the assumption that, left on their own, businesses' behavior will be socially irresponsible? As the market cannot force socially responsible behavior, then society must force the issue. To this end, a welfare policy aimed at affecting behavior operates on similar premises. It effectively calls upon society to compensate for the failures of private institutions that should have performed the socializing function.

On a practical level, liberals can make distinctions between what matters fall within the purview of the public interest and what matters do not. This, however, may be a more complicated task partly because it isn't for just liberals alone to define the public interest—it is the right of the polity as a whole to determine what constitutes the public interest. To categorically deny that conditions for the receipt of welfare benefits are in the public interest is myopic and may ultimately fail the test of reason. After all, if dependency is the result, is it not in the public interest to modify policies so that dependency will be broken? If laziness, or even general social breakdown, is the result, is it not similarly in the public interest to modify policies accordingly? In a democratic society, these are matters the community as a whole must decide.

Consider for a moment Walzer's contention that the primary enemy of justice is domination as opposed to inegalitarian distribution of goods. Of course, another way to state this is that the primary enemy of liberalism is servitude or lack of liberty, not an unequal distribution of wealth and income. At issue is membership in the community, for without it abuses are sure to follow. But in a democratic community, the community defines who may be admitted and who may not, which ultimately means it defines the terms of membership, or in a larger sense the terms of citizenship. While Walzer would suggest that prolonged unemployment effectively deprives individuals of membership because it represents "a kind of economic exile, a punishment that we are loathe to say that anyone deserves,"[72] it doesn't necessarily follow that conditions for welfare—a policy that Walzer at best believes will help, but will not confer self-respect—will in any way undermine membership. Participation is central to citizenship, and as Walzer argues, poverty should not have to be abolished before the poor can participate in the life of the community.[73] By this logic, requirements that recipients work, or any conditions for that matter, ought to be acceptable insofar as they serve to socialize individuals into the same patterns of general citizen participation as everyone else.[74] As the liberal tradition in America represents a trajectory of enhancing citizen participation, whatever measures serve to fulfill those objectives can be said to fall within the larger tradition. And even by the terms of the Lockean contract, participation is a prerequisite to consent.

When liberals assert rights without corresponding obligations, they forget that the liberal tradition in America rests on a conception of citizenship based on contract. Contract by its very nature requires obligation. Here public opinion cannot be ignored. In their survey of popular attitudes on inequality, Kluegel and Smith found that most Americans, despite some variation, subscribed to the "dominant ideology," that income inequalities were acceptable because opportunities existed for people to make it. In line with this notion that individuals are ultimately responsible for their own fate, most Americans, while they would not want children to starve, believe that welfare transfers without any work requirements are essentially contrary to those values they have grown up with.[75] And according to a study by Cook and Barrett, even though support for the general welfare system was found among the public and members of Congress, when specific programs were analyzed separately, there was considerable variation. Support for AFDC, for instance, tended to be less than for programs like medicare and social security.[76] It must be assumed, then, that in the minds of most, effective membership in the community requires some contribution to society as a precondition. In this case, that contribution is work.

Amnesia

The argument that the attachment of restrictions is coercive also suffers from amnesia. Much of contemporary liberal public philosophy in America revolves around Mill's harm principle. In the absence of any harm, government should not interfere. Human happiness, however, is predicated on the protection of two vital interests: autonomy and security. Mill was concerned that a significant expansion of welfare would foster dependence on the part of those who were in need. This would violate autonomy. But to not offer any provision in accordance with the dictates of laissez-faire would jeopardize security. Although he considered a right to welfare to be necessary to the survival and autonomy—the dignity and self-respect—of its recipients, he also felt compelled to attach conditions to that right that would otherwise negate that dignity and self-respect. As necessary as a right to welfare might be to survival and autonomy, it could never be absolute. Rather, it would have to be conditional on what the community would feel is necessary to prevent long-term harm to either the individual or the community.

At the same time, Mill made it clear that those who couldn't read, write, or do arithmetic or who paid no taxes and were on welfare should be denied the right to vote because they had not demonstrated the competence to make it on their own, sufficient to participate as full-fledged members of the community. They were to be excluded because they had not demonstrated even minimal interest in taking care of themselves, much less an interest in the general good.[77] Of course, this is no different from Walzer's community that defines its terms of membership. Two sets of consequences, then, must be weighed against each other: the benefits of assistance and the consequence of dependence that would be destructive to autonomy. For Mill, it is important that the position of the recipient be less desirable than that of the self-supporting laborer.[78] Locke, too, was of the mind that the able-bodied poor ought to be put to work, and forcibly if necessary.[79] While participation could be constructed in the very narrow act of voting in the spirit of republican government, it would appear that it has to be viewed within the broader context of socialization and the collective desire of people to work toward a common project.

Distorted Obsession with Authority

To hold that welfare programs that make demands of recipients are illiberal because they raise the specter of authoritarianism is to misunderstand what liberalism has specifically been opposed to. Even though Locke's primary concern was with arbitrary government, he certainly recognized that the state had the power to coerce. At issue was under what conditions coercion would be legitimate. Coercion could be legitimate if it was for the public interest. As discussed in chapter 2, the state could regulate, hence interfere, if it was for the public good. Preservation of the community according to a Lockean standard would also include its moral fabric. The classical liberal conception of contract did presuppose that individuals freely choose to submit to some type of authority.[80]

Therefore, it does not follow that work requirements would be authoritarian insofar as they would preclude the ability of recipients to make choices. It is questionable whether such requirements would erode the independence of the poor any more than it already has been eroded under the current welfare system. Insofar as the one in need must make application to the state for assistance, the case could be made that any requirements that would be attached to that assistance would be no different from the requirements imposed upon any party freely entering into a contractual arrangement. To state this in larger terms, to demand the benefits of citizenship requires that one bear part of the cost.[81] To say that the program is coercive because it penalizes failure to participate with the loss of benefits becomes somewhat dubious.

In essence, the work requirement effectively transforms the welfare apparatus into a form of pubic works, not dissimilar to the private labor market. Such penalties, then, might be viewed no differently from the typical employment situation, whereby someone failing to meet an employer's expectations is terminated. The fact that it raises the specter of authority hardly suffices to render it violative of liberal principles. As Flathman points out, adherence to the ideals of citizenship does require subordination to authority.[82]

The real issue is arbitrariness. What liberalism has specifically been opposed to is unchecked authority—that which can act arbitrarily. Nothing is necessarily wrong with work requirements so long as they apply to all recipients equally and are not arbitrarily applied and enforced. It isn't that we have not had work requirements, for we did with the WIN program, but the enforcement of WIN has in fact been arbitrary. As Mead made clear, some offices chose to enforce the requirements and others did not. Those who enforced them, were ultimately more successful in getting people off the welfare rolls.[83] If fair procedures exist, it cannot be maintained that work requirements are coercive, any more than it could be maintained that filing income tax returns or registering automobiles is coercive. On these grounds, Mead's and Kaus's requirements for work may actually be less exploitive than Murray's call for the elimination of programs. For this is implicit recognition that human dignity and integrity cannot be maintained through starvation. It is certainly less harsh. And at the same time, they may also show greater respect for the integrity of individuals. They, in fact, demand that individuals be treated equally, that no distinction can be drawn between the poor and the nonpoor. Or, at least, to be viewed as equals by one's peers, there must be participation in the common project.

Still, that there is nothing in liberalism that is necessarily violated through the imposition of conditions does not entirely dismiss the fact that a workfare policy, whose only purpose is to demonstrate to the public that the poor are fulfilling their obligations, is not necessarily autonomy enabling. That is, if workfare is framed out of cynicism and not a sincere commitment, it may not be in full accord with liberal purposes of human dignity. This is especially so if programs, in the process of socialization, do not also provide the poor with the skills and competence to continue being self-sufficient and productive members of society. Or at least it might not be conforming to Goodin's criteria. But is there also not another purpose that might be at stake? What about the moral fabric that binds society together? If maintenance of the work ethic, through whatever means, is necessary for the preservation of that fabric—that is, preserving society in Lockean language—is this not the goal we should be looking at in a liberal society?

Supported Workfare?

To a certain extent, the welfare policy debate, as it has come to be known, does illustrate the difficulty confronting liberals in defining their objectives. Let's suppose that both workfare in its pure form and welfare as transfer payments represent extremes, both of which could potentially be considered to distort liberal idealism. What about programs that attempt to meet the basic subsistence needs of the poor while also striving to foster greater self-sufficiency? The politics of welfare reform during both the Nixon and Carter administrations saw battle lines drawn between liberals and conservatives on precisely these issues. Conservatives were not willing to back policies that did not demand work and have a serious mechanism for enforcement. Liberals, however, were not willing to back a scheme that would result in such a diminution in benefits that it created the appearance (1) that we lacked compassion as a society and (2) that all they had fought for was now being undone. And it wasn't that liberals did not want recipients to work, only that they were not convinced that welfare mothers ought to be forced to work. Meanwhile, conservatives' expectations that recipients should work did not extend beyond limited work tests. They were not prepared to force recipients to work through authoritarian means; rather, they preferred to cut programs instead of use them for "conservative ends."[84]

Yet, both ends of the political spectrum agreed that reform was in fact necessary. Their approaches, however, differed. Liberals continued to believe that reform could be achieved through traditional modifications of incentives. Conservatives believed that the poor could be forced to work simply through the loss of programs. But they also came to believe that people had to be forced to behave according to certain norms. To this extent, both agreed that behavior had to be changed. But they differed as to the approach that needed to be taken. They also differed as to the nature of the behavior that was in question. Regarding the type of behavior that conservatives were finding offensive, liberals still seemed to stick to a doctrine of neutrality. Yet, given the intractable nature of these problems, is that realistic? In terms of policy, the real question is whether it is possible to find a scheme that satisfies the moral and ideological concerns of each. What about a workfare scheme that would back up its work requirements with job training and other support services?

Consider the case of the GAIN (Greater Avenues to Independence) program in California. GAIN was adopted in 1985 and has attracted perhaps the greatest attention of all state workfare programs. The program concentrates on an estimated 190,000 recipients in a state well known for its generous provision. At the heart of the program is job training, whereby caseworkers, on the basis of recipients' skills, negotiate training contracts, which are then binding on both the recipients and the welfare bureaucracy. Those still remaining unemployed upon completion of training are then required to work for the state—for no more than a year so as to pay off their benefits. But unlike the more punitive workfare programs, these workfare jobs are valued at the same hourly rates as average starting salaries in the state. Not only, then, are individuals trained to work in the workforce, but through their workfare, they acquire experience that might make them more attractive to prospective employers. Supervisors are also expected to know their workers well enough that they can write references. And should there be no job after a year of workfare, the job training cycle begins again. All eligible recipients must participate, and if they break the rules, they are penalized.[85] California officials have boasted success—of those individuals registered in the program, approximately thirty-eight thousand have found jobs because of the program.[86]

Similar to GAIN, Massachusetts has Employment and Training Choices (E.T.). Those electing to participate in E.T. meet with a caseworker to discuss background and needs, and should training be needed they are then referred to a career counselor. E.T. then provides participants with an array of options from which to choose: remedial education, vocational or higher education, training, supported work, or direct job search through the state's employment service.[87] E.T. too has had some success. Nightingale and others found for the 1986 to 1987 period that E.T. reduced the amount of time on AFDC by about 29 percent. For those participating in E.T. the average welfare spell was ten months, while it was fourteen for the comparison group. It also increased the employment rate among participants in the first six months of 1988 by 8 percent. After starting E.T. 44 percent were employed, compared with 36 percent for those who did not participate. Moreover, those who participated in E.T. during the 1986 to 1987 period had average earnings that were 32 percent higher over the first six months of 1988 than the earnings of those in the comparison group.[88]

In addition to job training, these programs also offer support services such as child care and counseling to welfare mothers so as to ease the transition from home to work. Massachusetts subsidizes child care as well as transportation during the first year of employment. While the federal government would only provide medicaid for four months after jobs are found, E.T. has in some cases extended it to fifteen.

Supported workfare would appear to appeal to both ends of the political spectrum. Because it also subsidizes work, it effectively removes whatever disincentive there may previously have been to work, thereby making welfare a less attractive alternative. More important, however, it departs from the underpinning assumptions of pure workfare. Contrary to conservatives' assumptions that these people would rather be on the dole doing nothing, it assumes people to be on welfare because they lack both resources and opportunities to work. As Kirp points out, "programs like GAIN presume that a sizable number of adults on welfare need neither discipline nor handouts but tangible opportunities to develop their talent." Programs such as these are aimed at those who it is assumed share the basic values. Even if participation in these programs doesn't always result in paying jobs, it does at least assist those "engaged in the struggle for independence, for full membership in the society, though not necessarily winning it."[89]

Based on the California model, coupled with the fact that modifications in the traditional incentive system have not always worked to get people off the dole, Congress passed the Family Support Act of 1988. It essentially reflected a consensus that while welfare policy should certainly attempt to ameliorate the harshness of poverty, it should also foster self-sufficiency, as well as teach responsibility. But it also took into account new social realities—mainly, more women in the labor force, more single mothers, and fathers failing to provide support.[90] At the same time, it also arose out of frustration over the course of national social policy in recent years, tempered with an awareness that states have made some strides with their own initiatives. Though the act mandates provisions to enforce paternal child support, it is the training component that truly sets the act apart from the workfare scheme of the early Reagan administration. Instead of aiming to get "value" out of AFDC recipients, the objectives of the Family Support Act are to get AFDC recipients who do not possess working skills but are caught up in the web of poverty and despair, and many of whom are single mothers, to sign up for training once their children are six months old. Specifically the act creates the Job Opportunities and Basic Skills Training (JOBS) program, which, in the words of former Health and Human Services Under-Secretary Constance Horne, "embodies a new consensus that the well-being of children depends not only on meeting their material needs but also on the parents' ability to become self-sufficient."[91] Those participating in the JOBS program are supposed to receive child care while in the program and transitional care upon entering the labor market.

The premises underlying the Family Support Act might very well be a point of departure for serious discussion of what types of policies best fit liberal objectives. The primary objection of conservatives like Mead, however, is that it is still voluntary. In this vein, it still reflects the same neutrality inherent in past reform efforts. Through further incentives, the objective is to induce people to voluntarily sign up for the training program. Still, the objectives might be seen as a good attempt to reach a welfare accord satisfactory to both conservative and liberal ends of the spectrum. Supported workfare might even address the issue of exploitation as it may be experienced by both recipients and nonrecipients alike. It not only ensures that society receives something back immediately, but also that society may receive an even greater return on its investment insofar as recipients may be off assistance indefinitely. In this regard, common ground is reached between those arguing the moral imperative of assisting those in need and those arguing the need for juridical standards. Does this not then conform to Goodin's criteria of doing what is good for people? Taxes targeted for welfare policy could no longer be regarded as a form of compulsory charity but as a more prudent long-term investment into the future. To this end, the Family Support Act may well be a point of departure for beginning the dialogue of how we can best achieve liberal principles of mutuality and commitment to the common project. But at best, it is only a point of departure. It still does not address how we alter the behavior of those society really considers to be deviant.

This ultimately is the dilemma that confronts liberalism: Can a liberal society teach people how to behave "appropriately" without imposing a moral absolute in the process? Is it ever the proper function of government to do this, or is this only a matter for the myriad of private institutions to legitimately address? On the other hand, given the history of liberalism in the United States—the tendency to justify intervention as compensation for the failure of private institutions to perform their functions—can liberalism afford to turn away from the real issues that need to be addressed?

Whither Neutrality?

To further liberal purposes on this issue would appear to require some strong medicine. That medicine would entail nothing less than the abandonment of neutrality. In order to construct a community in which human dignity and integrity are served, it is necessary to ensure that all members of the community understand the meaning of equality in terms of both their rights and obligations. They need to understand that there is a common project that holds the community together. At times this may actually require more statist policies aimed at achieving socialization. Paradoxically, coercion may have to be employed in order to achieve greater self-sufficiency. Yet, it isn't coercion in a literal sense, it is simply a harsher version of the incentive system. What the history of welfare reform demonstrates is that welfare policies predicated on neutrality not only have failed to fulfill their objectives, but also in many cases may have produced results clearly at odds with the philosophical premises of a liberal society. Still, it begs the question of whether human integrity and dignity are being fostered. The issues inherent to welfare policy ultimately raise the following question: Can a liberal state truly respect the dignity and integrity of the poor when it effectively assumes their poverty to be a function of their subculture and not simply a lack of employment opportunities? For the sake of philosophical consistency, how can government tell people how to behave as a condition for receiving welfare and at the same time allow them to make choices when it comes to the so-called bedroom issues?

It is important to remember that the welfare explosion was part of a larger and more expansive social rights revolution. While the civil rights movement was pulling liberal politics in one direction, there was yet another movement, not altogether unrelated, that appeared to be shoring up a fundamental tenet in liberal political philosophy: the concept of individualism and the requirement that government respect individual zones of privacy. To an extent, during the 1960s and into the 1970s, liberalism appeared to be moving in two different directions. In the economic realm, the trend was toward greater government involvement, as had been the case since the early part of the century. But in the social realm—the realm of personal privacy—the trend was moving the other way. The wall of separation between public and private, especially when it came to issues of speech, religious belief and expression, personal morality, and personal privacy regarding bedroom issues and reproductive freedom, was becoming ever thicker. Beginning in the 1960s, the Court made it clear that public prayer in the classroom, for instance, was no longer permissible because it violated the separation of church and state.[92] In the name of building an inclusive community, issues that had the potential to divide and effectively exclude had to be removed from public discourse. Not only was religion a question of voluntary association, as Locke had made clear in his *Letter Concerning Toleration*,[93] but also it was fundamentally a question of privacy.

The line between public and private became ever more clear first with *Griswold v. Connecticut* in 1965 and second with *Roe v. Wade* in 1973. In *Griswold*, the now famous contraception case, the Court established a right by married people to privacy. The Court suggested that although the Constitution did not specifically mention privacy, it did contain a penumbra where privacy is protected from government intrusion. The Connecticut statute banning contraception could not stand because the means by which the state would achieve its purpose would "sweep unnecessarily broadly and thereby invade the area of protected freedoms." Writing for the Court, Justice Douglas opined: "Would we allow the police to search the sacred precincts of marital bedrooms for telltale signs of the use of contraceptives? The very idea is repulsive to the notions of privacy surrounding the marriage relationship."[94] Within the bonds of marriage, there existed certain rights to privacy, and these rights essentially entailed no less than the personal liberty to decide not to have children every bit as much as they did to have children. But if we can step back from this case for a moment, we can also see quite clearly the parallel of the crux of Douglas's opinion and the fight to put an end to midnight raids. If we aren't going to allow the bedroom police to look for telltale signs of contraception, why would we allow the welfare police to look for telltale signs of men?

To an extent, *Griswold* captures well the liberal ideal of free conscience.[95] In essence, the Court was saying that government may not tell people how to live their lives. It may not tell them how to behave, especially if their behavior will not have any impact on the public. *Roe v. Wade* only reinforced this concept by asserting that the right to privacy included the right to terminate pregnancies during the first two trimesters. Only if the state had a compelling interest could it interfere with that right to privacy.[96] Not only was the Court reaffirming this notion that issues of personal behavior and conduct were out of the realm of public interference, but also it seemed to suggest that issues of contraception, abortion, and other bedroom issues were really matters of personal morality. If there was no discernible relationship between one's personal conduct and the public interest, government had to presume in favor of individual rights.

Arguably, the movement for one set of rights certainly provided political impetus to fight for others. These cases are about the right of Americans not to be told how to behave. If government should then come along and suggest that individuals do not know how to behave and must therefore be taught, liberals may well have good reason to be ambivalent, at a minimum. Certainly they should be concerned that after struggling to achieve certain rights protections, this is only a step backwards. Once the point is made that government may not tell people how to behave, to turn around and suggest that there is a class of people who do not know how but need to be instructed is to create invidious distinctions and a double standard. If liberals should then presume to tell a group of people how to behave because they are unfortunate enough to need public assistance, they would in effect be relegating those in need to the status of second-class citizens.

Yet, the fact may remain that, while certain choices people make in private may offend some, choices cannot really harm anyone in a tangible way. The issue in welfare policy is whether the public should be compelled to pay for the poor's life style, which the general public detests. Perhaps the case most instructive on this is the case dealing with public-funded abortions. In *Harris v. McRae*, on the issue of whether government had a responsibility to pay for medically necessary abortions with public monies, the Court asserted that it did not follow that because government could not prohibit certain things, it had an affirmative responsibility to provide them. It is for Congress to answer whether constitutionally protected freedom of choice warrants federal subsidy. The Court made it clear that a public-policy decision not to pay for that which individuals have a right to seek on their own does not impinge on their rights.[97] To put it another way, the public is under no obligation to subsidize what it might find to be offensive.

Perhaps the issue is not really as controversial as conservatives like Mead allege. Instead of telling people how to behave, we simply adopt Kaus's idea for an overhaul of the welfare state and model it along the same lines as the WPA of the New Deal. By simply requiring people to show up at job sites, we do not have to pass judgment on anybody. To this end, not only are the objectives of liberal society furthered, but also some semblance of neutrality is maintained. This, after all, is simply another version of the incentive system. They must work for their benefits or else they will starve. Though not falling totally short, it does fall somewhat short of forcing people to work. This may sound harsh, but liberalism does not require the type of responsiveness to the public that is necessarily charitable or compassionate. It requires, as Goodin argues, that we do what is good for people[98] and that we be responsive to the goals of society as contained in the Lockean ideal. In the end, it requires that we do what is necessary to maintain the social fabric of the community. If this is the criterion we are going to use, and we will effectively be paternalistic no matter what the policy specifics, we would do better to further the objectives of society. Those objectives—liberal purposes—require that individuals be autonomous.

Liberal objectives do require that whatever measures are adopted be aimed at preserving society while not causing harm in the process. It should be remembered that Locke considered welfare provision to ultimately undermine the public interest and that Mill similarly thought welfare as simple charitable giving to be potentially harmful. So harmful was it that Mill thought recipients should be denied an element of citizenship working people would not be denied. Indeed, the English Poor Law of 1834 offered social relief and security to those in need, but only if they were willing to effectively renounce their rights of citizenship. Relief was viewed as an alternative to citizenship, not as a right inherent to it.[99] To this end, Kaus's policy solution may well capture an element of neutrality that never existed in the distinction between the "worthy" and "unworthy" poor. At the same time, Kaus's proposal, while it may appear to recapture some lost neutrality, is more of a statist solution. In the minds of many it will be seen as straddling the line between coercive and noncoercive activity. Yet, his plan makes no moral judgments. Instead, it merely offers assistance to those willing to work. Those who aren't simply receive nothing. To this end, Kaus's policy proposal not only recaptures much of the foundations of New Deal liberalism lost during the welfare expansion of the 1960s, but also it aspires to many assumptions belying the initial regulatory framework. It relies on the same New Deal assumptions of work as the basis for individual integrity. It also assumes that this individual integrity is crucial to the social fabric because there must be participation in the common project. Ultimately, the Kaus solution assumes that, if necessary, government must teach people values, assist in their socialization, as compensation for private institutions' failure to do so. Although there is an element of neutrality here, it still lacks the moral neutrality found in the writings of Rawls, Dworkin, and Ackerman.[100] It would also appear to strike the same type of balance that Locke had in mind. Although the individual may well have been prior to society, one still had obligations to that society, as the nature of one's individualism was a function of one's experience with the environment—one's community—that one was socialized in.

5. *Public-Private Partnership*

THE history of liberalism in the twentieth century is essentially the history of state development. As we have already seen in the preceding policy chapters, new social complexity has necessitated new and more innovative solutions ultimately showing themselves to be less and less neutral. What this suggests is that in order to attempt a solution to serious economic and social problems government must make hard choices, determine which values have priority, and even abridge rights at times in the name of the greater good. It would appear that the type of neutrality that would effectively ensure an open framework for individuals to make choices has to be abandoned so as to achieve the liberal purposes of a community in which the locus is human dignity. Similarly, the evolving nature of liberalism illustrates how the concept of state has changed. In classical liberalism, the state was viewed as, perhaps, a necessary evil, and its power was to be feared. But during the New Deal the state came to be looked to as an answer to our problems.

New Deal liberalism was in large measure born out of a Burkean conservatism that to conserve the traditions of the past it would be necessary to reform in ways that at the time might be perceived as radical. The object was to get business back on its feet. Although the New Deal represented a departure from a classical conception of passive and limited government, the fundamental nature of the capitalist order was left intact. The goal was the preservation of the American system. Liberal means were being employed toward conservative ends.[1] To this end, New Deal liberalism represented a continuation of corporate liberalism, but it was more positive and extended beyond, with a new emphasis on administration.

For Dewey, in particular, liberal ideals were no longer a valid legitimation of capitalist society but a potential force for its deligitimation. For liberal values to be revitalized, and to become the basis of a democratic society, liberals would have to become alert to the historical circumstances in which their philosophy had developed. The key liberal value was individuality—liberty and freedom of "intelligence." Dewey was most eager to reconstruct the liberal value of liberty. Liberty was more than just an abstract principle; it was the power to do specific things. Questions about liberty were essentially questions about the distribution of power. As Dewey understood it, liberalism was committed to an end that was both enduring and flexible: the liberation of individuals so that they may be able to realize their capacities, and the creation of a social organization that would enable individuals, if not empower them, to achieve effective liberty and opportunity for personal growth.[2] What the Great Depression demonstrated, perhaps more so than the earlier trust crisis—the crisis precipitating corporate liberalism—was that there were forces other than political ones that would deprive individuals of effective liberty and opportunities for personal growth. The New Deal grew out of Franklin Roosevelt's brain trust, which in spirit was still corporate liberalism in that it sought to achieve an alternative to socialism. What the brain trust agreed on was that positive intervention in the marketplace was necessary to organize it collectively while also preserving principles of individualism. Here the objective was to achieve individualism through some state direction of capitalism. The state, by protecting the disadvantaged and advancing opportunity, could avoid a dictatorship of the proletariat.[3]

Classical liberalism has traditionally been associated with the night-watchman state and corporate liberalism with the regulatory state, but New Deal liberalism has been associated with the positive and administrative state. What became clear from the New Deal was that government could no longer sit around and regulate in a negative fashion so as to prevent harm to others, but that it would have to take positive steps to ensure that individuals would be able to function as they always had. Yet, if the state could be turned to for regulation, economic management, and the provision of welfare, what else could we expect from it? In reality, activism reflected the need to build on community principles in a world whose forces severely undermined the fabric of community—to in fact give some substance to the Lockean ideal.

During the 1930s, this activism assumed the form of public works programs designed to get the economy moving. Specifically, the issue was finding a way to boost confidence so that capitalists would invest. This issue would in fact animate many of the stabilization policies, already discussed in chapter 3, that would form the crux of American economic policy into the 1980s. So long as capitalists were investing here, the thrust of economic policies could be stabilization. But following the Second World War, the economic base of the country underwent transformation yet again. This time the trend was toward the postindustrial economy, predicated less on manufacturing and more on the service sector. American politics seemed to revolve around the question of growth—who could generate it and who could maintain it.[4] As long as growth appeared to be assured, public attention could potentially be turned toward nonmaterial matters.[5] Still, maintaining national prosperity would require considerably more. During the 1960s and into the mid-1970s, growth, it was assumed, could be maintained simply through stabilization policies, particularly fiscal and monetary ones. By the mid-1970s, following the oil shocks and the coming-of-age of our German and Japanese economic rivals, the language of policy changed as well—to that of investment. Investment, while always important, was simply assumed through the other stabilization policies. It was also assumed through various adjustments in the tax code aimed at offering businesses incentive to invest by effectively leaving more available cash in their hands.

In recent years, however, policy makers have no longer been able to assume that investment would simply follow modifications in monetary and tax policies but have actually had to court it. Policy officials at different levels of government have discovered that greater effectiveness might be achieved if they would take a more active approach toward getting private investment. Instead of passively waiting for business interests to seize upon new incentives in the tax code, public officials would actively court them and attempt to conclude quasi-contractual arrangements. This policy has come to be known as the new public-private partnership.

The public-private partnership consists of a willingness on the part of public officials to actively work in partnership with private industry for the attainment of mutually beneficial objectives. David Osborne, for instance, suggests that it is paradigmatic of a new liberalism.[6] This new liberalism is one that sees prosperity being rooted in cooperative relations between public and private concerns. In addition to its being a policy of choice in recent years among state and local officials, the nature of its implementation is especially critical to our discussion of liberalism. For, in a couple of instances where it was tried, it did illuminate the fundamental challenges confronting the policy maker who needs to consider radical steps to address complex problems but still attempt to maintain a measure of neutrality. These challenges arise insofar as they may evoke images of a strong state that can act arbitrarily against the interests of citizens. If it is an example of some form of centralized planning, it may be an example of government that does not necessarily treat all its citizens equally. While new public-private partnerships may flow logically from the precedents of liberal evolution, the central question is whether they might not also press against many of the core principles of liberalism.

The public-private partnership was first formulated as a policy approach in 1978 by the Carter administration to assist urban officials in their economic revitalization efforts and was intended to be used in conjunction with traditional fiscal and monetary policy tools.[7] To some extent, these partnerships may simply represent new strategies or approaches to traditional state-sponsored incentives in a state that, as Lindblom observes, cannot command anybody to do anything but can only induce them to.[8] They do, however, represent a departure from the past. They essentially consist of arrangements between public and private officials, whereby both have agreed to work in partnership for the attainment of mutually beneficial objectives. Although the idea of partnership is nothing new, these recent partnerships are significant because of their explicitness.

James O'Connor, for instance, argues the existence of an implicit partnership between the public and private sectors, a presumption that capitalists would make prudent investments, which would generate jobs and economic opportunities, whereas the public sector would make both capital and social investments, so as to ease the burden on capitalists. By easing this burden, the public sector would effectively ensure economic opportunities for its residents. Capital investments would include the physical economic infrastructure, such as roads, bridges, and water and land improvements, as well as urban renewal. Social investments would include education, research, and development, as well as administrative services. While public investments would ensure growth opportunities for constituents, they would also result in effective cost savings for business.[9] This implicit partnership of which O'Connor speaks then constitutes the *old partnership*. It is a partnership very much assumed by the classical version of liberalism.[10]

The *new partnership*, however, differs. It is a product of liberalism's evolution from the passive to the positive state. The new partnership typifies the positive state in that government is actively attempting to promote opportunities. It is not a by-product of a regulatory framework in which government's function is essentially negative—that is, the mediation of conflict and the prevention of undue harm to others. Nor is it an example of stabilization policies in which government is performing a maintenance function. Rather, government is using the arsenal of public policy to stimulate investment, even if government should at times need to be a coinvestor or a source of capital. No longer is government the passive cheerleader creating an environment conducive to investment—the "favorable business climate"—but an active participant courting it. Public officials act as salespeople; they sell their communities as good places to do business.[11] No longer does government sit by, passively performing traditional tasks of creating environments conducive to investment, as suggested by O'Connor, but works with business in efforts to ascertain just what specifically each other's respective needs are and how the two can work together for their attainment. As new competitive realities have resulted in greater capital mobility and economic dislocation, policy makers have had to address the following question: What can the public sector do either to maintain industry or to better meet the needs of industry?

Public-private partnerships are important because they attempt to address many of the problems associated with economic transformation. In this respect, they also reflect a liberal state's policy trajectory in conformity with increasing social complexity. They are an outgrowth of the postindustrial service-sector economy in which government has to play a more active role. In chapter 3, we discussed plant-closing policy and corporatism. On one level, public-private partnerships may appear somewhat corporatist in form, insofar as they involve a quasi-contractual arrangement between business and government. But in that they may not involve labor in discussions at all, or that the issues they address are not solely restricted to wage and price levels, they may not completely fit the traditional corporatist paradigm. Invariably, however, they will be a response to the effects of plant closure. In part, they are second-best approaches to the problems caused by capital mobility and economic dislocation, insofar as effective plant-closing legislation would effectively sit outside the philosophic bounds of neutral-based liberalism. The question is whether this approach also does not raise a set of challenges to the point that a public philosophy framed in the name of liberalism ends up losing touch with its underpinning philosophic precepts, especially those grounded in neutrality. They are specifically arrangements designed to either revitalize sagging economies or prevent key employers from departing or going bankrupt. Two cases that clearly touch on these issues are the General Motors Poletown plant and the United States' bailout of Chrysler Corporation. To put it more bluntly, these arrangements are public attempts to alter the choices that individuals, operating within the confines of the liberal framework, are presumed to have for the sake of the community's interest—to preserve society.

Poletown

The Poletown case involved an agreement between General Motors (GM) and the city of Detroit. GM had informed the local authorities of its intentions to close two of its plants and relocate elsewhere, but the company would be willing to consider building two new Cadillac plants in Detroit in exchange for certain concessions. GM would construct these plants if the city of Detroit would undertake to acquire the properties (through the powers of eminent domain), clear them, and then prepare the site for construction. This was to be in addition to the traditional litany of tax abatements.[12] GM, however, wasn't just asking for the city to locate a site, but to specifically acquire and prepare the neighborhood of Poletown, a close-knit ethnic community. To accommodate GM, then, Detroit officials were forced to raise huge sums of money from both the state and federal governments. This was to involve no less than public officials becoming active investors, albeit silent, in what always had been, and would continue to be, a private enterprise.

But the partnership wasn't just a question of public investment; rather, it involved the wholesale destruction of a community for the sake of maintaining a large employer. The central question is whether, through their actions, Detroit officials may have been taking activism too far. Did this precedent carry with it a set of expectations that public officials would enter into similar arrangements with others, and that all private actors need to do is make their demands known? On one level, it may create precedent for future partnerships, and ones established on business terms. On another level, such partnerships flow from the precedents of the administrative state. What principally set modern liberalism, as it took shape during the New Deal, apart from its classical ancestor was administration. Administration would essentially serve to mediate the harshness of impersonal forces, thereby erecting a wall of protection around the interests of society at large. Modern liberalism was also set apart because of greater centralization of state activity.

The issue of administration is essentially this: Can large government be watched—its power checked—as small government can? This was essentially the rationale for neutrality, as it would find expression in limited government. Ironically, however, administration was a continuation of neutrality. Lowi, in particular, has shown that the most negative consequence was the congressional delegation of authority, which ultimately resulted in a degeneration into "interest-group liberalism." Congress would adopt policies in broad outline by passing general legislation and would then authorize the appropriate agencies and departments in the executive branch to fill in the details. Through these delegations, Congress not only alleviated itself of responsibility but also undermined the whole process of deliberation and, ultimately, accountability. Because liberal governments wouldn't be able to order values, because that would connote a state showing preference for one good over another, the whole issue could effectively be circumvented through delegations of authority to those agencies isolated from popular pressures. But these agencies didn't assume the responsibility for the ordering of values; rather, they simply distributed to each and all. As a result, the door was then open for different interests to approach these administrative agencies and departments with even greater expectations that their interests would be served, which in turn only led to greater reliance on administration.[13]

This trend, then, was only the beginning of what Cass Sunstein calls a rights revolution, the creation of legal entitlements by Congress to a variety of protections and largess. This New Deal constitutionalism and rights revolution contributed to a number of problems the original Constitution sought to remedy. One purpose of the original was to ensure both deliberation and accountability in government. Yet, regulatory statutes, at least in the form of broad-based delegations, often fail to provide either.[14] Even though these delegations were occurring at the national level, the ensuing brand of politics was to set the standard for interests to approach administrative agencies at other levels, and with full expectations that their demands would be met. In order for these delegations to have occurred, the administrative foundations had to be in place, which, as a result of the corporate phase, they were.

Expectations effectively became entitlements. Not only is the precedent established for government intervention—to possibly encroach upon our rights—but the precedent is established for government to serve as the panacea for all of society's ailments. As government gives more, we respond by demanding more. The first casualty, then, is our own self-reliance. As Sunstein puts it, through statute we have been liberated from risk.[15] We look to government for the answers. Government will solve our problems.

At issue in Poletown, then, is whether, in spite of the precedent of administration, those actions taken by public officials were legitimate. Were their specific actions going to further liberal purposes? Clearly, public officials would justify their actions on grounds of necessity, that affirmative steps must be taken to at least preserve economic stability, if not to go further and generate economic growth. However, this justification may only serve to rationalize their failure to consider the consequences of their actions. The first issue to consider is whether this case can be said to clear liberalism's neutrality principle, or, for that matter, whether it possibly could have.

The second issue, then, is whether it in any way accords with liberal purposes. This issue could turn out to be more complex because determination of whether it corresponds with liberal purposes is compounded by the question of how we best achieve them. If investment in the community is deemed to be in accordance with those purposes, is private industry the appropriate vehicle for the realization of those purposes? At the same time, they may also be a reaffirmation of the virtues of relying on private actors, through the choices they make, to generate prosperity. It isn't so much that the principle has changed any, only that assistance by government is needed. But then, even during the classical period, business relied on some degree of assistance. The extent of that assistance was always contingent on the nature of the economy.

Liberal governments have typically had to rely on the willingness of those with resources to invest, which requires that promotional policies be based on incentives and not on command. For a government that cannot coerce can only get people to do things through induction.[16] As much as this has been the reality, it does conceivably create the appearance of a business-government alliance in which the bane of government's existence is to serve the interests of business. The relationship between money and politics in the American political system has perhaps reinforced the image that big business interests will always get the attention of government officials, while ordinary citizens receive short shrift.[17]

Instrumentalism?

The proper first question is, did GM receive preferential treatment at the expense of the general community? One measure of neutrality might be within the context of instrumentalism, in which the measure would consist of the following question: Is the state being used as an instrument for the attainment of private objectives? The measure is essentially Marxist, beginning with the assumption that all public policy is in the service of the economic interests that ultimately rule. The instrumentalist, then, points to cases in which this can be proven true. Against this measure, the general concept of public-private partnership might be held to be instrumentalist on the grounds that it furthers the interests of business by virtue of the alliance it creates. For the alliance it forges isn't neutral regarding a particular good. The fact that such partnerships usually consist of the same set of actors—government and business—means that government is more likely to embrace the concerns of business than the concerns of others.[18] But does this necessarily prove anything?

To establish an alliance with those parties possessing the resources to invest doesn't necessarily prove the state apparatus to be an instrument of the private sector. As Fred Block argues, for a structural argument to be viable it must do two things: First, it must show what structural constraints operate to reduce the likelihood that state managers will act against the general interests of capitalists. Second, it must also explain why there is a tendency to pursue policies that are in the general interests of capital. "It is not sufficient to explain why the state avoids anticapitalists policies; it is necessary to explain why the state has served to rationalize capitalism."[19] Therefore, it would have to be established that this alliance is just one of many in a pattern of preferential treatment toward business. It would also have to be clear in this pattern of preferential treatment that business always triumphed over the interests of the public at large and that policies antithetical to business interests were never pursued. For a policy to be truly instrumentalist, it would have to be clear that there was neither an intended nor actual benefit to the larger public, but that it only accrued to that small group petitioning special accommodation.

Against this measure of instrumentalism, however, this particular partnership may not easily fit. Even though GM basically dictated the terms, it isn't clear that Detroit officials necessarily pursued this policy because they thought it would be in the best interests of GM. Perhaps they truly believed that it would really aid the Detroit economy, otherwise in a state of utter decay. Still, this doesn't altogether dismiss the issue of instrumentalism, for there might still be a variation of it that bears on the general principle of neutrality. It has already been noted that the neutrality principle would require that all relevant parties be included in the decision-making process. Exclusion from the process results in an infringement of their rights, as they haven't been afforded equal respect and treatment. In this case the concerns of others were never taken into account; rather, it was assumed that only by working with business instead of against it would socially optimal objectives be achieved. If it should be argued that their actions could be justified through some form of public discussion—the dialogue—none took place. Instead, it would appear that the precedent of administration effectively precluded the need for any discussion on the assumption that policy experts would make appropriate decisions in the best interests of the community. The standard set by the delegation of authority only legitimized a bypass of those institutions in which debate would most likely occur.

Has a particular conception of the good really been recognized? The case could certainly be made that if it doesn't violate anybody's rights and some social purpose is served, it is a legitimate state action. This is certainly a position that Dworkin would take.[20] It might be deemed to be in the service of liberal objectives in that it is framed with the aim of preserving society. The problem with this, however, is that in the absence of a public discussion on what constitutes social purpose, neutrality is violated insofar as public officials made an arbitrary decision based on assumption. Any assertion that rights haven't been violated, then, becomes dubious. Either the notion of rights flows logically from the principle of neutrality, or the idea of neutrality becomes an interesting device for protecting rights. The injunction against favoring A's conception of the good over that of B's is put forth on the presumption that if A's is favored, then B's rights must have been violated. B, it must be presumed, simply did not receive equal respect and treatment to A. In this case, then, it would be obvious that the neutrality principle had in fact been violated.

Now the question is whether the above hypothetical scenario is transferable to Poletown. Did all parties in Poletown receive equal respect and treatment? In this case, whole communities were destroyed and families were dislocated through the city's power of eminent domain. This case did not involve the impartial selection of a site but preference for a specific site. Was the effect of liberalism's gradual move toward greater administration, as it would manifest itself in interest-group liberalism, only signaling to GM that it could approach local authorities and expect that its demands would in fact be met? In the end, only six thousand jobs were created.[21] At what costs, then, was this partnership achieved? Perhaps the troubling question in all this is, why Poletown? Just because GM demanded this particular location, did public officials have to be blindly obedient? Did they not have a responsibility to the larger community to look for another suitable site—one that, perhaps, would not have been as costly to the community?

Though the laws of eminent domain require just compensation as the means by which property owners' rights will be protected, the perennial question of what is just does loom large. Glendon argues that the significance of Poletown lies in the fact that it resulted in a further erosion of property. Individual members of the community were essentially powerless to invoke their rights to property against the state's power of eminent domain. The community had an interest, and one not dissimilar to many other communities that have suffered the pangs of economic transformation.[22] If the community residents were powerless in the political arena and subsequently powerless in lower courts, does this case then shed any light on Locke's concept of property? Does this then constitute a case whereby the public interest in Locke's scheme—as defined in terms of preservation of society—supersedes the interests of property? There is, however, still a problem here. This assumes that property is an end of the Lockean liberal contract when, in fact, as has already been pointed out in chapter 2, it has a more functional purpose.

In the end, it would appear that property not only triumphed over community but also, ultimately, rode roughshod over it. GM, the epitome of a propertied interest in this country, was effectively able to dictate to the community. Had the community not abided by its demands, GM would have exercised its ultimate property right—freedom of mobility, which is clearly derived from the principle of freedom of choice—and abandoned the community altogether. In this vein, to even talk of this case as a diminution of property rights is perhaps to miss the point. The Marxists would be more correct in arguing that this is a classic case of a powerful corporate interest riding roughshod over little people. Or, as Samuel Bowles and Herbert Gintis might suggest, this case well represents a contradiction in modern political thought. Here is a company essentially exploiting the traditional norms of capitalist markets that are rooted in liberalism, while defying democratic principles that are equally rooted in the same liberalism.[23] In short, Detroit officials succumbed to the threat of a capital strike.[24]

Still, the key question remains as to whether it is sufficient to buy out the community's rights with just compensation, especially when it isn't clear if a price tag can be attached to the value of community. Though the choice of a public-private partnership as a tool may be a matter for policy experts to decide, because they may understand what works, the issue of what is good for the community in terms of value is for all to decide, because that is a question of the general public interest. For pragmatic reasons we may defer to policy makers for the resolution of specific problems, but we as a liberal democratic polity do not, or certainly should not, surrender our ultimate right to make decisions of monumental significance.[25] At the very least, the community should have been entitled to a voice. This greater benefit cannot be defined in terms of what is good or what contributes to the greatest happiness for the greatest number, and this is the fundamental problem with administration predicated on neutral procedures. It is ill-equipped to make these decisions, yet deference to it effectively legitimizes it as a decision-making body. Whereas administration was intended to bring forth the implementation of policy on the basis of impartial rules and procedures, the effect, as the Poletown case demonstrates, was clearly different. If administration was intended to achieve neutrality through the isolation of policy from politics, Poletown only illustrates how the principle was violated.

Still, the issue of representation cannot be dismissed lightly. Poletown might well speak to the dilemmas experienced by many a local politician. The dilemma, as put forth by Paul Peterson, is that local officials who want to maintain popular support must create growth opportunities.

They must pursue developmental policies, projects that will attract investment dollars. But to do that, they might have to court outside interests. It is often those outside the city who might have the resources to invest, and hence they must be appealed to if economic opportunities are to be generated.[26] This, of course, raises the question of who local officials are representing. Are they representing their immediate constituents, those who elected them? Or are they representing the outside money interests, whose only influence is capital as opposed to the ballot box? When a local government undertakes to bulldoze a neighborhood for the sake of accommodating a business interest and only six thousand jobs are created, one seriously has to question who exactly is being represented by this government. Moreover, if Locke's tract on property is to be properly understood as a basis for empowering individuals, there is still a problem. At a minimum, it suggests that procedures must be followed. It isn't at all clear that there were procedures for those individual homeowners who wanted to preserve their community except for the narrow ones of traditional eminent domain laws. When they tried to contest the "takings" in court, they were simply laughed out.[27] This would seem to suggest that definition of the public interest was really only one-sided. Unquestionably, the public interest was defined as what would best maintain a jobs base. Preservation of local communities, and particularly the fabric comprising those communities, would be no more than a secondary concern. It is not at all clear that this is what Locke had in mind when he talked about the requirement of government to preserve society.

Contract?

Another issue this case raises is that of contract. Are arrangements arrived at with public officials analogous to a contractual agreement? This case certainly raises some interesting questions concerning the meaning of the social contract. A social contract implies the existence of mutual expectations between communities and capital. Indeed, the traditional social contract, as both business and community leaders have understood it, is no different than the implicit partnership as described by O'Connor. Yet, in Poletown the partnership extended beyond unstated assumptions and expectations. Rather than intuitive understanding, a company explicitly made its demands known to the community and then expected compliance under threat of disinvestment. On one level, it might be conceded that the company is not obliged to guarantee workers jobs because that would presuppose a right to work. The crucial question is, why shouldn't such an agreement guarantee a right to a job? Or, why shouldn't there be a guaranteed right to work?

Jon Elster, for instance, distinguishes between the right to work and the right to a job. The right to work would be asserted as a positive right insofar as those living in a democratic polity enjoy the legal right to choose to (or not to) work. This would correspond to the metaphysical impossibility of actually coercing one into not working. This would be in contrast to negative rights aimed at protecting individuals from coercion either from the state or others. The positive right to work, however, is not to be taken in the same way as guaranteeing employment. Within the context of a right to work, such a right might simply be defined as a right against the employer, which "can at most be the right to retain a job that one already holds."[28] In the case of a public-private partnership, such a right might have to be defined as a right by an employee to hold a job that was initially created by the partnership agreement.

Could a public-private partnership result in a new understanding of property? Glendon argues that Poletown made it clear that residents did not have property rights against the supposed interests of the larger community. What about the employer who enters into such an arrangement? Does this employer not effectively lose property rights too? If, through the contract, the employees acquire rights to their jobs, is the effect not to diminish the property rights of the employer? Just as property may only be seized with just compensation, a right to a job that the partnership would create would similarly require a form of compensation as well. An employer would no longer have sole control over the property, but would have to buy out the employees should the employer desire to disinvest at a later date. In effect, the newly created right to a job makes the employees partners in the ownership and control of the property.

Although management, as a senior partner, might ultimately retain the right to disinvest and move elsewhere, it is now required to provide compensation. Yet, the fact that workers have acquired such rights might also entitle them to challenge such a decision and possibly get an injunction against the disinvestment decision. It isn't too difficult to see that arrangements that effectively abridge the rights of managers by granting workers rights in their jobs might be viewed as a "taking" under the Fifth Amendment. Does this not affect the traditional bundle of property rights? Does the partnership not effectively transfer a degree of control from management to workers?

If the act of entering into a contract with the community does entitle its members to jobs, what then are the limits to what the company might owe the community? To an extent, a contract is effectively being drawn that obliges companies to abstain from following the maxims of capitalism: to pursue whatever investment opportunities might yield the highest return. In a larger sense, the contract is asking the company to negate a fundamental core principle in liberalism: economic self-interest. Pursuit of self-interest in economic terms—or capital mobility—is akin to freedom of choice. Are we not asking actors in a liberal state to sacrifice the means for certain ends? Are we even sure that those ends necessarily fulfill liberal purposes that a sacrifice of the means can even be justified?

On another level, however, there is a case to be made that the public's role in this partnership, especially the investment of public resources, entitles the community to some form of return in the event the company might ultimately decide to close its doors. For the community didn't just create a favorable business climate—it bore a cost that may not have been worth the actual benefit. Thus the issue emerging from this case is, as it would be from any public-private partnership, just what does the company owe to the community? Even though local authorities were willing to bend over backwards to attract investment dollars, there were absolutely no guarantees that GM wouldn't opt to close its doors at a later date. GM, in short, did not promise the city of Detroit anything.[29]

The issue of contract, however, is more than simply a philosophical academic enterprise. Specific conditions were established. It was not just a question of providing a good place to do business. To discuss the matter of contract is to address the larger philosophical question of political obligation and apply it to specific circumstance. A strong case can be made that the company does have an obligation to the community because it freely entered into a contract. What obligates the company is simply that it offered its consent.[30] If, as a consequence of that consent, the employer suffers a diminution of property, it has to be accepted that the employer understood such a diminution would be the price to pay for the possibility of deriving future benefit. Even a literal reading of Locke's exhortation for government to preserve property would undoubtedly yield the same conclusion. The key fact remains that the contract was voluntary. Private actors were not coerced into it.

What about a quasi-contract, in which exchange relations are not clearly stated? It isn't clear that Poletown was a formal agreement in the sense that two parties actually sat down and signed an agreement that could be referred to as a contract, perhaps at a later date in court. However, employing O'Connor's measure, it might be said that a set of mutual understandings and expectations existed, from which may have emerged a sense of social obligation. Staughton Lynd, for instance, notes that when steelworkers in a federal district courtroom in Pittsburgh challenged a plant closing in Youngstown, the judge alluded to an implicit social contract based on the fact that a set of understandings and expectations arose out of the long-time presence of steel in the community.[31] As steel was the basis for the community's being, there at least may have existed the moral foundations for a corporate obligation to the community. Even though a moral obligation differs from a legal one, the fact that as much was said suggests a form of social contract that may arise on the basis of the assumptions people have made, as well as what they have come to expect.[32]

Under the new modern partnership, however, these understandings and expectations are couched in terms of explicit conditional promises: If the community provides X, the company will return Y. But in the absence of any corporate guarantees to the community, the impression does exist that public officials are serving corporate interests at the expense of the community. For the community isn't really demanding anything from capital but is hoping that if it accedes to the demands of capital, capital will in fact provide Y. Though we call this a partnership, it by most standards would be considered a one-sided arrangement, hardly the basis for a freely negotiated contractual arrangement guaranteeing mutuality of costs and benefits. An issue that looms ever large is, just what is the recourse of the community when companies renege on their agreements? Can a corporation be ordered to stay because of its contractual obligations?

In a Michigan state court in January 1993, the issue was resolved in favor of the community. GM was ordered to keep its plants operating because the community of Ypsilanti did offer benefits to the company in the first place. The plant had been targeted for closure as part of a restructuring arrangement that was to result in the closure of over twenty-one plants in the United States and Canada and the loss of over seventy-four thousand jobs. The issue of exploitation, similar to the one raised in the preceding chapter, would again have to be addressed. If public officials make public-private partnerships so attractive to business leaders that they are willing to enter into them, are they not also putting them into a position where their freedom can be limited and coercion can be used? If GM is being ordered to remain open, it is effectively being coerced. Yet, the state court's ruling didn't appear to be in any way related to the constitutional issue of "takings." The court did not say that the community had a right to force GM to remain in business—an effective restriction on absolute property rights—because it furthers the public interest in accordance with those principles underlying the laws of eminent domain. Although the case may well raise the larger specter of seizure, the court's ruling appears to have been much narrower.

The court's decision appears to have been confined to the parameters of a freely negotiated public-private partnership. The basis for its ruling was that a contract of sorts existed and that GM's departure was effectively a breach of contract. If two parties freely entered into a contract, expecting to derive mutual benefit, it can hardly be deemed a violation of any neutral principle if the party in breach is then ordered to maintain it. It would appear that the neutrality of the state is actually being maintained in that preference is being displayed for neither party. The Court is doing nothing more than respecting the concept of contract. The contract was freely entered into, and as such it carries with it a set of mutual obligations.[33] Moreover, the whole concept of contract would have to be said to presuppose that those parties entering into it knew and understood the conditions up front. Insofar as this may be true, it could not even be maintained that the state's actions are in any way—or that they have the potential to be—arbitrary. The state court's ruling, however, was short lived, as it was subsequently overturned by the state's court of appeals.

Still, there is a larger philosophical question. Can one be forced to do something against one's will for the larger public interest? In the last chapter, we tentatively broached the issue when we talked about forcing welfare recipients to work for their benefits and to conform to social standards of appropriate conduct. But is there not still a difference? To force one to work in exchange for benefits is really no more than a tightening up of the incentive system. Presumably individuals who are forced to work will in the process receive the proper socialization. In short, we are also justifying whatever coercion there is for the benefit of the recipients, as it supposedly teaches them how to function in the larger society. But, in the end, that individual cannot really be coerced into working. There may be consequences for not working, but the individual cannot really be coerced into doing so. If, however, we force companies to remain in a particular location, just what benefit is it to them? What consequences are we willing to impose for companies' failure to invest or remain in business against their will? Of course, it was the state's offer of incentives that induced them to enter into the agreement in the first place. In truth, they have already been socialized according to the rules of capitalism. Are we not in effect changing the rules on them in the middle of the game?

Even if we feel no sorrow for the wealthy corporation, is there still not a dangerous message here? Does the precedent not occasion the possibility that communities will outlaw capital mobility whenever it deems the departure of a firm to be contrary to the public interest? Of course, no community will readily admit that any company's departure in any way furthers its interest. Perhaps the issue in this type of arrangement is just what the limits are to communities invoking the public interest at the expense of individual rights. In terms of neutrality-based liberalism, images of a slippery slope are evoked, whereby the precedent for exploitation fuels perceptions of arbitrary exercises of power, whether they be public or private. The fact remains that because the precedent has been created, an opening exists.

To a certain extent, the nature of the world economy, and the place of the American economy within it, does seriously force us to revisit Madison's dilemma. Although we are not talking about interest groups specifically, we are talking about whether individual liberty can always be compatible with the public interest. When Madison discusses the causes of faction in Federalist Paper No. 10, he acknowledges that their cause is specifically a function of liberty—freedom to organize. As simple as it might be to ban liberty so as to preclude the formation of factions—which are deemed to be antithetical to the public interest at all times—Madison concludes the cure to be worse than the disease itself.[34] Are we not being asked to grapple with a similar question? If we want to live in a society in which individuals can make choices, do we not have to bear some of the consequences of those choices, however unpleasant they may be? Madison had rightly concluded that this was the price we pay for liberty. At best we can control the effects of factions. Similarly, we attempt to control the effects of the choices we live with if liberty is to have any real meaning. Public-private partnerships are essentially controls on the consequences flowing from the choices people in the economic marketplace have made. In some cases, choices may have been made freely, whereas in other cases, they may have been forced by a variety of conditions beyond a person's control. But is a public-private partnership along the lines of Poletown a good example of control?

The Chrysler Bailout

The Chrysler case, by contrast, not only took place at the national level, but also illustrated the other side of the neutrality principle—the consequences that attend when that opening has occurred. Chrysler points to the specter of an interventionist and perhaps corporatist state willing to violate the very foundations of a market economy, thereby speaking to some of the very fears and concerns of classical liberalism that are also at the heart of neutrality. Those fears were that once the state would begin to meddle in people's lives, it would then be in a position to encroach upon their rights and ultimately abridge their freedom, their capacity to act on their own conceptions of what is good. This was essentially the reason why government had to be limited to nothing more than the mediation of conflict or the prevention of harm.

On the verge of bankruptcy, Chrysler approached the Carter administration in search of loan assistance. In spite of the heated debate over the appropriateness of government interference in the presumed normal operations of capitalist markets, the federal government came forward with public assistance. Assistance was forthcoming largely because the collapse of Chrysler would have immediately affected not only those working for Chrysler itself, but also those both selling and servicing Chrysler products, as well as those working in major supplier firms. Yet, the federal government wasn't about to bail it out without strings attached.

According to Reich and Donahue, what the Chrysler episode demonstrated was that a large corporation was really nothing more than a network of claims and obligations by various constituencies. What the government's partnership with Chrysler was able to ensure was that some type of agreement would be arrived at between Chrysler and its constituents. Ultimately what was needed from all parties involved was a share in the sacrifice. Labor would have to be willing to make concessions in exchange for which they would be given shares in the company. Creditors and suppliers would have to be willing to hold back on their demands for payment. Unwillingness on their part would result in the government's refusal to provide the loans, which would ultimately force Chrysler to declare bankruptcy, and all parties would lose.[35] To an extent, Chrysler could be seen as the precursor to a sophisticated industrial policy in which government invests its resources into those industries deemed to be strong and allows the weaker ones to die out.[36] The Chrysler episode is probably more typical of the type of crisis management that has formed the catalyst for most liberal policy making. Industrial policy, by contrast, tends to involve systematic centralized planning. In that sacrifice was being required of all parties, there were clearly some striking similarities to corporatism. The critical difference, however, was that government was now the stronger partner.

Though Chrysler wasn't a classic example of industrial policy, the precedent it created certainly does touch on the general debate. For Chrysler essentially evoked the same ambivalence toward state-directed enterprise that was raised during the antitrust debates at the beginning of the century, which marked the corporate period of liberalism. It was during that period that intervention, even in the form of regulation, because it was so radically different from the past, was a movement toward state-directed enterprise.[37] Proponents of the bailout would argue the public interest of saving a major corporation insofar as it maintains jobs; preserves a federal, state, and local tax base; and keeps people off the welfare rolls. Lee Iacocca, Chrysler's chairman, argued the bailout to be in the public interest on the grounds that the collapse of a major corporation would be more costly to the public than the immediate costs of the bailout. Moreover, it was unconscionable in his view that one of the Big Three automakers—a Fortune 500 company—could be allowed to fold.[38] But despite the persuasive arguments of Chrysler officials that the company should be bailed out, the arguments for allowing the company to fold were equally persuasive.

First, there was the market principle, that in a free competitive economy there will be winners and losers and Chrysler's failure clearly indicated its inability to compete. Second was the question of Chrysler management. The evidence suggested that Chrysler had perhaps been mismanaged and overextended and now it wanted the community to come to its rescue.[39] More to the point, however, did the Chrysler bailout only create a precedent for future bailouts? By bailing Chrysler out, was the federal government sending the wrong signals? Although this wasn't the first federal bailout of a corporation,[40] questions of where it would end were always present. At issue is once government gets into the business of bailing companies out, does it not potentially occasion the possibility that it might intervene preemptively in business affairs in efforts to prevent future bailouts?

Though instrumentalists will again point to the alliance forged, the peripheral observation fails to account for the heated debate that at times appeared as though it would be resolved against Chrysler. The instrumentalist argument fails to account for much of the opposition to the bailout from the business community, which opposed it for reasons of principle. Moreover, an instrumentalist critique simply fails to explain the reticence of government to have entered into the partnership in the first place. Rather, the principal issue of concern is the precedent it creates, and it is the issue of precedence that has a direct bearing on the neutrality principle. By coming to the rescue, was government signaling to others that they too could expect similar accommodation? Was government not in effect creating a new entitlement? Insofar as the effects of the general rights revolution were to immunize people from risk, it would come as no surprise that corporations would seek the same immunity.

Government could supposedly make distinctions, pick and choose which companies it will bail out and which ones it will not, but on what basis does it do this? If it does make distinctions, certainly it could be said to be in violation of the neutrality principle as it is effectively showing preference to one company over another. Does this not also become the basis for centralized planning, thereby reinforcing concerns about industrial policy?[41] How can government truly remain neutral if by precedent it becomes incumbent upon it to bail out companies on the verge of bankruptcy? If, by Chrysler's argument, many of its financial problems stemmed from an increase in foreign competition, the bailout becomes even more suspect in relation to the neutrality principle. Though the bailout clearly assists members of the greater Chrysler family—all those who earn a living by virtue of either direct or indirect associations with the company—it doesn't assist consumers who have obviously made their feelings known in their preference for foreign cars. Why should the interests of the greater Chrysler family take precedence over the interests of consumers? Like Poletown, it would appear that the foundations for this partnership also lie in the legacy of administration, in which case this might be another example of interest-group liberalism.

But if Chrysler was failing because of the choices its managers made, should government be forced to compensate for their poor choices? In other words, what are the limits to which government should be willing to immunize people from risk? Risk, after all, is part and parcel of choice.[42] At the same time, if government does not do anything, it effectively forces innocent people to bear the costs of the choices for which they had no responsibility. Has this not essentially been the liberal justification for public intervention generally and welfare provision specifically? If there are negative consequences arising from intervention due to so-called forces beyond our control, Chrysler may well be an example. More important, episodes like this bear considerable similarity to plant closings in that they show how narrow democracy in this country really is. In that companies can do what they please irrespective of community interests, we can clearly see the limitations to purely political definitions of democracy.[43]

Moreover, if government must bail out a Chrysler because the choices of a few have resulted in serious consequences for a larger community, there would appear to be a powerful argument for economic democracy.[44] At a minimum, the argument would be to attach priority to the interests of the community over those of individuals. Although this isn't antithetical to liberalism, even Lockean liberalism, it does run contrary to the American version of liberalism, which has conceived of individualism in terms of rights against the state.

The problem with administration here is, who decides when intervention to save a company, in the name of the larger public interest, is necessary? When the state can make that decision and the precedent is established, the precedent then occasions the possibility for arbitrary exercises of state power. Does this situation not occasion the possibility that, because the state is offering assistance, it may circumscribe behavior as well? While the federal government brought all parties together, it also imposed a set of conditions on Chrysler management, thereby limiting its managerial discretion as a precondition to receiving assistance.

The principle behind neutrality isn't so much the protection of specific interests, but the protection of all, whether they are propertied or not. For only through the protection of certain rights can individuals be assured equal respect and treatment. The ultimate rationale, then, for preserving the basic integrity of the neutrality measure is a principled one, for a state that can act arbitrarily in some circumstances can do so in others, to the extent where a discussion of rights, liberty, free choice, the guiding principles of the liberal tradition, become totally bereft of any real meaning. On the other hand, if partnerships like Poletown and Chrysler are deemed necessary for the preservation of society, can they ever be accomplished according to neutral principles? It would appear that policies of this sort illustrate well the nature of zero-sum politics.

The obvious question arising from the argument that a bailout may in some cases be necessary for the preservation of society is, by what criteria do we determine who gets bailed out and who does not? Why is it necessarily better to bail out a company because it happens to be one of the Big Three automakers? Such decisions are obviously policy decisions and need to be resolved in a public forum. But as we all disagree over the virtues of specific plans, let alone larger goals, would we be able to truly make the hard choices if they were to always be subject to the liberal form of dialogue? This ultimately becomes the core of the liberal dilemma.

The Challenge

The challenge in public-private partnerships—especially in the form they took in both Poletown and Chrysler—is that administration, the legacy of modern liberalism as well as the foundations of these policies, finds itself in conflict with underlying liberal principles, especially neutrality. One issue in these types of partnerships is whether problems that require these types of approaches can ever be framed according to neutrality. The principle of neutrality as a measure has a virtue in that it is intended to maintain the integrity of the framework that will treat individuals equally. To the extent that it may succeed in this endeavor, neutrality is then intended not only to ensure accountability on the part of public authorities to citizens, but also to prevent the arbitrary exercise of power.

Even if we concede that neutrality is ultimately irrelevant because it is essentially a myth, the implementation of these partnerships still forces us to confront the legitimacy of the authority that decided to enter into them. We are forced to confront the dangers inherent in too much deference to and reliance on administration. It isn't that dialogue not only may have legitimized the partnership against the neutrality measure, but also that it would have erected democratic checks on the abuses of administration. This ultimately is more important, as the former is merely abstract while the latter is more concrete. In the absence of this dialogue, then, the issue of whose best interests public officials were catering to does loom large. Even though instrumentalism may not be a valid critique, it forces us nonetheless to address the question of whose interests are being served. And the perception that interest groups run the country continues to loom ever large.

Lowi's solution to the problem of interest groups was juridical democracy, which would essentially be a return to procedure. Not only would it be a response to interest-group liberalism, but it would effectively restore the basic tenets of the liberal philosophy that were effectively lost as a function of interest groups and the inability of the state to make substantive prioritization of values. In a juridical democracy, the emphasis would be on formal law and procedure operating within institutions. Yet, this juridical democracy would also build a public philosophy around the state.[45] But just what procedures? It sounds good to invoke procedure in the abstract, but there also comes a point at the end of the day when one actually has to devise specific procedures and apply them. This task isn't nearly as easy.

Can we be sure that each claim presenting itself through dialogue will be able to transcend individual interests and rise to the occasion of making hard choices so as to preserve society? How many people would be so self-effacing as to willingly sacrifice their houses for the sake of a so-called community interest? While Americans are well known for wanting to derive benefits while passing costs on to others, through Lowi's model of distributive politics,[46] the model does have another side to it. They are equally suspicious of those who tell them that if they sacrifice they will benefit. Typically, they believe that they will sacrifice and others will benefit.

Even though liberalism has traditionally distinguished between public (political) and private (economic), there was always the presumption that the basis for public policy would be the democratic process, that through traditional channels of communication with elected representatives, policy would achieve legitimacy. One has to question the legitimacy of public officials acting on the basis of what they assume the public wants, even if these officials can ultimately be removed from office should it turn out that their assumptions were wrong. While voting the rascals out is a version of dialogue to be sure, it is only post hoc. Rather, the argument might be made that if an express policy that could have a profound public impact is to be adopted, it should then be subject to a full public discussion. Only by remaining strictly accountable in a forum that allows divergent points of views to be expressed is the neutrality principle adhered to.

If Lowi's juridical democracy might be said to form the essence of the dialogue, other problems are surely bound to arise. First and foremost, it is highly unlikely that we will get agreement. So in the end nothing will get done. True enough, it does remove the debate from the bureaucracy and lodges it back in the legislative bodies, where in theory it belongs. But to what end? If juridical democracy is to consist of a precise set of principles determining who gets bailed out, when, and why—or what types of firms the community will enter into partnerships with—there is probably no getting around the fact that preferences will effectively be displayed for some at the expense of others and in clear violation of the Dworkinian and Rawlsian standard of moral neutrality. There is, perhaps, no getting around the zero-sum nature of American society generally, and American politics especially.[47] These are precisely the concerns that are expressed by opponents of industrial policy who charge that in the end everything is centrally planned and ultimately nobody has freedom of choice.

The democratic process, however, may not always further liberal purposes. This is the central dilemma in modern liberalism today. As society becomes more complex, government must respond. If government responses are to be legitimate, they must effectively be based on the consent of the public. The democratic process is the only effective means of ensuring this legitimacy. Yet, the democratic process in America, especially as it is conceived on the basis of broad representative consensus, prevents effective solutions to serious problems. The system, as it was designed, was intended to protect individual interests, not to ensure efficient or necessarily effective government.[48] Given this, it is easier to rely on the precedents of administrators and bypass the dialogue. In part, the whole premise of limited government was that, since an open political system would make it difficult to get agreement, it would be best for the public to stay out of private affairs. Yet, doing nothing is no longer a viable alternative. The implementation of some of these partnerships does perhaps lend credibility to the notion that government, when it gets involved, only fouls things up.

Traditionally, liberalism emphasized procedure because of its inability to determine which substantive choices would take priority over other substantive choices. Because of its neutrality on questions of "good" and "just," liberalism merely assumed that if procedures were fair and just, so too would be the outcome. One way of resolving the dilemma might be to reassert procedure, even if for the discussion of substantive goals. Serious attempts to reconstruct liberalism would require not only that substantive issues of good and just be debated in public and decided on the basis of consensus, but also that the earlier emphasis on procedure be reasserted. Political institutions would then be required to assume greater responsibility. Clearly there are weaknesses with this, as the robustness of the process might not yield policy that violates the neutrality measure any less than the administrative process does. Nevertheless, as this would still restore policy making to a forum open to the presentation of competing claims, it would serve to legitimize the decision-making process even if the effect had not been neutral. The point I have been attempting to make thus far is that since neutrality doesn't really exist, nor has it ever, we might simply do better not to even try to approximate it. The violation comes from reliance on administrative precedent, which in turn stems inevitably from neutrality.

Ultimately, there is a challenge in public-private partnerships that needs to be addressed. Given that greater efforts have to be made to maintain material prosperity, can it be achieved without some form of centralized planning? Perhaps the real danger in these partnerships, if any can be said to exist, is that they seriously call into question the ability of the marketplace on its own to motivate people to invest. Prior regulation merely demonstrated that markets are susceptible to failure, for which some compensation would be required as a form of counterweight. But the new partnership actually cuts to the core of market theory, that individuals cannot always be relied upon to invest and create opportunities for prosperity. On one level, this may appear to defy liberalism's fundamental rational-activist assumptions. Yet, it isn't that they cannot be relied upon to invest, only that they cannot be relied upon to invest here. The real issue is what constitutes the national or community interest. The rational activism that could be relied upon to build a nation may no longer be sufficient to sustain it.

Whereas the community interest would require the maintenance of an economic base, individual actors may find their own interests to be furthered by disinvesting here and employing their resources elsewhere. As a political ideology, liberalism always assumed that if individuals were free to make their own choices or, in economic terms, pursue their self-interests, society as a whole would prosper. The fact that we may have to resort to the new public-private partnership—largely because the old one is failing—not only shows those assumptions to be obsolete, but also raises the question as to whether the doctrine that has guided us for so long still furthers the national interest. As society becomes more complex, does its preservation not require increasingly more and more restrictions on freedom of choice?

The doctrine that has been at the heart of the nation's development could also, if not reconstructed around principles of community, ultimately be the source of its undevelopment. What policies like public-private partnerships, corporatism, plant-closing laws, monetarism, and regulation all share in common is that they are the responses to the choices some individual or group has been able to make. Often they were made in the absence of any real constraint and in total ignorance of possible consequences to the surrounding community. If made with any such knowledge, they could always be justified on the central presumption of individualism, that if there are no laws to prevent one from doing something, one may do it because one must assume that it is acceptable to do so. As the trajectory of liberal policy making takes us increasingly in the direction of policies cutting to the core of liberal principles, the question is whether there comes a point when those choices or the ability to make them has to be checked or regulated. This is the fundamental dilemma, and, until it is addressed, liberalism may not be able to be restructured in any meaningful way.

6. *Privacy Issues*

RAWLS distinguishes between neutrality regarding concrete policy aimed at solving problems and neutrality regarding moral comprehensive doctrines. When talking about questions of what constitutes the good life, the state must adhere rigidly to a stance of neutrality. Were one group's particular moral doctrine to prevail, and in fact be imposed on others, society would effectively become intolerant of diversity and would cease to be broadly inclusive. Rather, it would become exclusive. Because issues of privacy involve life-style choices, they do fall under the rubric of comprehensive moral doctrines, whereas issues of economic policy do not.[1] And yet, issues of economic policy do speak to the larger question of what the role of government ought to be in society and hence in our daily lives. To make distinctions would, on a peripheral level at least, appear to be splitting hairs. Libertarians would surely argue that once government gets involved in one realm of activity, it can surely get involved in another.

For modern liberalism, however, there appears to be a paradox, one ultimately pressing at the heart of community. Liberals might disingenuously argue that neutrality in economic issues need not be achieved because these issues don't really impinge on our ability to make life-style choices—that is, our ability to be ourselves in conformity with the dictates of moral agency. On the contrary, they merely affect the integrity of the framework that will enable us to continue relying on our agency. But privacy issues do speak to the essence of individualism, which is no less than the essence of agency. Consequently, liberals often insist that those matters concerning personal privacy, or those matters affecting our fundamental rights—those rights that are essential for securing what Justice Cardozo once referred to as "ordered liberty"[2]—strictly adhere to principles of moral neutrality. Moreover, the distinction can find legitimacy on the grounds that what one does in the marketplace will affect others, whereas what one does in privacy will not. The same potential for harm doesn't exist in the realm of privacy as it does in the marketplace. What remains to be seen is whether this proposition is actually true.

On matters of privacy, there would appear to be a balkanization of community, or at least that is the impression often portrayed by conservatives. Because government cannot make moral choices, it ought not to maintain any common standards of morality, principally because we in a liberal society cannot agree on just what those standards might be. While neutrality has had to be abandoned for liberal purposes on policies concerning material goods, it is still the ideal to be achieved when it comes to matters of conscience. Consequently, the liberal framework should tolerate a diversity of religious positions, political forms of expression, and alternative life styles. In other words, the liberal ideal of "leave me alone" is to be respected.[3] This shouldn't, however, necessarily be confused with atomization.

It is this dichotomous relationship that appears to have given liberalism in recent years an image of being bereft of value. At issue, then, is if the preservation of society requires greater reliance on community—even at the expense of some forms of individualism—just what are the limits to that community? More to the point, however, can we justify a liberalism calling for greater community in one area while allowing for greater atomism in another? If neutrality must be abandoned in favor of "liberal purposes" in the material realm, why does it necessarily follow that greater neutrality will further those same purposes in the realm of privacy? What I hope to show in this chapter is that when we consider a set of policies that pull in the opposite direction of those we have been considering thus far, we ultimately achieve some refinement of Mill's harm principle as well as Locke's exhortation to preserve society. But such a refinement involves viewing harm in terms of physical or material threats to our well-being. Ironically, these are the same arguments used by conservatives to justify fewer regulations on business. Still, it begs the question of whether a community can be held together by nothing more than the need to prevent harm to others or whether the community also requires a common bonding. At issue, ultimately, is what does it mean to talk about an inclusive community. These issues press against the very meaning of our common project.

Religion?

The "liberal idea," as Flathman calls it,[4] is perhaps best captured in Locke's *Letter*. If individuals are free to think for themselves, and conceive of their own "goods" as an essential part of their individualism, it follows logically that they can pick and choose which gods, if any at all, they will believe in and live their lives accordingly. Since there is no such thing as objective truth, one must seek one's own truth. Consequently, the liberal state that is tolerant of diversity must be tolerant of religious diversity. Religious diversity, for all intents and purposes, has been at the heart of liberalism since its inception, especially as it was in response to the absolutism and clericalism of particular religious orthodoxies out of which liberalism as an ideology was born.

Locke's rejection of Adamicism in both his refutation of Filmer and his larger argument contained in the *Essay* is a response to the Enthusiasts—those fundamentalist preachers who were part of the established religious order in England. As Aaron suggests, Locke might have simply regarded his own life as a passage from the age of Enthusiasm to one of

Reason.[5] As much as the *Letter* may have had a political purpose—to fight against the intentions of King Charles II to impose Catholicism on the country—it clearly laid out a larger principle of toleration. Locke made it clear that religion as an institution was essentially voluntary, which meant that matters of religious faith had to be private. Implicit, of course, is the notion that tolerance is ultimately what makes for political stability and social tranquility. This was by no means lost on James Madison and the other framers of the Constitution when they recognized that if the fledgling American nation was to truly escape history, it would have to be not only a land where religion could be practiced freely, but also a land where many religious groups could practice their respective faiths unencumbered by others.[6] This required that government be neutral on all matters concerning faith. The establishment clause of the First Amendment was intended not only to ensure freedom of religion but also to ensure that politics would not be influenced by the absolutes of any religious faiths. The establishment clause thus contains the dual purpose of ensuring that neither religion nor politics will be corrupted by each other.

Regarding religion, the liberal state in the United States has become increasingly more neutral over the last forty to fifty years. School prayer cases before the Supreme Court have resulted in a greater wall of separation between church and state. Before the 1960s, beginning a school day with a moment of prayer was commonplace. Since then, school prayer has been considered a violation of First Amendment rights to practice free religion. More precisely, it has been regarded as a right by minorities, whether they be believers of something different or nonbelievers, not to have the majority faith imposed upon them, or, more correctly, not to be forced to believe at all— the essence of individuality.

In 1962 the Court addressed the constitutionality of nondenominational prayer in *Engel v. Vitale*. At issue was the New York State board of regents' requirement that the following prayer be recited at the beginning of each school day in the presence of a teacher: "Almighty God, we acknowledge our dependence upon Thee, and we beg Thy blessings upon us, our parents, our teachers and our Country." Speaking for the Supreme Court, Justice Black asserted that "the State of New York has adopted a practice wholly inconsistent with the Establishment Clause. There can, of course, be no doubt that New York's program of daily classroom invocation of God's blessings as prescribed in the Regent's prayer is a religious activity. It is a solemn avowal of divine faith and supplication for the blessings of the Almighty." Black went on to point out that the First Amendment was specifically designed to guarantee that neither the power nor the prestige of the government would be used to "control, support, or influence" the types of prayers that the people can say.[7] The express purpose of the establishment clause was to isolate people's religious faith from the vicissitudes of prevailing public opinion and politics. The Fourteenth Amendment, as far as the Court was concerned, only served to reinforce the intent and design of the First Amendment in this particular case.[8]

It is perhaps true that once an opening exists, in the form of a prayer, the potential is there for future groups to bend and modify it so that it fits their purposes. Yet, this prayer was nondenominational! Was it imposing a particular religious viewpoint on anyone? Was it the same as saying that A's religious beliefs have merit, or more merit than B's, and therefore the state will show preference for A's? Was it not also stating a preference for all believers, whoever they were? The state, by adopting a prayer at all, was in fact expressing a belief in God, a belief that it expected all children would express belief in as well. Or perhaps more to the point, they would be expected to affirm a commitment to a concept of God in which they might not believe. To do so would not only defeat the purpose of a liberal education—the process by which all points of view are weighed against each other as the basis upon which a conclusion can independently be drawn—but would deny the legitimacy of their individuality, the right to think differently and resist conformity. The school, in short, was putting forth a religious value, with the effect being to leave the nonbeliever isolated from the rest of the group—to say that this person who does not believe does not belong. To define membership in a community by a public recitation of a prayer was to be no different than imposing a type of conformity on those who in fact chose to be different. Although the Court was well aware that the prayer was not the same as a total establishment of religion, the prayer's effective establishment of a particular standard for inclusion was by no means lost on the Court either.

The definition of communal membership is fundamentally important, for only a year later, the Court took up the case of *Abington School District v. Schempp*. The state of Pennsylvania had required: "At least ten verses from the Holy Bible shall be read, without comment, at the opening of each public school day. Any child shall be excused from such Bible reading, or attending such Bible reading, upon written request of his parent or guardian."[9] Speaking for the Court, Justice Clark asserted:

> The wholesome "neutrality" of which this Court's cases speak . . . stems from a recognition of the teachings of history that powerful sects or groups might bring about a fusion of government and religious functions or a concert or dependency of one upon the other to the end that official support of the State or Federal Government would be placed behind the tenets of one or of all orthodoxies. This the Establishment Clause prohibits. And a further reason for neutrality is found in the Free Exercise Clause, which recognized the value of religious training, teaching, and observance, and, more particularly, the right of every person to freely choose his own course with reference thereto, free of any compulsion from the state.[10]

Although the state maintained that the purpose of Bible reading had been to foster moral values, in part as a counterweight to the increasing materialism of the times, the fact that such readings were taken from the Bible, particularly the King James Version, was sufficient in and of itself to establish that this exercise was an instrument of religion. Moreover, the Court was not at all ready to accept the argument that the prohibition of a religious exercise to which a majority consented thus infringes upon that majority's right to free exercise of religion. The Court said, "While the Free Exercise Clause clearly prohibits the use of state action to deny the rights of free exercise to *anyone*, it has never meant that a majority could use the machinery of the state to practice its beliefs."[11]

Justice Clark made it clear that religion in American society had an exalted place and was not to be invaded by the state. The state could only maintain a legitimate commitment to that exalted position from a position of neutrality. In a larger sense, however, Justice Clark seemed to be intimating that a majority seeking to use the political process, predicated on the principle of consent through majority rule, to have a religious exercise in the name of its own free exercise of religion was effectively excluding those who did not subscribe to that view. In this vein, both *Schempp* and *Vitale* have to be viewed as statements on the meaning of community that is inclusive, as opposed to exclusive.

The effect of both the *Schempp* and *Vitale* decisions was to make it clear that on matters of religious faith—or faith at all for that matter—the state was in fact required to be completely neutral. Still, how does one address the thorny question of differentials in education, that is, disparities between public school education on the one hand and church-based education on the other? Suppose a school district desired to ensure that the secular education in church-based schools would be equivalent to that of the public schools through a subsidy to church-based schools. Would this be the same as imposing a moral position on others? In *Lemon v. Kurtzman*, the Court took up the issue of Rhode Island's Salary Supplement Act. Based on legislative findings that the quality of secular education in parochial schools was in jeopardy because of the rising salaries needed to attract competent teachers, the act authorized a supplement to be paid directly to the teachers of secular subjects in nonpublic elementary schools.

Although the stated purpose of the state legislation was to enhance the quality of secular education in all schools, at issue was whether the state wasn't, in the process, violating the religious freedom of others by effectively forcing them to subsidize religious education through their tax dollars. The Court maintained that Rhode Island's law did create an entanglement between church and state. Even if teachers were subsidized directly, the Court found it hard to believe that a teacher, whose employment was controlled by a religious structure, would not teach a secular subject without some religious content. The state could not ensure that subsidized teachers would not inculcate religion.[12]

The *Lemon* case, to a large extent, represents a response to the 1947 case of *Everson v. Board of Education*, in which the issue was the provision of public transportation to all schools, including church-based ones. This case arose from a New Jersey statute authorizing local school districts to make rules and contracts for transportation of their children to and from school. In this case, the local school board authorized reimbursement to parents of monies expended by them for transportation on public buses. Parents who were sending their children to Catholic schools were being reimbursed as well. Were taxpayers being asked to subsidize religious education by providing free transportation to those attending parochial schools? And yet, all parents received the reimbursement, regardless of where they sent their children.

Speaking for the Court, Justice Black maintained that the state was not contributing money to the schools, nor was it in any way supporting them. Rather, it was a neutral policy aimed at helping parents transport their children safely to school, regardless of their religious orientation. More important, however, Black clearly enunciated the standard upon which cases concerning religious freedom were to be decided. "The First Amendment has erected a wall between church and state. That wall must be kept high and impregnable."[13] Ever high as that wall was to be kept, it had not been breached in this particular case. What *Lemon* did was qualify what would constitute a breach, as it enunciated the following principles: (1) the statute in question must have a secular legislative purpose; (2) its principal or primary effect must be one that neither advances nor inhibits religion; and (3) the statute must not foster "an excessive government entanglement with religion."[14] It is essentially the *Lemon* test that is used to determine whether a school policy or legislative action in any way violates First Amendment principles of separation of church and state.

Still, this begs the question. If both *Vitale* and *Schempp* served to establish criteria for defining an inclusive community, why couldn't the subsidy of secular education for those attending parochial schools not be viewed as an attempt to maintain a broadly inclusive community? The objective of public education, after all, is to ensure that each is taught equally. The implicit meaning of *Vitale* and *Schempp* is that inclusive community does in fact require tolerance for diversity, that unless each person's moral worth is recognized, on equal terms, there can be no prospect of maintaining a community at all. Cannot one, then, argue that unless the needs of each group can be met, diversity is not being tolerated? The message of *Lemon* is clear: if you want a quality secular education, you must attend the public school, but check your religion at the door. Is this necessarily tolerance for diversity? If it isn't, is the state really being neutral?

As much as this is an effective statement on the liberal position of moral neutrality, and perhaps taken directly from the pages of Locke's

Letter, a nagging question still persists: Under the rubric of religious freedom, is it not then possible to wall oneself off from the community? What if religious faith and expression does form the basis of the community? What if it is on the basis of religious faith that the core of the community's values are formed? What, then, does this wall of separation do to the structure of community? By asserting the need for a wall of separation, the Court was clearly placing matters of religion under the purview of privacy. How one views and practices religion is essentially a question of privacy because it involves delving into the recesses of one's own mind. Justice Black had been quite clear on this in *Vitale* when he said, "The Establishment Clause thus stands as an expression of principle on the part of the Founders of our Constitution that religion is too personal, too sacred, too holy, to permit its 'unhallowed perversion' by a civil magistrate."[15]

This is no different from the liberal idea of freedom of conscience. To subscribe to a particular religious faith or not is to subscribe to a particular moral conception of the good. To interfere with the privacy of one's faith is to effectively limit the choices people can make and ultimately be intolerant of diversity. These points had been made earlier by the Court when it decided that the choice of parents to send their children to parochial schools, as opposed to public ones, was nothing less than a right in privacy. In both *Pierce v. Society of Sisters* and *Meyer v. Nebraska* the Court asserted the rights of individuals in privacy to decide how to live their lives and how best to raise their children, according to whatever precepts—religious and otherwise—they considered to accord with their life styles.[16]

The wall of separation serves to maintain equality by excluding from the public domain those issues that are truly divisive and effectively make for an exclusive community. To this end, it can certainly be said to conform to the Rawlsian position that the state must remain neutral regarding comprehensive moral doctrines. The general society becomes inclusive insofar as issues calling attention to differences between people are effectively removed.[17] Such a wall, then, has to be viewed no differently than erecting a buffer between the state and the choices people make regarding how best they are going to live their lives. The choice of a religion, after all, is one of life style. To impose one's faith on another is to impose one's morality on another. This essentially violates the basic injunction not to show preference for A over B because to do so would essentially be the same as not giving each equal respect and treatment.[18] If we are to create an inclusive community revolving around those principles in liberalism, our starting point must, by definition, be the equality of all individuals.

However, is there not a fabric that must also be relied upon to hold the community together? On what basis, then, does there exist a community? If, for example, a nondenominational prayer, or even a moment of silence, would be considered a basis upon which to build a sense of community, the Supreme Court has made it clear that this still violates the First Amendment. Can the argument be made that prayer of any sort forms the basis of a community? By asking this question I am not asking whether everybody should be forced to believe in God, as that is a metaphysical impossibility, but whether the act of prayer does not in some way constitute a common and shared experience.

What if a community should want to have a prayer experience, not for the purposes of fostering a particular religious position but because the act of praying constitutes a communal experience? That is, a time when everybody can come together and affirm a common commitment to something. An example of this might be the observance in Israel of Remembrance Day. On this day, a siren is sounded throughout the country and, regardless of where people are or what they are doing, they stop to observe a moment of silence in memory of all those who lost their lives fighting for the nation's security. On this day, which is just one day before Israeli Independence Day, are not members of the community effectively being brought together, if for no other purpose than to affirm a common bond?

What if this communal experience is essential to preserving society? In other words, this prayer experience is not to foster a religious purpose but a secular legislative one. In order for society to be maintained, is there not some common faith that must be maintained? Perhaps the common criticism of liberalism, as it is predicated on a conception of moral neutrality, is that if all can freely choose their respective goods and government is to maintain neutrality, what is the common thread that holds society together?[19] What binds us together as a nation? Commitment to the framework may partly bind us together, but that commitment is only to procedure. Are there no commonly shared values that form the basis of a faith?

Sanford Levinson suggests that America's commitment to the Constitution and its values forms the basis of a secular faith. It is this constitutional faith that holds the nation together.[20] It may well be that this constitutional faith takes the place of religious faith, principally because we cannot agree as to which religious faith we will subscribe. It does provide a set of community values to which we can subscribe. But then, what is the substantive difference between a civil religion—which a constitutional faith is—and a theological one? After all, if we should begin our school day with recitation of the Pledge of Allegiance, are we not in effect engaging in a common prayer of sorts? What difference does it make whether we pray for that which the flag symbolizes or to a "God Almighty?" The reason we recite the pledge is so that we can affirm a common heritage. It is, in short, a communal experience. Yet, there is a secular purpose: to express pride and loyalty to the nation and its ideals as symbolized by that flag. Why, then, isn't recitation of a nondenominational prayer viewed in the same terms? To ask these questions may ultimately be to ask whether it is possible as a society to come together in the form of communal affirmation without violating people's rights to privacy.

This question, perhaps, cuts to the core of calls for moments of silence at the beginning of a school day. Even if some groups do have a hidden political agenda, is there not this larger philosophical question that must be addressed? A moment of silence, while it raises the specter of a slippery slope for some, does tread the line between respecting individuals' zones of privacy and actually encroaching upon them. Once specific words are required for recitation during that moment, the line has actually been crossed. On this point, we might have a refinement of Mill's harm principle, but it is a very thin line. The moment of silence is ambiguous. That is, can a moment of silence actually hurt someone? The presumption would appear to be that actual prayers, as ecumenical as they may be, do have the potential to hurt people—they have the potential to restrict people's freedom of thought and conscience, and, ultimately, their liberty.

This trajectory is clearly visible in *Wallace v. Jaffree*, decided in 1985. This case involved a statute that began as nothing more than a simple moment of silence but through two successive amendments ended up requiring the actual recitation of a prayer. In 1978, the state of Alabama required a one-minute period of silence in all public schools for the purpose of meditation. In 1981, the statute was amended to allow for meditation or voluntary prayer. In 1982, the statute was amended again to allow for teachers to lead "willing students" in a prescribed prayer to "Almighty God . . . the Creator and Supreme Judge of the World."[21] It would appear from this trajectory that the state was intending to encourage religious activity. Nevertheless, the district court upheld the constitutionality of these statutes on the grounds that Alabama did possess the right to establish a state religion if it so desired, and that the federal Constitution imposed no obstacles to a state religion.

Upon deciding this case, the Supreme Court had no desire to comment at length on how the district court had reached the conclusion it had. Rather, it sufficed for the Court to unanimously affirm the court of appeals' reversal of the district court, and to note in passing that the position of the district court was correct until the Fourteenth Amendment got in the way. More substantively, however, the Court, in the opinion of Justice Stevens, asserted: "The legislative intent to return prayer to the public schools is, of course, quite different from merely protecting every student's right to engage in voluntary prayer during an appropriate moment of silence during the school day. The 1978 statute already protected that right, containing nothing that prevented any student from engaging in voluntary prayer during a silent minute of meditation." As Alabama could offer no compelling secular purpose for amending the statute to encourage religious activity, the Court simply concluded that the endorsement of prayer activity was the legislative intent behind the law.[22]

On one level, this case clearly demonstrates that the slippery slope often invoked as the reason for not putting so much as a chip in the wall is a very real possibility. True neutrality, then, would require that no moment of silence be observed because of the precedent it creates. On another level, the Court intimated that had Alabama simply stopped with the 1978 statute, there would have been no real violation of one's privacy rights. In short, it is the actual transformation of silence into some institutional prayer that strips religion, or whatever activity it is, of its privacy. The action becomes public, and with its exposure comes the potential for individuals to be forced into conformity through the sheer force of peer pressure. This point had been made abundantly clear over forty years earlier by Justice Jackson when he said:

> If there is any fixed star in our constitutional constellation, it is that no official, high or petty, can prescribe what shall be orthodox in politics, nationalism, religion, or other matters of opinion or force citizens to confess by word or act their faith therein.[23]

Could we not then infer that the Court was suggesting that the moment of silence might actually be acceptable because it constitutes a time when everybody, though they might not be thinking the same things, are doing the same thing? Silence, in other words, becomes the shared experience of the community. It also affords everyone the right to maintain privacy while simultaneously participating in a community experience.

The principal argument for the wall of separation would appear to be that it is essential for the maintenance of an inclusive community. But doesn't an uncompromising commitment to this wall create an absolute that can exclude as much as it includes? If everybody, from behind this wall, can assert individual uniqueness, and even use it to draw distinctions, does it not also become a basis for fracturing the community along religious lines? Two cases in particular that appear to have this effect are *Wisconsin v. Yoder* and *Edwards v. Aguillard*. To an extent, the first case is more troubling than the second because it directly cuts to the bone of the issue of one's being able to wall oneself off from the community in the name of religious freedom. The second merely deals with another side of inclusion.

Yoder involved a state's compulsory school attendance law and the right of an individual, based on free exercise of religion, to be exempt from attending school. The respondents in this case were members of the Old Order Amish religion and had refused to send their children to school past the eighth grade. The law required that children attend school till they were sixteen. The reason for not sending their children to school was the belief that attendance at a high school, whether it be public or private, was contrary to the Amish religion and way of life. By sending their children to high school, they believed that they would not only expose themselves to danger of censure of the church community, but also endanger their own salvation and that of their children. The values that would be taught were considered to be in marked variance with Amish values. "Formal high school education beyond the eighth grade is contrary to Amish beliefs . . . because it takes the children away from their community, physically and emotionally, during the crucial and formative adolescent period of life. During this period, the children must acquire Amish attitudes favoring manual work and self-reliance and the specific skills needed to perform the adult role of an Amish farmer or housewife. They must learn to enjoy labor." Elementary education, however, wasn't objectionable because the Amish did agree that their children needed to learn basic skills so as to read the Bible, be good farmers, and deal with the non-Amish when necessary. For the Court's position, compulsory school education did have a threat of undermining the Amish community and its religious practices. Speaking for the Court, Chief Justice Burger opined, "We can accept it as settled, therefore, that however strong the State's interest in universal compulsory education, it is by no means absolute to the exclusion of all other interests."[24]

Was the chief justice not missing the point here? The purpose of compulsory education was to ensure that children would be able to obtain the necessary skills so that they can become relatively self-sufficient. If it should turn out that these people cannot earn a living as farmers and lack appropriate skills to obtain other employment because they stayed out of school on religious principle, will they not then become burdens to the community? Compulsory education's other purpose, as it came of age during the New Deal period, was to ensure that children would not be taken out of school so they could go to work in the sweatshops and be exploited. This much had been acknowledged when Burger mentioned the provisions of the Federal Fair Labor Standards Act of 1938.[25] Instead of saying that the Amish were entitled to create their own high school in conformity with their own values, the Court simply excused them from their communal responsibility. Would it not have been wiser, better for society, had the Court attempted to balance the two competing claims—a legitimate secular purpose and free exercise of religion?

The Court never really explained why a high school education necessarily had to be incompatible with the Amish's free exercise of religion. The purpose was not to threaten the values of a particular group. Was the Court not in effect saying that the ultimate meaning of neutrality, especially as it finds form in this wall of separation, is to be able to wall yourself off from the community? If work forms the principal norm of inclusion in society for adults, does school not form the principal norm of inclusion for children? What if all groups sought to wall themselves off from the community? What commonality would there be? School, it must be presumed, does form a basis for some commonality. Even Locke maintained that religious toleration was to be maintained only if it did not undermine society. Where, then, does one draw the line? If one group can claim religious exemption, can't they all? What is troubling about this decision from the standpoint of community is that the law was not aimed at discriminating against anyone. Rather, it applied across the board to all, regardless of their faiths. If anything, the minimum floor it sought to create by requiring students to stay in school until age sixteen could be said to be in keeping with a concept of inclusive community. If anything, the line was drawn at maintaining an equal standard.

Justice Douglas, in his dissent, presented the problem rather poignantly when he asked that if religion was an individual matter, what right did parents have to decide for their children? As Douglas put it:

> It is the future of the student, not the future of the parents, that is imperiled by today's decision. If a parent keeps his child out of school beyond the grade school, then the child will be forever barred from entry into the new and amazing world of diversity that we have today. The child may decide that that is the preferred course, or he may rebel. It is the student's judgment, not his parents', that is essential if we are to give full meaning to what we have said about the Bill of Rights and of the right of students to be masters of their own destiny. If he is harnessed to the Amish way of life by those in authority over him and if his education is truncated, his entire life may be stunted and deformed. The child, therefore, should be given an opportunity to be heard before the State gives the exemption which we honor today.[26]

By allowing these children to be kept out of school, was the Court not in effect sanctioning a form of discrimination? These children were effectively being denied those tools essential for selecting the type of life style that would best suit them later on in life. Were they not being denied the bases upon which they would be able to make choices in accordance with liberal principles? If the purpose of a liberal community is to create a framework in which individuals can reach their fullest potential as an expression of their individuality, how were they to do this if they were being denied access to a marketplace of alternative and competing ideals that would ultimately enable them to do so? Paradoxically, liberal principles were being employed to serve what can only be viewed as ultimately illiberal ends. On what basis, then, has the objective of an inclusive community been served? Although this case found its justification in a liberal understanding of a wall of separation, it seriously presses against the question of whether liberal purposes were being served.

The point here is that allowing children to stay out of school ultimately causes them to be disadvantaged—they do not possess the same tools that everyone else does, tools that might be necessary for carving out their respective niches in life. This is all the more true if these children should grow up and then decide to abandon the Amish way of life. In the race for life, they perhaps are just as disadvantaged as if they themselves had been forced to go to racially segregated schools under the old authority of *Plessy v. Ferguson*. The effect, as was made abundantly clear in *Brown v. Board of Education*,[27] is to leave these people unequal. While the end result is to further the liberal objective of personal liberty, it ultimately negates the other objective that is just as important: equality. It is this emphasis on personal liberty, as important as it may be, that, for Walzer, liberals have been misguided. Liberalism, as a doctrine that prizes privacy, should be as much about equality as it is about liberty.[28] The Court in *Yoder* certainly affirmed a commitment to liberty, individualism, and even diversity, but did it for equality? Perversely, the Amish did recognize that individualism is nothing if not a product of the community that shapes it. Only by remaining under the tight control of their communities could their children be the individuals they wanted them to be.

Whereas this case involved the right of a group to wall itself off from the rest of the community on the basis of religious freedom, *Edwards* involved a group of people who thought they were being excluded from the community precisely because of where the wall of separation had been erected. This case involved Louisiana's Balanced Treatment for Creation-Science and Evolution-Science in Public School Instruction Act (Creationism Act). The Creationism Act forbade the teaching of the theory of evolution in public schools unless accompanied by instruction in "creation science." Although neither was required to be taught, one could not be taught without the other. The act was challenged as a violation of the establishment clause. Louisiana, of course, defended it on the grounds that it protects the secular interest of academic freedom. Speaking for the Court, Justice Brennan said: "Even if academic freedom is read to mean 'teaching all of the evidence' with respect to the origin of human beings, the Act does not further this purpose. The goal of providing a more comprehensive science curriculum is not furthered either by outlawing the teaching of evolution or by requiring the teaching of creation science."[29]

The Court maintained that the act displayed "discriminatory preference" for the teaching of creationism and against the teaching of evolution. Had Louisiana wanted to maximize the comprehensiveness and effectiveness of science education, it would have encouraged the teaching of all scientific theories about the origins of humankind. There was no question in the Court's mind that the act violated the establishment clause because it sought to employ the symbolic and financial support of government for the achievement of a religious purpose. What about the argument that by teaching one position without offering some equal time to the other side another group of citizens was being excluded? Perhaps Justice Scalia summed it up well in his dissent when he stated rather tersely:

> In sum, even if one concedes, for the sake of argument, that a majority of the Louisiana Legislature voted for the Balanced Treatment Act partly in order to foster (rather than merely eliminate discrimination against) Christian fundamentalist beliefs, our cases establish that that alone would not suffice to invalidate the Act, so long as there was a genuine secular purpose as well. We have, moreover, no adequate basis for disbelieving the secular purpose set forth in the Act itself, or for concluding that it is a sham enacted to conceal the legislators' violation of their oaths of office. I am astonished by the Court's unprecedented readiness to reach such a conclusion,

> which I can only attribute to an intellectual predisposition created by the facts and the legend of *Scopes v. State* . . . an instinctive reaction that any governmentally imposed requirements bearing upon the teaching of evolution must be a manifestation of Christian fundamentalist repression. In this case, however, it seems to me the Court's position is the repressive one.[30]

Aside from the issue of religious freedom, there would also appear to be the issue of free expression. Is a community fostered when people are put into a position where they have to fear that what they say and do will offend others? For Scalia's position, this case was nothing more than an exercise of "Scopes-in-reverse." As there was no objective evidence to support evolution, or none to discredit creationism, evolution had to be regarded as no more and no less of a belief than was creationism. Scalia's basic point was that we simply do not know conclusively to say what constitutes truth. If it should be conceded that Scalia is perhaps partial to the teaching of creationism because of his own religious convictions, the humility that his dissent displays toward the question of truth is really at the heart of liberalism's freedom of conscience. That is, there can be no absolute conceptions of anything because there is no such thing as objective truth. As free-thinking individuals, we each possess our own truths. But this is also at the heart of Locke's theory of language, that because there is no such thing as a universal language, we all have the ability to conceive of things as we will.

Ultimately, a wall of separation intended to preserve the basic integrity of individualism may end up eroding that individualism when individuals come to fear the consequences of their thoughts, words, and actions.[31] The issue puts the liberal state in a quandary. Tolerance, after all, would require that all perspectives be taught, regardless of how offensive they might be to some. The only constraint is that they not cause harm to others. At the same time, should the liberal state tolerate thought or measures, though they may be framed with the community in mind, that are ultimately intended to create a society that is not tolerant but exclusive of those deemed not to belong? In other words, should the liberal state tolerate beliefs that could lead to its own destruction? It would appear that on this point Locke and Mill might diverge. Again, recall that Locke did not believe that Catholics should be tolerated because of their allegiance to a foreign potentate.[32] As mentioned already, the Court in *Wallace* seemed to suggest that the thin line was actually drawn on silence. Do the words of Justice Jackson not come back to haunt us here?

Even if a case could be made that the previous cases were aimed at declaring the neutrality of the state on matters of religious preference and morality, where was that neutrality here? Is the teaching of evolution and the exclusion of creationism not effectively the same as expressing preference for one group over another? Nevertheless, there is an inconsistency with *Yoder*. If we can take from its meaning that identifiable communities can define values and take steps to protect them, then why can't this community, so defined, do the same thing? Are communities not, as Walzer argues, the ones who define the terms of their membership? This is the principal good that communities distribute.[33] Yet, religion is nothing more than the outer surface. Ultimately, what holds a community together is its common morality. But from whence, then, does this common morality come if not from either one religious ethic or an amalgam of several religious ethics?

Nevertheless, the traditional liberal commitment to religious freedom does beg the question of a common morality. The issue is fundamental because it goes to the heart of individual conscience. From the standpoint of Mill's harm principle—which is as much a foundation for pulling the community together as it is for protecting individuals from it—the privacy of religious faith cannot be said to cause harm to others in quite the same way as one's pursuing private profits might. Though religious freedom touches on the issue, those issues that really penetrate to the core of community may well be some of the tougher privacy issues—those that do press against competing conceptions of morality—like abortion, pornography, and homosexual rights. But it is also important to bear in mind that the history of liberalism is the struggle against the tyranny of religious authority—absolute clericalism—where the basis of membership was determined solely on the content of one's beliefs.

Reproductive Freedom

When critics of liberalism seek to identify a point in time when the moral fabric of society began to deteriorate, they often point to the famous 1965 contraception case of *Griswold v. Connecticut.* On one level, it was a deterioration because it marked the beginning of a process in which the Court began to create rights not explicitly provided for in the Constitution. It was only eight years later, with *Roe v. Wade,* that the right to privacy would take on a whole new dimension. Critics of *Roe* have been all too quick to point out that the Constitution does not contain any explicit rights to privacy.[34] Yet, the Court's application of privacy to the bedroom, in part, appealed to the same precedents that informed its decisions on religious freedom. Those rights to privacy that entitled parents to decide how to live and raise their children had to be the same when it came to making decisions about reproduction and other bedroom issues.[35]

In *Griswold,* the Court suggested that although the Constitution may not specifically mention privacy, it does contain a penumbra where privacy is protected from government intrusion. The Connecticut statute banning contraception could not stand because it interfered with the rights of a married couple to make private decisions not only regarding how many children they would have but also, ultimately, regarding life style.[36] This right was only expanded in *Eisenstadt v. Baird,* where the Court said that the same rights to privacy that existed in the marital relationship also applied to unmarried individuals. As the marital relationship was nothing more than a union of two individuals, it was not an entity with a mind and heart of its own. "If the right of privacy means anything, it is the right of the individual, married or single, to be free from unwarranted government intrusion into matters so fundamentally affecting a person as the decision whether to bear or beget a child."[37]

Essentially, then, the Court was touching on the issue of life-style choice, as the number of children, or any children at all, would have a bearing. Moreover, from the standpoint of harm, could the decision not to have children really be said to hurt others? If it offended anybody at all, it offended their conceptions of morality based on their own respective religious teachings. One wonders whether this was really a question of privacy or simply another version of religious freedom, the right to be free from the religious precepts others would seek to impose. Still, *Roe* was to take the right in privacy yet one step further.

The Court would say that the Fourteenth Amendment's concept of personal liberty, as well as the Ninth Amendment's reservation of rights to the people, was "broad enough to encompass a woman's decision whether or not to terminate her pregnancy. The detriment that the State would impose upon the pregnant woman by denying this choice altogether is apparent."[38] The trajectory from *Griswold* to this point would appear to be clear. Implicit in *Griswold* was the notion that if contraception was an issue of privacy in marriage, then the decision not to get pregnant was actually a joint decision between husband and wife. By suggesting that contraception was a right to privacy for individuals, the Court in *Eisenstadt* effectively acknowledged that the decision not to get pregnant was no longer a shared decision, as it had been in *Griswold*, but a matter to be left to the sole discretion of the woman. Nobody could have an interest in this issue but the individual in question.

In *Roe*, however, the Court asserted that the right to decide not to have children went beyond simply preventing conception to terminating the pregnancy after conception. The right of personal privacy as it had been enunciated in *Griswold* and *Eisenstadt* would also include the abortion decision. To a large extent, *Roe* only built on the acknowledgment in *Eisenstadt* that the decision is not a shared one but a private one, which only the woman herself could make. Yet, the right was not an unqualified right but would have to be considered against important state interests in regulation. Never in *Roe* did the Court say abortion was an absolute right, for it did assert the right of the state to regulate on the basis of "compelling state interests."[39]

To put this in terms of either Mill's harm principle or Locke's preservation of society, the state could regulate at the point at which harm would be caused to somebody, or when the interests of society would be undermined. What wasn't clear, however, was what the state would protect from harm. Theoretically, it was the health of the mother. Historically, abortion laws had been promulgated in order to protect women from unlicensed practitioners and scheming abortionists who had no training. In many cases, legislatures adopted these laws at the requests of the emerging medical profession, which was itself attempting to establish universal professional norms and standards.[40] The Court did in effect rule out the possibility of invoking harm to protect the rights of fetuses because it stated clearly that the fetus was not a person. But if it wasn't a person during the first trimester, why was it any more of one during the second and third trimesters?

While *Roe* aimed to protect the rights of individuals to make choices, it didn't adequately address the issue of protecting life as that might be considered a community interest. As far as the Court was concerned, the state would have no such interest during the first trimester of pregnancy on the grounds that the fetus did not constitute a person entitled to the privileges and immunities as any other. The state could regulate during the second trimester so as to protect the mother's health. The state could protect the life of the unborn during the third trimester unless the life of the mother was at stake. But the Court also asserted that neither a state nor a local government could overcome a women's right "by adopting one theory of life," that is, that life begins at conception.[41] Nevertheless, the fact remains that the state could regulate, and presumably it would be up to the state to decide what a compelling state interest would be.

Critics of *Roe* have charged that the reasoning of the case was based on a conception of substantive due process that was by no means the intent of the Fourteenth Amendment. They allege that it was based on a substantive due process doctrine that had been repudiated in *Lochner,* the case in which an active Supreme Court judiciary struck down a New York State regulation limiting bakers' hours to ten hours daily and sixty hours weekly on the grounds that it violated individual liberty of contract.[42] Yet, the Court claims to disavow *Lochner.*[43] The argument is that the Court read into the orbit of constitutional protection certain values that were neither suggested by the Constitution nor alluded to by the framers of the Constitution. For Robert Bork, *Roe* symbolized the greatest judicial usurpation of democratic prerogative in the twentieth century. *Roe* was only possible because *Griswold* created a right that had not previously existed. *Griswold* was not a constitutional issue, but a cultural one—an attempt to escape the values of a particular cultural mind-set. The intent of the framers was not for the Courts to create rights, but for the legislators to make such decisions and the Court to implement those decisions made through the legislative process.[44] The purpose of the Fourteenth Amendment is to protect procedural due process. But what if *Roe* does share something with *Lochner? Lochner* merely reflected the wisdom that the exercise of state police power should bear some reasonable relationship to public ends. What is the end involved in violating privacy? The answer, of course, would depend on what one does in privacy.

The argument for violating privacy may look as follows: Though it might be conceded that the public does not have a sufficient welfare interest to interfere with reproductive freedom in the first instance (contraception), it may in the second (abortion) on the grounds that life already conceived is being protected. That the public does not have an interest in protecting the life of the unborn is nothing more than a moral value judgment. Value judgments need to be worked out in the public arena. But is this sufficient? The fear of leaving this issue to the public realm is that a majority would attempt to impose its moral judgments on those who do not share that morality. If choice is a right that we all possess, not just regarding abortion but in any matter, should the Court not protect that right? Yet, if we can decide the issue in the public realm, whatever solution is realized, albeit in the form of a compromise, will tend to be more broadly representative of the community and, consequently, more inclusive.

In his famous footnote to *U.S. v. Carolene Products Co.*, Justice Stone suggested that prejudice might constitute a special condition "which tends seriously to curtail the operation of those political processes ordinarily to be relied upon to protect minorities, and which may call for a correspondingly more searching judicial inquiry." The Court might then be acting within its proper sphere of authority if it were to protect such minorities under the Fourteenth Amendment's equal protection clause.[45] By implication, if abortion restrictions reflect the morality of a majority, even as arrived at through the political process, those minorities not subscribing to this view ought to be able to seek protection from the Court. If we were to say that the Court here is protecting a minority, then how is it overextending itself?

To answer the question is to also ask just what are the legitimate rights of the minority? And here, we are still left with a definitional problem. If the intent is the protection of life, the *Carolene Products* footnote does not apply. But in the absence of a clear consensus of what life is or whether life is the same as a person (that is, we all disagree),[46] the footnote would appear to be quite apt. That is, minorities ought to be able to seek protection for their position on the grounds that not only are their rights going to be protected, but also a larger principle of tolerance will be adhered to.[47] Nevertheless, the questions still remains: on what basis is the right to choose protected? And, in this regard, substantive due process worked well to justify it nicely. Although critics will still assert substantive due process to be wrong—that no basis for it exists in the Constitution—others assert that the denial of it is a misnomer. Even the concern for procedure must embody some substantive conception of value. After all, to invoke procedure, as opposed to moral choices, is to make a substantive value choice.[48]

Michael Perry, for instance, finds it highly significant that despite the apparent demise of *Lochner*, the discrediting of economic due process, the Court never really abandoned substantive due process. The Fourteenth Amendment was intended to place federal constitutional limits on state legislative limits. The Court has always held the state police power to be limited by those rights that were considered purely and exclusively private. That the Court has not abandoned the substantive due process doctrine indicates "the continuing constitutional vitality of the notion that a state may not invade an individual's life, liberty, or property interests without good reason." It is a staple of American constitutional jurisprudence that the police power is limited, "inherently by and to their pursuit of the public welfare." Such limitations are recurrent and basic themes of American constitutional theory.[49] So if *Roe* is based on substantive due process, it could simply be said to reflect a developed theory of fundamental rights against the state. If procedure is to be invoked, this theory must come first.[50]

Still, this begs the question: What if a majority of citizens do not share the view that abortion regulation is not necessarily an invasion of one's life, liberty, or property interests without good reason? Are we not then creating a situation whereby the minority holds the larger community hostage to its conception of rights? If policies can effectively be made through judicial fiat, it becomes impossible for the community to determine its own circumstances through an operationalization of modern-day Lockean consent theory. On the contrary, the case might be made that a court making such determinations in defiance of community values is actually constructing the circumstances ripe for the invocation of resistance theory.

What about the concerns of a majority, as that majority might be said to reflect community? It is this issue that constitutes a serious dilemma in democratic society. On the issue of abortion, we may find that two fundamental principles of liberalism—consent and individualism—find themselves at odds with one another. On the one hand, requirements for consent as the basis of continuing government legitimacy would require broad consensus and a degree of majoritarianism. Liberalism requires this consent as an affirmation of support for governing institutions and for the conferring of legitimacy upon them. On the other hand, liberalism requires that individuals' zones of privacy be respected because that is the only way they can be free to make their own choices with respect to their own conceptions of what constitutes good.

Abortion may be a troubling issue because, in large measure, it takes a private issue and effectively makes it public. In contrast to simple contraception, which can be utilized in the privacy of one's bedroom without specific knowledge by the larger community, abortion usually is performed in a facility open to anybody. One must go to an abortion clinic and seek the assistance of a medical professional. Abortion is not the anonymous act that contraception is. Even if the case can be made that the decision by person A to have an abortion does not cause actual harm to abortion protesters—group B—other than an offense to their religious or moral sensibilities, group B can still point to a facility in which the abortions occur, witness people coming and going, and easily conclude that it is occurring within their midst. Should it turn out that group B is equally opposed to contraception on the same grounds, it cannot identify who, where, and when.

In a series of abortion-funding cases, the Court sought to draw the line between public and private more precisely. In *Maher v. Roe*, the Court maintained that an obligation to protect a woman's right to choose was not the same thing as an affirmative responsibility to ensure that those who could not afford abortions received them at the expense of the state.[51] The Court only reaffirmed this position in *Harris v. McRae*, in which the constitutionality of the Hyde amendment was being determined. The Hyde amendment sought to relieve states of any obligations under medicaid funding to fund medically necessary abortions, for which a federal reimbursement was unavailable. The Court made it clear that freedom of choice did not entitle one to a federal subsidy.[52]

The Court seemed to be taking a narrow view of access. In terms of rights protection, the Court was recognizing them to be no more than trumps for which legal obstacles to their realization could not be erected. Interference, then, was not defined as "effective" barriers arising from disadvantaged economic circumstances but as legal barriers to access. While it was recognizing the right of women to decide—that is, the right to choose—it was not extending that right to include a state's obligation to ensure that all women would be able take advantage of it. But in terms of privacy, the Court was suggesting that if privacy meant freedom from public intrusion, it also meant that one making private decisions could not solicit the aid of the public. The Court would hold only to this narrow interpretation in *City of Akron v. Akron Center for Reproductive Health Inc.* The Court held waiting periods and parental notification, as well as hospital requirements, to be effective impediments to a woman's ability to choose. The Court concluded that such restrictions would effectively inhibit the vast majority of abortions after the first trimester. From the Court's standpoint, the state failed to demonstrate a compelling state interest. And more to the point, it failed to show how a woman's right to choose was being protected.[53] Rather than viewing this case as a deviation from *Harris* and *Maher*, the Court was merely subscribing to a technical definition of what it would mean to "interfere" with one's rights. On the contrary, all these cases taken together suggest that privacy rights are still protected, but their scope is limited to a strict separation between public and private. In theory, the Court continued to adhere to its distinction between public and private that was enunciated in these two cases and would also become critical later in *Webster v. Reproductive Health Services.*

By implication, the Court was suggesting that so long as abortions were a matter of private choice, and assuming they were paid for by the individuals themselves, the state could not restrict access by erecting burdensome barriers. At issue was not the cutoff of funds to which the individual had no rights but regulations affecting access to that which individuals did have rights to. The position was only reinforced in *Thorn-*

burgh v. American College of Obstetricians and Gynecologists. Here the bone of contention was the requirement that the physician performing the abortion furnish printed materials, as well as a second physician be consulted. The Court asserted that the "States are not free, under the guise of protecting maternal health or potential life, to intimidate women into continuing pregnancies."[54] As far as the Court was concerned, the printed-materials requirement represented nothing less than an attempt by the Commonwealth of Pennsylvania to interject its own message discouraging abortion into the privacy of the traditional physician-patient relationship. This was all the more true given that the printed material was nonmedical. Once again, the Court was assuming that abortion was a private matter and in no way involved any relationship to the public.

The ultimate statement on the nature of the public-private relationship was made in *Webster.* This case involved regulations prohibiting the use of public funds, employees, and facilities to either perform or assist in nontherapeutic abortions. Hence, physicians affiliated with public hospitals could not perform abortions. But a public facility was defined loosely to include any hospital receiving any public funds, which might include medicaid and medicare reimbursements. The regulations also contained the typical restrictions of informed consent, in which the physician would be required to apprise women of certain facts, as well as a post-sixteen-week hospital requirement. In addition, and perhaps most controversially, the preamble to the regulations contained a definition of life as beginning at conception. While the other regulations could be seen as falling within the purview of *Maher* and *Harris*, the preamble seemed to present a direct challenge to *Roe*, insofar as the state appeared to be adopting one theory of life over another. However, as far as the Court was concerned, the preamble was not really a part of the legislation but was separate. Even if it was part of the legislation, it was not altering the basic definition of a person that was established in *Roe*, that is, the fetal viability standard. Rather, the preamble was merely a value judgment, and *Roe* never implied any limitations of a state's authority to make a value judgment favoring childbirth over abortion.[55]

What the Court did not address, however, was the implication of states defining life at conception. Here it would appear as though the

Court were opening the door for states to promulgate new abortion regulations even during the first trimester on the basis of a "compelling state interest." As the legislative record has shown since *Webster*, that is precisely what happened. Regarding the use of public facilities, the Court merely echoed its earlier rulings in *Maher* and *Harris* by asserting that the due process clause generally did not confer any affirmative right to government assistance. Yet, the Court maintained that it was still upholding the basic integrity of *Roe*, that a woman still had a right to choose, though that right was no longer fundamental. Instead, states could regulate so long as no "absolute" barriers to access were created. But what exactly could a woman choose?

By upholding the preamble, the Court in effect said that even though a woman's right to choose could not be denied, the state could, as a function of its value judgment, effectively brand those who would choose abortion. By defining life as beginning at conception, a state could effectively imply that those who choose abortion are committing murder. If so, do we have equal respect and treatment in which the state ought not to embrace one party's conception of the good over another?[56] Overall, the Court was maintaining the same narrow distinction between public and private it had constructed in the preceding cases. In fact, it was making the distinction even narrower by being strict in the construction of private and fairly broad in the construction of public. What the Court was in effect saying was that if a woman decides to have an abortion, she may decide in private and have it in private, but she may not involve the public in any way, even if she is paying for it herself. The obvious concern here is that the meaning of public was so overarching; one has to wonder if any facility defined as *private* even existed. In effect, the Court was saying that although the right to choose was to be adhered to, the state could erect sufficient barriers to the realization of that right so long as the case was made that these barriers were necessary to keep the public out of private affairs—and so long as it wasn't creating an absolute barrier.

One has to wonder if cases like *Webster* do anything to further the interests of community. On the one hand, they allow individual communities greater latitude in addressing the issue. On the other hand, they may actually succeed in sharpening the battle lines. We certainly are not of one mind that fetuses are persons. We may recognize that the three-trimester standard in *Roe* is no longer credible given advances in medical technology, as Justice O'Connor's dissent in *City of Akron* made abundantly clear.[57] If there is any community arising from *Webster*, it is the common consensus that *Roe* and what it protects are in deep trouble. *Webster* only underscored the fragility of *Roe* on several grounds. Constitutionally, it illustrated that *Roe* was on extremely shaky ground.

What makes *Roe* fragile, then, is not the assertion of a right to privacy, but the basis upon which the Court determined that abortion constituted such a right. The Court had reasoned that abortion was essentially no different from contraception because what was being terminated wasn't a person. That it was life wasn't substantively different from the prevention of life, but it wasn't a person because it wasn't viable. Yet, if viability occurs earlier, does not also the definition of a person? If the definition of personhood is then contingent on the current state of medical technology, so too is the right to choose. Similarly, if the right were to become altered, it could no longer receive protection under the equal protection clause. The right is conditional and by no means secure. What is significant about *Webster* is not that it rolls back a right already established, but that it hints at the fragility of *Roe* by implicitly acknowledging conceptions of life to be contingent on an array of circumstances and not that it is a priori. If the Court was not acknowledging that groups differ on the meaning of life, why assert that a state could construct its own conception? If the Court was departing from *Roe* at all, it was perhaps in its own humility saying that we do not know enough to state categorically what is a life and what is not.

It is telling that the Court did not say that abortion was wrong. If wrong, the Court should simply ban it. Insofar as the Court might allow states to decide, it certainly was not acknowledging the presence of a pro-life position in the Constitution. But there are consequences that are problematic. For instance, if a state may define life as beginning at conception, is the Court not suggesting that a state, according to its own value judgments, can define abortion as murder while another does not? If abortion can be viewed as murder, it must treat the murder of the fetus no differently than it treats the murder of anybody else.[58] But if such distinctions can exist among states, then the notion that the fetus is a person is being severely undermined. As it currently stands, one cannot deliberately kill someone and be said to be acting illegally in state A while legally in state B. Yet, this is precisely the implication we can draw from the Court's acceptance of the preamble to Missouri's abortion law. Moreover, if there is a foundation of community to be inferred from this ruling, it is as shaky as the rights created by *Roe*. One cannot build a sense of community around a conception of where life begins. Any sense of community, or community standard, revolving around a fetal viability standard is only bound to be fragile.

The fact that different states have attempted to approach this issue differently only demonstrates that we do not all share the same morality. That different states have attempted to allow for a variety of exceptions to abortion restrictions only indicates the inconsistency of the pro-life position. For instance, a state calling for bans on abortions except for incidences of rape and incest is making a dubious distinction between categories of life. If a woman gets pregnant because she freely chose to engage in sexual relations, the fetus is a life that cannot be aborted. But if she became pregnant because sex was forced upon her, the fetus is not a life? Certainly the fetus cannot be any less of a life because of the means by which conception occurred. If this distinction does reflect a compromised pro-life position, do we not have yet another violation of the equal protection clause? Are we not then setting up invidious classifications for fetuses? If anything, this distinction may represent less of a commitment to life than it does a commitment to a particular morality regarding sexual practice. As Tribe rightly points out, the opposition to abortion other than for rape and incest simply "reflects a sense that women must pay for engaging in 'consensual sex.'"[59] Insofar as this is true, women's groups are correct when they argue abortion and choice to be a matter of control. Or, because only women can get pregnant, the effect of restrictive abortion laws is to create a "totalitarian intervention into a woman's life."[60]

The liberal position on abortion is still problematic, regardless of which position is staked out. Tribe largely is correct when he presents the issue as a clash between absolutes in which compromise is highly unlikely. It would seem that no matter what is done, the end result is a no-win situation. If an absolute position is taken regarding choice—one may choose at all times and for whatever reason—battle lines are forged around each group's conception of morality. And it is this respective morality—the basis upon which they were socialized—that forms the basis upon which they will view the world. It must be remembered that the open framework that liberalism requires so that each individual can make choices does allow for each to present claims. This is, after all, the Madisonian dilemma—the price we pay for liberty. The irony is that the structure that is put in place to allow for individuals and groups to enjoy liberty can ultimately be the basis upon which their liberty will be restricted.

The position that abortion is a clash between absolutes is not shared by all. As Glendon demonstrates through comparative legal analysis, other Western democracies have found a middle ground between the absolutism of the pro-lifers and the atomistic individualism of the pro-choicers. The problem is that the atomistic individualistic message emanating from *Eisenstadt* and *Roe* no less reflects the individualistic foundations underpinning American culture. Her proposition for compromise is to view abortion regulation not necessarily as a restriction of women's liberty but within a larger context of other laws relating to mothers and children. "If the state is once again to restrict the availability of abortion and to affirm the value of unborn life, it should in all fairness strive to help those who bear and raise children, not only during pregnancy but also after childbirth." In essence, her proposition is to make childbearing an attractive alternative.[61] In a larger sense, she is proposing to build an inclusive community around political compromise.[62] Compromise, because it requires broad consensus, ends up broadly representing the entire community and is, ultimately, more inclusive. If abortion—perhaps one of the most divisive issues in contemporary American politics—can be resolved only through political compromise—by the community itself—it is inevitable that we must conclude that community cannot be built on neutrality. On the contrary, a community is constructed on the shared values of its members. In the end, the community must be built on common aspirations and not merely a desire to prevent harm from one or a few. Community, in short, cannot simply be the creature of necessity.

Still, if liberals compromise, not only is the framework in which individuals can make choices effectively narrowed, but there will always be a group who feels that restrictions on its choices are a function of the morality imposed by others. What the abortion issue clearly dramatizes is that there really is no such thing as a political compromise that does not in some way reflect the moral position of some individual or some group. Even if we could distinguish between rights and fundamental rights in correspondence with Cardozo's position in *Palko*, we still have not satisfied everybody, nor have we removed the issue from politics. The fact still remains that abortion does involve a clash between two competing conceptions of fundamental rights: those of the mother and those of her unborn child, whom many regard as a life whether the law chooses to recognize it as a person or not. But more than any other issue, abortion forces us to seriously address the question of whether true community can be maintained through neutrality.

And yet, a reversal of *Roe*, as *Webster* portends, and an effective return of the issue to the states isn't satisfactory either, as each state can effectively do as it wants. Not only are the choices of individuals then subject to the will of local, and perhaps provincial, majorities, but a national standard aimed at preserving a sense of unified citizenship effectively is lost. Abortion, as with any number of heated moral issues, illustrates just how fractured the national community is. There is no national unity when it comes to these issues, nor was there ever. What *Roe* did do was establish a uniform standard that, if nothing else, ensured equality of citizenship across state boundary lines. The problem is that hard cases like abortion, which constitutionally turn deeply on questions of states' rights, cut to the core of the meaning of national citizenship. If each state can decide this issue for itself, does each citizen of the United States enjoy the same rights to equal respect and treatment? In other words, a return to the states effectively calls into question the type of liberalism we are emphasizing. On the one hand, it results in diversity in that each state within a broadly liberal framework can decide. But by living in different states, we are not all equal within the broadly liberal framework.

The essence of equal citizenship could be said to be the dignity of full membership in society. Equal citizenship might be said to parallel Dworkin's liberal conception of equality, whereby the state is expected to give each individual equal respect and treatment. Does this not then fall within the purview of "life, liberty, and the pursuit of happiness"? As

Kenneth Karst explains, "the principle presumptively forbids the organized society to treat an individual either as a member of an inferior or dependent caste or as a nonparticipant."[63] It would follow logically, then, that citizen A enjoys the same rights and is entitled to the same protections as citizen B regardless of racial, sexual, and other classificatory differences. This essentially has been the basis upon which the equal protection clause has been applied. To require equality under this standard is to require that those similarly situated be treated similarly. If individuals are to be treated differently, then it must be justified by reference to some public value.[64] But it should also follow logically that citizen A would enjoy the same rights and would be entitled to the same privileges and immunities as citizen B regardless of which state A happens to live in. That is, there cannot be legislative differences. If the states were to fall under the principle of equality, as it was envisaged by those who framed the Fourteenth Amendment,[65] one state may not recognize one good that another does not, for the effect would otherwise be inequality. Which is to say, if the Fourteenth Amendment is intended to create a national standard for citizenship (that is, anybody being born in the United States), the rights one enjoys should not vary from state to state.

Though the Fourteenth Amendment creates this standard, the federal structure of the Constitution still presumes in favor of states' rights unless it is demonstrably clear that individual rights have been violated. It is a principle the Court affirmed in the *Slaughter-House Cases*, the first opportunity to give the Fourteenth Amendment judicial construction. The Court acknowledged that "privileges and immunities" applied to all citizens born in the United States but declined to define just what those privileges and immunities were. Generally, the privileges and immunities clause has been interpreted to mean that state legislators cannot treat those from out of state differently than they do their own residents. It was intended to ensure that those citizens passing from state A to state B would enjoy the same rights as those already enjoyed in state B.[66] It has not been interpreted to mean, however, that one passing from B, where rights are more extensive, to A, where they are less extensive, can enjoy those rights enjoyed in B.

The Court in *Slaughter-House* effectively narrowed the applicability of the equal protection clause by saying that, in the absence of a federal definition of privileges and immunities, the states were presumed to have the right to define them for their own citizens, in which case the equal protection clause would not apply.[67] Consequently, then, the Fourteenth Amendment has been limited by the prerequisite of rights. Here is where the specter of *Roe* being overturned presents a problem, for the effect would be for states to decide for themselves the legality of abortion on the grounds that no such right exists, or at least no national one. In its current application, the equal protection clause is limited by the preexistence of a right—or at least that the fundamental right to privacy encompasses the abortion decision.

Let us consider this scenario for a minute. If an abortion essentially involves a woman being able to make choices for herself regarding control of her body, and disparities exist between the states, then women in state A do not enjoy the same rights as do women in state B. Women coming from A, where abortions may be banned, into B, where they may be legal, are entitled to have an abortion. While in B, a woman could not be denied because she happened to be a legal resident of A. Yet, a woman from B could not go into A and enjoy the same rights she enjoyed in B. Has she not just surrendered some of her rights as a function of crossing state boundary lines? If this scenario does not necessarily violate the Court's traditional construction of equal protection, doesn't it violate the spirit? Could we not suppose that the equal protection clause contains a penumbra? This would be especially so if we take the Constitution to represent the aspirations of the political community, not just what judges say it means.[68]

The problem here is that the equal protection clause, as it has been constructed, assumes that the classifications that would violate this standard are either based on sex, race, or wealth. It does not assume the classifications to be based on state boundary lines. That is, within a given state, for instance, it would not be acceptable to prohibit abortions for one class of women while permitting them for another. That would be a violation of the equal protection clause. But this state could prohibit abortion for all women, and the only basis on which it could distinguish among them is if there is a compelling interest—some public value. As an example, women falling into the class of those who became pregnant as a function of rape or incest would be permitted to have an abortion whereas those who did not fall into that category would not. Presumably, this distinction could be justified, but, as noted earlier, such a distinction is dubious.

Although this scenario does not constitute discrimination on the basis of invidious classification, it effectively does so on the basis of an arbitrary state boundary line. Why then should we treat women differently because they are victims of geography? If women can be treated differently solely because of the state in which they reside, and they are presumed to be equal citizens of the larger republic, do we not then have a problem with how the equal protection clause has been applied thus far? Also, it fails to account for a possible scenario in which state citizenship will directly challenge national citizenship. Consider the following: Let's suppose that state A were to pass an absolute ban on abortion with full knowledge that its neighboring states had unrestricted access. What if this state, as part of its general policy of prohibiting abortions for its citizens, was to prohibit pregnant women from leaving the state on the presumption that once outside they might seek to have an abortion? The basis for such a restriction is that since abortion is a crime in state A, the state therefore has a right to take steps to ensure that its citizens do not commit crimes. But even the conventional understanding of the privileges and immunities clause, which informs the limited understanding of the equal protection clause, holds that as part of national citizenship, citizens of the United States may freely travel across state boundary lines. Which citizenship, then, has priority?

Here is where the prospect of states deciding this issue again touches on the meaning of citizenship. The effect is for the citizen of state A to have inherently fewer rights than the citizen of state B. This effectively means that citizens of the national society do not possess the same rights. The effect is to have unequal citizenship. The issue is also important because, on another level, abortion may well reflect the conflict between competing conceptions of community. That is, are we to conceive of community in national terms or more parochial ones? Yet, liberal evolution since the New Deal essentially has been about the construction of a national community. That is, a community in which more and more people would be equal, at least in material terms. But they would also be equal in their ability to have access. Community was thus constituted by creating a national tent in which disparities among people, especially given differences among states, would be diminished.

What is the compromise? Is compromise possible? From a policy point of view, education may be the key. Sex education might actually reduce the number of abortions performed—because most are the result of unintended pregnancies. This, however, offends people just as much. Libertarians do not believe that schools should be teaching about those matters that are essentially private. Certain conservatives view it as an encroachment of the public sector into the private realm of the family. Religious groups, too, are offended, as they see sex education as essentially encouraging promiscuity. To encourage people to have sex is anything but neutral. It would appear that abortion may actually differ from religious freedom, as it does not offer us clear refinement of Mill's harm principle. But it does challenge us to seriously consider what are our purposes as a liberal community. Ultimately, it may force us to articulate clearly what means are essential to the preservation of society. If the issue is so divisive that it effectively polarizes the community—and we see more and more of this as antiabortion protests grow increasingly more violent—are we furthering liberal purposes if we stand absolutely steadfast to a position of no compromise out of perhaps a misplaced commitment to a liberal ideal of neutrality?

Opposing Common Standards

Issues of morality and politics with potential to fracture the community do not end with abortion. Issues of pornography, gay rights, and even the right to die also press against common conceptions of morality, or what we might simply deem to be community standards of appropriate behavior. If the issue is privacy, and it is measured against Mill's standard of what causes harm to others, it ought to follow logically that gay sex ought to be permissible because it is private. Should what two people do in the privacy of their bedrooms be deemed offensive to others? Can it really undermine society? Similarly, individuals opting to die—desiring to have life-support machines turned off—ought to have that right because it is essentially a matter of privacy. Lastly, if individuals seek to watch pornography at home, that would be considered an issue of privacy as well. Yet, the same groups that desire to ban abortion, and maybe even contraception, on the grounds that it is morally offensive, often seek to limit these rights on the same grounds.

Let's suppose that from both *Griswold* and *Roe* come what we can call our common understandings of what it means to have privacy. If one can in privacy make choices regarding conceptions of good and life style, those same decisions made in privacy ought to extend into areas of homosexuality, quality of life, and home entertainment. The Court has not been consistent on this. In *Bowers v. Hardwick*, the Supreme Court ruled that Georgia's sodomy law was not an unconstitutional abridgment of personal privacy because the law was steeped in centuries of Western tradition predicated on the common morality contained in the Judeo-Christian ethic.[69] If considered within the narrow confines of the equal protection clause, it may be conceded that this ruling really wasn't out of sync with other cases given that the law applied to homosexuals and heterosexuals alike.[70] In broader terms, however, why wasn't the same common morality invoked to uphold both contraceptive and abortion decisions? Rather, the Court saw nothing unreasonable about a sodomy law on the books in approximately twenty-five states, despite its own acknowledgment that such laws were utterly unenforceable. Is there really a common morality? Does that common morality basically assume we are all heterosexual and mostly married individuals? Have we just lost neutrality, or can a compelling case be made that homosexuality represents a set of values harmful to the community?

The Court did maintain a commitment to privacy when it recognized a limited right to die in *Cruzan v. Director, Missouri Dept. of Health*. The Court had determined that the state could require a continuation of life support and the use of feeding equipment as part of its compelling state interest in protecting life. However, the Court suggested that had the family had convincing proof of Nancy Cruzan's wishes to have life support terminated, the state would have to abide by the wishes of the family. All the Court really said was that the state of Missouri had a right to require clear and convincing proof of her desires. In the absence of such proof, the state did not have to accept the family's decision on her behalf. What the Court did say was had there been a living will in which Cruzan had made known her wishes in the event that she would wind up in a vegetative state, that would have sufficed as proof.[71]

Was the Court not in effect suggesting that the right to die was one of privacy? Yet, if this had no harmful impact on the larger society, why then did homosexual behavior? Clearly a symmetry exists between *Cruzan* and *Roe*, and maybe even *Webster*, but there is none between *Cruzan* and *Hardwick*. Should society encourage the right to die? Can we be certain that such patients will never wake up, or that some new technology won't be developed in the short term that will ultimately result in their awakening? Of course, the other side is to ask whether it isn't really in the best interests of society to encourage living wills so that individuals will not needlessly and artificially have to be kept alive at a cost to society at large. But then who decides?

If we are to understand Locke and Mill properly, the critical concern is the interests of society. While Mill in his utilitarianism assumes that individual liberties will ultimately serve the greatest happiness for the greatest number, Locke presumes in favor of the individual but not at the expense of the public interest. The ruling in *Cruzan* might be said to have effectively accomplished that. The community interest of protecting life was maintained by insisting on a living will, which would demonstrate "clear and convincing evidence." The interest in demanding proof was to ensure that one simply could not opt to end somebody else's life. Only that individual could make that choice. As Chief Justice Rehnquist put it:

> We believe that Missouri may permissibly place an increased risk of an erroneous decision on those seeking to terminate an incompetent individual's life-sustaining treatment. An erroneous decision not to terminate results in a maintenance of the status quo; the possibility of subsequent developments such as advancements in medical science, the discovery of new evidence regarding the patient's intent, changes in the law, or simply the unexpected death of the patient despite the administration of life-sustaining treatment, at least create the potential that a wrong decision will eventually be corrected or its impact mitigated. An erroneous decision to withdraw life-sustaining treatment, however, is not susceptible of correction.[72]

Pornography

The last issue to be considered under the general category of privacy issues is pornography. The issue of pornography is more problematic than it might appear. On one level, it ought to fall into the category of free speech. In the minds of many, however, it isn't protected speech because it serves no useful political purpose. It simply is considered to be obscene. On another level, there is increasingly the view that pornography is actually harmful to society, not because of the moral sensibilities of some that it offends, but because it may actually encourage violent behavior toward women. Hence when the line is crossed from simply being entertained to engaging in unsocial and even violent behavior, Mill's harm principle might justifiably be invoked.

To date, the issue of pornography has not really been addressed with the same absoluteness that has attended cases concerning religious freedom. Local communities have more or less been at liberty to determine what they consider obscene and what they do not. On one level, there is the issue of privacy in terms of what one chooses to read or watch in the privacy of one's own home. On this matter, *Stanley v. Georgia* has been dispositive. The Court in *Stanley* held it as an essential right in privacy that one be able to read as one pleases, no matter how obscene the material might be, in the privacy of one's home. This wasn't only a question of First Amendment rights to free speech, but of the "right to be free, except in very limited circumstances, from unwanted governmental intrusion into one's privacy." Speaking for the Court, Justice Marshall stated: "If the First Amendment means anything, it means that a State has no business telling a man, sitting alone in his own home, what books he may read or what films he may watch. Our whole constitutional heritage rebels at the thought of giving government the power to control men's minds."[73]

But on another level, while it was clear that one's home is one's castle, this case really didn't address itself to the issue of "adult" material in public places. *Stanley* is essentially a testament to the strict separation between public and private. Community standards, whatever they might be, simply could not be permitted to intrude on one's privacy in one's own home. The Court, however, has not been willing to equate the privacy of home relied upon in *Stanley* with a zone of privacy following a distributor or consumer of materials wherever he or she goes. In *Paris Adult Theatre I v. Slaton*, the Court made it clear that the idea of a "privacy" right and place of accommodation are mutually exclusive.[74] Rather, the Court has preferred to defer the matter to local communities to decide the issue according to their own standards. On this, one of the principal cases is still the 1973 *Miller v. California* decision. Involved was an individual who was conducting a mass mailing campaign to advertise the sale of illustrated books euphemistically called adult material. At issue was the constitutionality of California's obscenity statute. Speaking for the Court, Chief Justice Warren Burger asserted, "A state offense must also be limited to works which, taken as a whole, appeal to the prurient interest in sex, which portray sexual conduct in a patently offensive way, and which taken as a whole, do not have serious literary, artistic, political, or scientific value."[75]

While the issue of "prurient interest" was certainly important for determining when free expression would be classified as obscene, the question of "serious literary, artistic, political, or scientific value" was critical to determining just what would fall under the rubric of First Amendment protection. Given that adult material might be considered by some to contain no value, the Court was perfectly willing to leave the matter up to states for their own respective determinations. As the Court stated:

> Under a national Constitution, fundamental First Amendment limitations on the powers of the States do not vary from community to community, but this does not mean that there are or should be, fixed uniform national standards of precisely what appeals to the "prurient interest" or is "patently offensive." These are essentially of fact, and our Nation is simply too big and diverse for this Court to reasonably expect that such standards could be articulated for all 50 States in a single formulation, even assuming the prerequisite consensus exists. When triers of fact are asked to decide whether "the average person applying contemporary community standards" would consider certain materials "prurient," it would be unrealistic to require that the answer be based on some abstract formulation.[76]

The Court wasn't necessarily sustaining the lower court's ruling, nor was the Court reversing it, but it was vacating and remanding it for further consideration under the test of community standards. But how do we determine what type of speech serves a useful purpose? One person's art is another's pornography, as was so trenchantly pointed out by Justice Douglas's dissenting remarks: "What shocks me may be sustenance for my neighbor. What causes one person to boil up in rage over one pamphlet or movie may reflect only his neurosis, not shared by others."[77] Yet, the Court's position on pornography, at least as evidenced by the contrast between *Stanley* on the one hand and *Paris Adult Theatre* and *Miller* on the other, would appear to toe the strict separation between public and private that Galston considers to be essential to a "purposive" liberalism.[78]

Conclusion

Ultimately, we are led to ask whether issues concerning reproductive freedom and those that simply fall under the category of opposing common standards should be treated the same. From the vantage point of neutrality, the state is not except in those cases deemed essential to the maintenance of an inclusive democratic state. The implication would appear to be clear: Those issues not deemed essential are not part of the constellation of fundamental rights essential to the maintenance of "ordered liberty" and thus must yield to community standards, whatever they may be. Many liberals would argue that control over our bodies is essential to the maintenance of human integrity. Some of the same liberals, however, might be inclined to argue that certain pornographic material ought to be banned because it serves no useful purpose and may encourage violent behavior. If the result of pornographic material is to lead to greater incidence of rape, incest, battered wives and lovers, and general sexual harassment, the case could rightfully be made in line with both Mill and Locke that such material ought to be banned so as to protect individuals from harm and ultimately preserve society. There may also be the issue of how women are portrayed, that they are not being treated equally if, under the cloak of free artistic expression, they are being degraded.

Still, there is a problem here. If we are arguing that pornographic material can lead to certain types of behavior, are we not then assuming that individuals are not capable of making moral determinations as to what is right and wrong? What has happened to the liberal assumption of freedom of choice? By this reasoning, the teaching of certain political ideologies, or even religious ones, should not be permitted because it may incite people to behave in inappropriate ways. If liberals actually take this view, they may be doing greater damage to their own underpinning foundations. The issue remains of what needs to be done to maintain a strong, cohesive community. Liberals have more or less divided their spheres of activities into absolutes. In the economic realm, they have simply assumed that economic activity does cause harm, and therefore it needs to be subject to public monitoring and sometimes control so as to maintain human integrity. In the realm of privacy, however, they have argued that what one does in the privacy of one's bedroom cannot seriously harm another at all. Rather, it simply offends people's sensibilities, which is no reason to prohibit it, as Mill himself made abundantly clear. The reason for the First Amendment is, after all, to protect people's rights to offend. Ultimately, this is what it means to tolerate diversity.

Still, there has to be some middle ground because no community that must tolerate diversity but still be cohesive can be formed on the basis of absolutes. To a large extent, *Miller* does provide a framework because it invokes community standards. True enough, it could lead to standards predicated on emotion, not on rationality. But the community is at least being called upon to determine what is of value. Who but the community can determine what those standards are? This is all the more true if we are to talk about being in accord with liberal purposes. Still, the integrity of a framework that allows for individuals to make choices in conformity with their own conceptions of good must be maintained. This is a tough balancing act, but it can be done if we can distinguish between those rights that are fundamental and those that are not. In this regard, *Miller* is not all that dissimilar to *Palko*. Ultimately, however, the irony in modern liberalism is that it is the material issues that appear to lead toward policy solutions cutting to the core of its underpinning philosophic foundations. But it is the absolute commitment to neutrality on these social issues that can seriously undermine the community. In the end it isn't entirely clear that it is a truly neutral position. For by maintaining an absolute commitment to atomistic individualism—as the abortion issue shows—the effect is not to tolerate conflicting opinion. Truthfully, the issue needs to be referred to dialogue. The inevitable result is compromise. Although the end result will not be neutral, the process was nonetheless open.

The bottom line, however, would appear to be that the community has to define its own standards and, ultimately, its own objectives. This can involve no less than a substantive debate of community values. In short, the community cannot hope to construct a community in conformity with liberal purposes unless it can come together to define just what those purposes are. Ultimately, this requires an abandonment of neutrality as both a basis for policy formulation and as a measure of policy effectiveness. The refinement of Mill may well come down to the following: If the community is to prevent harm to itself, it cannot afford to maintain an unbridgeable commitment to moral neutrality. It has to engage in values discourse. This clearly begins in the early stages of policy formulation,[79] but it must extend into policy analysis as well. This, as we will see in the next chapter, has clear implications for the methodology we employ in policy evaluation.

7. *Toward a New Methodology of Policy Analysis*

My arguments to this point have suggested that neutrality not only is an impossibility when it comes to formulating solutions to gripping social and economic problems but also may not necessarily correspond to those purposes the ideal liberal community would like to achieve. Rather, policies pursued by the liberal state must be measured in light of liberal purposes, as captured in the Lockean ideal, of individualism within a community structure that promotes individualism and equality—as the basis for individual integrity—and a firm sense of community in which obligations are understood. Do policies forged in the name of the liberal state meet the demands that those purposes would impose? If we take stock for a moment, the implication would be as follows: Policy, as it constitutes a mode of expression and action by the state, must at a minimum respect human agency. Ideally, it will strive to help individuals reach their full potential. But it cannot abdicate its moral responsibility by assuming the laissez-faire position, that an environment imposing the least restrictions on individual liberty will achieve this. Rather, it must recognize that there is a common project, that this project must be served, and that service to it is intertwined with human agency. Programs that strengthen the community will strengthen the individual. But service to the community perhaps requires more adaptability to changing circumstances and not necessarily waiting until a point of crisis because this is viewed as the best means by which individual rights can be protected against the abuses of an intrusive community. The criteria must be whether policy serves to bring about a broadly inclusive community that will further the ends of tolerance, mutuality, and the common project. This requires nothing short of a new methodology of evaluation—evaluation that seeks to join together empirical analysis with underpinning philosophical analysis. It would, in fact, be a methodology that explores the larger philosophical issues inherent to policy, at the stages of both formulation and implementation.

The purpose of this inquiry, after all, has been to expose the gap between the objectives of policy, as they have often been formulated according to liberal criteria, and the results that occur due to their actual implementation. When critics desire to point out the flaws in liberalism, they often point to the effects, which are not necessarily the intended objectives. By exploring those issues that arise from policy in the liberal state, it has similarly been my hope to find a theoretical foundation upon which liberalism would be reconstructed. If liberalism is to be reconstructed, policy produced in its name must yield effects congruent with its intended goals. This can require no less than a substantive discussion of values, not only in the political stages of formulation but also in the more administrative stages of evaluation.

As this is the prescription, the obvious must then stand out: liberal theory predicated on neutrality wouldn't demand such a methodology. On the contrary, it demands neutral procedures that rely on a separation of facts from values. For the most part, policy evaluation has sought to separate the two. There are perhaps two reasons for this, both of which may have been influenced by how the liberal tradition in America—grounded in neutrality—has been understood, and neither of which is mutually exclusive. The first has to do with the reforms of the Progressive

Era, which sought to separate politics from administration in an effort to remove politics from the implementation of public policy, and thereby achieve both efficiency and equity in its distribution. The second has to do with the desire to make the general discipline of political science into a science. Political science, during the early part of the century, sought to separate itself from the disciplines of history and philosophy by approaching political phenomena through a more empirical set of lenses. As an outgrowth of the behavioral revolution,[1] the methodology of much of the policy literature has focused on quantitative approaches.

As those who were essentially part of administration, policy analysts weren't supposed to be concerned with questions of values, for they were essentially issues of politics. Instead, policy analysts were supposed to be isolated from politics and concerned only with the implementation of policy. They were to ensure that the delivery of public services would be efficient and impartial. In their obligation to be neutral, they weren't supposed to even ask about whether policy had any relationship to community values; they were only to ask whether it worked. The principal question in this chapter is whether policy analysis would not be better served through more subjectivity? That is, why not measure policy against the larger philosophical issues bound to arise when measures of any type are adopted to satisfy a social purpose? The problem with neutrality is that it erroneously presupposes that one can separate one's understanding of facts from one's values, whereas in reality one's assessment of facts may be affected by one's own set of values. Moreover, attempts to maintain this mythic dichotomy may further limit policy understanding. Even if neutrality-based procedures tell us in a narrow sense whether a policy works, can they answer the larger question of whether the overarching purposes of society are being furthered?

My purpose in this chapter is to inquire as to whether we might not achieve greater understanding by combining elements of this traditional model with yet another: inquiry into the philosophical issues inherent to policy, as well as inquiry into the philosophic principles underpinning the structure of society's political organization and its ensuing politics. Indeed, the approach to policy taken in the preceding chapters has been leading in this direction. Such a combination, then, could form the basis of a new methodology of policy analysis. In turn, a new methodology might then form a theoretical foundation for a reconstructed liberalism. Therefore, I intend to present a new methodology for policy analysis that will yoke together empirical policy concerns with those of normative political theory. What I am suggesting is that the type of questions I have been raising about specific policies in the preceding chapters can form the basis of a general methodological framework for policy evaluation. In large measure, my thesis in this chapter is predicated on the fallacy of the fact-value dichotomy. My assumptions of fallacy flow from the same premises underlying the fallacy of liberal neutrality. As no society that is attempting to accommodate a multitude of diverse but competing interests can ever achieve true and absolute neutrality, policy analysis must similarly begin with the proposition that no society can separate its policies from its philosophic foundations, that is, the core principles underpinning the structure of its politics. It is a misnomer to think that policy can be neutrally formulated and applied without some cognizance of history.[2] If policy can be said to represent the goals and aspirations of the community, why should the analyst not be cognizant of them? Rather, a methodology that can maintain consistency between the policies a society pursues and its philosophic foundations can ultimately serve to bridge the gap between the intended goals of a society and the actual results.

Traditional Analysis

Prior to exploring such a methodology, it would behoove us to understand just what the traditional model has involved and why it simply will not do. In large measure, it is a model of rational activism that assumes once the goals of society have been identified, the choice of correct policy ought to flow easily so that society can achieve optimum social benefit.[3] The essence is reason, and it therefore assumes that facts and values can be separated and that this separation will be rigidly adhered to.[4] This is because the separation is predicated on positivist assumptions that value judgments are essentially emotional responses to life conditions. As they are subjective, they cannot be verified. The whole task of rational choice is to effect a substitution of reason for arbitrary personal decision.[5] As values are perceived, they then cannot be observed. Facts, by contrast, can. As Anderson notes, virtually all of contemporary policy theory has in common a positivist or "emotivist" theory of evaluation. Values cannot be justified in terms of their objective criteria. Consequently, then, they must be regarded as "preferences." The standard by which policy must be judged must be internally consistent. Criteria must be clearly and hierarchically ranked.[6]

The fact-value dichotomy would also appear to serve another function that can be traced back to the Progressive Era. As the objective was to separate politics from administration, it effectively allows the analyst to stay out of politics, and it does this by replacing politics with knowledge.[7] The analyst is able to maintain an air of professionalism and doesn't have to worry about tailoring analysis to the desires of particular constituencies. Rather, the analyst only has to be concerned with whether the policy works. The goal is to maintain neutrality in evaluating policy by producing impartial results. By concentrating on the simple question of whether it works, the policy analyst is able to avoid the larger and more subjective questions of what groups are going to benefit and which ones are going to lose, and whether these benefits and losses are even justifiable, let alone desirable. Herein may lie the problem. Even good neutral policy has to be mindful of costs and consequences. How can we know whether the policy is good or bad? Or whether it is even just? What it doesn't address, however, is the goodness or badness of those issues.

What the fact-value dichotomy has effectively done is remove policy evaluation from public discussion. Public discussion, by contrast, would only violate the sense of appropriate isolation. By virtue of the fact that the administration of policy and its subsequent analysis is bureaucratized, the structure of bureaucracy naturally militates against what Weber considered to be "value rationality" in favor of "instrumental rationality." As Weber conceived of value rationality as being concerned with the ultimate worthiness of an end, a bureaucracy serving instrumental purposes—implementation of policy—could not embody this value rationality. Instead, it could only embody the instrumental rationality—the means by which the end would be attained.[8] For the introduction of value rationality into administration would only lead to inefficiencies. Yet, the hard substantive questions of whether the policy in question is "just" or whether it is in conformity with underpinning social values are avoided under the fallacious assumption that so-called neutral policy analysis is also nonideological.[9] This also enables the policy analyst to maintain the illusion of being not a politician but a technocrat. Moreover, it theoretically absolves the analyst, in the name of the state, of having to make value preferences, which would amount to an effective assignment of priority to a particular conception of good. Public discussion is not considered necessary because the deference to professional expertise will supposedly produce good and correct policy. Perhaps as important, because deference is an inevitable by-product of the bureaucratization of society and specialization, it cannot be supposed that the polity as a whole has the competence to make a judgment. In terms of professional survival, however, it has been necessary to perpetuate this myth.[10]

Nevertheless, there is a fundamental problem with relying on technocracy. All too often technocratic responses may enable the analyst to think that comprehensive analytical models are available that can then be applied to different sets of circumstances. Neutrality dictates that a universal set of measures be devised that can be applied to all situations. But are situations the same? The technocratic response would appear to overlook the fact that policy formulation was presumably based on the specifics of circumstances that a society is attempting to remedy. Moreover, it ignores the reality that politics, especially in a democratic society, did play a role in the formulation of policy. If politics played a role in the formulation of policy, is it realistic to think that politics will not be present in its analysis? While such assumptions may miss the internal politics of an agency, it certainly misses the fact that the information supplied by so-called neutral agents will always be used for partisan politics. It may also assume too much from our analyst, as it assumes analysts to be empty vessels. Yet, all individuals are socialized and come to particular problems with their own individualized value systems. Though not intending to be partisan, analysts' evaluations of policy will certainly be affected by general world views, if albeit at a subconscious level. This much should have become clear from Locke's discussion of language development in chapter 2.

Nevertheless, the traditional model assumes that policy can be evaluated while neutrality also is maintained. But more than assumption, the model requires it. The result has been a methodology that is primarily quantitative and of a formal statistical quality. Policy analysis has thus primarily been quantitative, as opposed to qualitative. What is observed cannot easily be argued about. What is good, can be. It is easy to develop a set of criteria for what can be observed. Statistical measures may be universal. But can a set of criteria be developed for determining what is good? And what about the problem of how things are interpreted? To even conceive of a good in the analysis is to allow irrationality to creep in, for the rational activist denies values as knowledge. This is not to say that values will not have a part to play, but that they will be considered by the politicians. The policy analyst is simply a professional who supplies information for later scrutiny by others—which can then include subjective judgment. Moreover, this accords with the liberal exhortation to be neutral. Because there is no objective criteria for measuring right, wrong, good, and bad, these concepts amount to nothing more than value judgments expressive of a preference. As policy makers ought not to express preferences—because that would amount to not treating everybody equally—they should rely on neutral and objective measures.

This neutral model of evaluation, then, typically leads to scientific paradigms that are empirically based. Policy analysis might then be said to consist of two components: measuring effectiveness and measuring efficiency. In measuring effectiveness, the object has been to determine the extent to which policy has achieved the benefits it was supposed to plus whatever unanticipated benefits may have arisen. In measuring efficiency, the object has been to determine the extent to which those objectives were able to be achieved at minimal cost, especially monetary costs.[11] In establishing effectiveness, the analyst would like to establish a causal relationship between the policy adopted and the intended results. Insofar as a causal relationship might be established, the policy might then be said to be effective.

The first component would then consist of a research design intended to test the causality between independent (policy) and dependent (outcome) variables, as well as control for extraneous variables that would affect that causality. In setting up a research design, the policy analyst typically would attempt to duplicate a controlled laboratory setting in the real world, which is affected by any number of variables beyond our control. Through the use of control groups and randomization, it can be discerned whether the program was responsible for the outcomes or something else was. The basis for evaluation is strictly empirical.[12] As scientific as this approach may be, it still assumes there are generalized models that can be applied to any number of situations. And it is for the purpose of developing these generalized models that there is a fact-value dichotomy.

The second component often will consist of a cost-benefit analysis, which in many cases has come to be the fundamental paradigm of policy analysis. The focus of this type of analysis has been on the allocation of public funds. Policy alternatives are usually analyzed in terms of their cost-effectiveness.[13] A cost-benefit analysis, in simple terms, generally entails arraying the benefits of a program against its costs, and if the benefits exceed the costs, the program is then said to be efficient.[14] Though such analysis may be informative in private enterprise, where new product developments or production processes are ultimately to be measured by how much additional profit will be netted, it may still miss the fact that many public programs are simply intangible and hence cannot easily be quantified. Although cost-benefit analyses in the public sector have involved, in many cases, the substitution of "effectiveness" for "benefit," there is still the problem of just how such a determination is made. Are we all necessarily speaking the same language?

If we return to chapter 5 for a moment and recall the discussion of public-private partnerships, the first question that should have come to mind is, just what were the benefits supposed to have been? As much as job creation can be quantified, can the costs—especially as they may entail the destruction of communities and the disruption of people's lives—be quantified? How many jobs created are enough to justify the costs? Yet, until we can adequately answer this question, there is no real basis upon which we can evaluate the policy. At the root of such an analysis is the formulation of a subjective judgment as to whether the benefits truly justify the costs, or whether such costs can ever really be quantified as to ever justify them. The real issue that policy analysts, according to a traditional model, would not have been able to address is whether a price tag can ever be put on the cohesiveness of the community. Yet, discussion is precisely what was needed. Were we to look at the problem within the context of Lowi's critique of the administrative state, it is most likely that these hard questions were never really considered. On the contrary, all that was of any importance was that jobs were being created, and six thousand in a depressed area is in itself respectable enough. As far as the intangibles were concerned, responsibility was delegated elsewhere. The point is that serious discussion of policy involves serious consideration of the consequences.[15]

What cases like Poletown show is that the process of policy evaluation isn't as neat as it would appear from the traditional model. Rather, it is quite messy. They raise a number of issues that the typical policy analyst doesn't address. On the contrary, they are usually more likely to be addressed by the political theorist, who is concerned with just what the appropriate role of government—and, by extension, policy—is in society. For the typical analyst, according to a traditional model, the issues are quite narrow despite the broadness of the ramifications. Consider, then, the following scenario: The president announces that he will introduce a program to increase literacy and that he intends to spend approximately $2 billion for it. On one level, a traditional cost-benefit analysis could be employed, by tallying up the costs of the program against the observed benefits. When considering the costs, the analyst will most likely consider the social costs of doing nothing, in addition to considering the actual program costs. We might estimate these costs according to lost tax revenue and greater public assistance. While bearing in mind that the program does cost $2 billion, we want to look at data on welfare costs and tax revenue both before and after policy implementation. If, as a result of our program, the participants have found employment, thereby abandoning public assistance rolls and increasing the tax base, we could say the program has accomplished results.

If we can compare numbers, we should thus conclude that the program was efficient insofar as the benefits exceeded the costs. Even if through sophisticated statistical measures a causal link has been established between the program and greater reading, what have we in the end really learned about the value of the program? Has the program really been effective in a much larger sense? For, on another level, the measure of effectiveness would be the number of people who will learn to read as a result of the program and the level at which they will read. Hence, this simple analysis has not really told us what we are getting for our money. The question still remains as to how efficient the program really is. As MacRae points out, cost-benefit analyses are likely to ignore a cost that cannot easily be assigned monetary value because an analysis may also discount future benefits and costs to obtain their present value.[16] The point about quantitative studies is that they look nice—the results can easily fit into tables, whereas qualitative judgments cannot.

For an expenditure of $2 billion, we should know how many people will benefit and at what level they will read. If these are variables figuring into evaluations of effectiveness, do we not then require the analyst to make a judgment? Suppose our choice is among the following alternatives: (1) For $2 billion, one million people will learn to read at the seventh-grade level; (2) for $2 billion, five hundred thousand people will be able to pick up Shakespeare; (3) for the same money, a number of persons between five hundred thousand and one million will learn to read at a level between seventh grade and Shakespeare; or (4) more than one million will learn to read at less than a seventh-grade level.

Many analysts might easily conclude that as desirable as reading Shakespeare might be, one million people reading at a seventh-grade level is sufficient to enable them to function in the workplace. Even if we conclude that one million more readers at a seventh-grade level is optimal, why not conclude that more readers at less than seventh grade is even more so? Such a conclusion might be especially conceivable if it is clear that the level would not be that much less. But is not a value judgment being made? If in the process of administering a reading test, it is unclear as to whether one falls into a seventh-grade level or a sixth-grade level, a judgment is being made. Even if the basis for a judgment is said to be objective, the outcome may be affected by the test itself. Criteria may differ from test to test. Does the selection of tests not represent a value judgment—a deliberate intention to show something? Yet, here is where so-called neutral analysts do make value judgments. The use of different statistical measures will have different implications. There is the whole issue of bias involved in determining whether it would be preferable to have a Type I versus a Type II error. A Type I error is when the tested hypothesis is falsely rejected. This would occur when the sample result falls into a certain set of parameters that would dictate rejection even though the hypothesis turns out to be true. A Type II error is when the hypothesis isn't rejected even though it happens to be false.

When the sample result doesn't fall into those parameters that would dictate rejection, a Type II error is made even though some of the hypothesis may be true.[17] The researcher consciously selects which type of error is acceptable based solely on determining the parameters of the sample.

Of course, there is a slippery slope here, for how much is one willing to lower the level in order to encompass more participants? But aside from this, how do we even know that the better readers will not be of greater value to society? Is there no intrinsic value to reading Shakespeare that would justify government expense? Let's simply say that the criteria in a Lockean sense is that the government, in its determination of policy, will be accountable to and responsive to the needs of the community. By so doing, it serves to preserve the public interest. On what basis, however, do we determine whether and to what extent government is being accountable and responsive if we aren't basing it on some value presuppositions? Purists arguing for the higher reading level might conclude that if the result will not be reading at the Shakespearean level, there is no justification for the program at all. Even these value judgments obscure a definitional, albeit critical, question: How many people reading is enough to justify the program and determine whether it is effective? That people are learning to read ought to indicate that the program works, it does not tell us how well it works. Is effectiveness not then measured by this question as well? Do more people reading enhance community values, and which ones do they enhance?

Even if we can find an arbitrary cutoff to determine effectiveness, we still lack a sense of purpose. Why should society teach people to read? If society should teach reading for the intrinsic value of reading, then shouldn't success be measured by whether individuals can read the most sophisticated texts? Do we teach people to read because reading is an essential tool toward a particular end? Though the answers to each of these questions will surely differ, the fact that they exist at all tells us that the policy, whatever its specific purpose, is in the service of some underpinning values. Whether society values functional citizens so they will be independent or knowledgeable individuals so they will be well-informed citizens—neither of which is mutually exclusive—society does value something. If there were no values driving the program, there would be no need for the program.

The problem with this type of divorce from underpinning values is that the policy analyst might lose sight of overall purpose. Though this type of separation makes analysis manageable for the analyst, it overlooks the fact that public policy is essentially a political arrangement "designed for the practical world of social action where facts and values are inextricably interwoven."[18] As Stone notes, public policy "is about communities trying to achieve something as communities," in spite of the fact that there is generally conflict within communities over what its goals should be.[19] Contained within public policy, then, is some consensus of what constitutes the public interest. It would be difficult to conceive of the public interest as some conception apart from some commonly held values. This means that the public interest could not really be conceived as something devoid of a sense of right and wrong. The point is that in determining what constitutes effectiveness, the policy maker does have to make a value judgment. And though the facts might well be out there, how they are interpreted will be affected by the value systems each analyst brings to bear. Insofar as we are all products of our environment, it is naive to think that the policy analyst has not been similarly socialized into a particular cultural milieu.[20] Facts, then, aren't merely facts. They are simple notions we have all come to recognize, through the process of socialization, in the same way.

This has precisely been the problem with welfare policy. Again, the debate over welfare policy has often centered on whether the War on Poverty of the 1960s was won or lost. While one group has said yes because fewer people live below the poverty line now than before,[21] the other has said no, alleging social policy to have hurt the underclass by fostering greater dependency and encouraging further family disintegration.[22] While the two groups might be answering the question, they aren't answering the same one. The fact that fewer people might be living in poverty does not say a whole lot unless we have a sense of why poverty is bad. Why, in other words, is it necessary to fight such a war? If the only purpose was to increase the number of persons living above the poverty line, the first group might claim a small victory and argue the policy to have been effective. The objective, after all, was to reduce poverty, or at the very least to create the appearance of such. But if it was hoped that by providing the resources, the policy would decrease dependency and enable individuals to be independent and self-sufficient, the second group would be correct to suggest failure. For the question in need of answering is whether the policy furthered any sense of social welfare. Within the context of liberal purposes, did these policies further liberal aims of individual self-sufficiency and integrity? What we discovered in chapter 4 was that not only did it fail to foster these objectives, but it failed to demand that recipients participate in the common project, as defined by work. Because social welfare is subject to interpretation, it may be myopic to think that consideration of values can be absent from policy analysis. How, then, would our policy analyst relying on a neutral cost-effective mechanism answer the second group?

Yet, it is the second group that would appear to be speaking to a larger issue. That is, why even mention independence and self-sufficiency at all if they are not considered to be pivotal social values? To answer the first group is to ask whether the policy or program works in a technical sense. Though indeed it might be useful to know, this has little explanatory value. By contrast, to answer the second group is to ask whether the policy furthers a larger social purpose. To answer this question, the policy analyst would have to abandon his or her mythic neutrality and explore just what those values are. This would require discerning just what the society's underpinning values are. The policy analyst must then explore the theoretical presuppositions.[23]

Theoretical presuppositions must be explored because public policy is essentially a value-laden enterprise. And the methodology of separating facts from values only distorts the basic purpose, that policy is essentially the vehicle for the attainment of communal ends.[24] Policy is implemented in a particular social and cultural context. As Weber writes, "Normative standards of value can and must be the objects of dispute in a discussion of a problem of social policy because the problem lies in the domain of the general cultural values."[25] The more general the problem of concern, the broader its cultural significance. Unless we have this discussion of value, how are we to know whether our policy is truly serving the community? And if we cannot know this, what true purpose does policy evaluation really serve?

Robert Goodin, too, argues that no evaluation of policy is possible without some sort of theory of value. The problem with the fact-value dichotomy is that it connotes monolithic policy responses that can then be applied to any situation. Though similarities may exist, this certainly misses the fact that each society has its own unique attributes and characteristics. Policy, then, must be thought of as being culturally specific. Responsible policy, then, must be based on some theoretical understanding of the system into which it is intended to intervene. No optimal size exists for a policy intervention in perfectly general terms.[26] It would then seem that by perpetuating the mythic dichotomy, we lose sight not only of the purpose of policy, but also the purpose of evaluation: to improve policy so that it better serves the needs of the community. The object, after all, is to make for a better community. And the objective of policy in the liberal community, it will be recalled, is to preserve, protect, and promote a community conducive to individualism but equally respectful of the dignity of all individuals. This cannot be done without establishing the strong foundations of community. Yet, these purposes must bear some relationship to past traditions.

Moreover, it is because of common perceptions of liberalism in recent years that this is essential. The principal criticism has often been, it will be recalled, that many of the policies pursued are often perceived as being out of touch with mainstream values of society. However, not only is it that values bear little connection, but the whole philosophy of liberalism, with its emphasis on individuals, often results in a subversion of community concerns. Recall that the common critique of liberalism often depicts it as a society consisting of atomistic individuals who are disconnected from their environment. As such, they can make claims against the community—to the point where individuals assume priority, and community is nothing more that the sum total of individual interests.[27] When it comes to policy, this assessment often suggests that policy is pursued on an ad hoc basis, often aimed at addressing the concerns of specific groups because each has a need that must be met. Moreover, whatever policy does emerge, it is the product of competing interest groups with the result generally being that the one with the greater resources gets its way.[28] Liberalism, in this vein, lacks a clear, comprehensive view of what is good for society as a whole. Yet, as the discussion in chapter 2 makes clear, liberalism, especially as it is grounded in the Lockean ideal, does have a comprehensive view of what is good for society as a whole. The traditional model does inevitably lead to a policy program that will inevitably be constrained by the need to be mindful of individual rights, and the requirement that those rights must be protected.

If, for instance, the conservative critique of welfare policy in recent years does at all speak to a larger problem in American society, it is that liberalism, which has not only guided our constitutional structure but also much of our policy and positive state, is now impoverished. If it isn't an adequate response to liberal shortcomings, it is certainly the reaction to a policy program that has failed to achieve its desired results. But it isn't impoverished because conservatives say it is. It is impoverished because liberals have failed to show the connection between their policies and the values of the community. And they couldn't do this by relying on neutrality. Karl Popper argues that the primary enemies of the open society are those reactionaries who desire to recapture a more traditional and tribalistic one, that it is the shock of transition that sparks the rise of reactionary movements.[29] This is a critical point given that the principal goal of a liberal society is that it ultimately be an open one. This requires that it be responsive and constantly in a state of transition so that it can remain open. But unless liberalism is able to demonstrate the relationship between this constant transition and the traditions it is supposed to exemplify, the reactionary movements, as they may best be reflected in contemporary critiques of liberalism, will succeed in defining liberalism as they see it and not necessarily as it really is. I am certainly not about to suggest that conservative critics seek to impose authoritarianism—although some believe that authoritarian or coercive measures may be essential for addressing some gripping social problems[30]—but they do bespeak the gap between goals and actual results. The implications would thus appear to be clear: If the gap is to be narrowed, we must focus less on results and more on values and assess the results in light of the community's values. In other words, the measurement of policy is whether the results are in accord with values and whether they advance the goals of the community.

The problem is that policy cannot be framed in strict adherence to neutral procedures with total disregard for the community. Policy predicated on neutrality presupposes that it can be applied to any society with similar objective circumstances. Respective social cultures are irrelevant.

It would appear to suggest a one-size-fits-all approach to policy. But communities do differ. More fundamentally, however, policy formulated in such a way that it is disconnected from the values of the community is only bound to invite criticism. By evaluating policy in accordance with society's underpinning philosophic foundations, policy could be better formulated so that it is more consistent with the Lockean ideal. In the end, this might serve to narrow the gap between the liberal political philosophy, as it is grounded in the community-minded conception of the Lockean ideal, and liberal public policy aimed at furthering the public interest. Liberalism would effectively be reconstructed because policy framed in its name would be in greater harmony with community interests. The point is this: Policy cannot conform to the values of society unless a serious discussion of society's values has been undertaken. Reconstructing liberalism in the end requires the joining together again of facts and values.

A New Methodology

The need to reconstruct liberal theory—the public philosophy—does perhaps raise the question of just what the goals of the policy analyst ought to be. As suggested in chapter 2, Locke would subscribe to the idea that fact and value do in fact need to be yoked together because all knowledge is based on experience. We know what we know because of the experiences we have had, and the experiences we have had are ultimately a function of our respective socialization. Therefore, it would be-hoove the analyst to abandon the mythic dichotomy and incorporate serious discussion of values into analysis. The basis for a new methodology—which might be referred to as *issues-oriented policy analysis*—lies in bridging the gap between facts and values, which in turn requires no less than the yoking together of empirical policy concerns with normative political theory. It is not simply a matter of bridging the gap between quantitative and qualitative approaches. It is not, as King, Keohane, and Verba suggest, simply a matter of style that is methodologically and substantively unimportant.[31] This new methodology would not go as far as to abandon the scientific method characteristic of traditional analysis but would attempt to place it in a larger context. As MacRae argues, reliable scientific knowledge can coexist with rational ethical discourse, and "that scientific propositions and ethical assertions, while clearly distinguishable, may be fruitfully combined in academic disciplines concerned with the study of man and society."[32] Or, as Mark Sagoff suggests, public policy must be based on communitarian or public values. The application of a cost-benefit formula cannot in a democracy replace public discussion of ideas. For what counts in public policy is a conception of the good society—that is, value—not simply what works.[33]

If policy analysis is for the purpose of improving policy making, it must consider more prominently the role of ideas. As Reich argues, policy making—of which analysis might then be considered an extension—ought to be more than the discovery of what satisfies public desires, but it "should entail the creation of contexts in which people can critically evaluate and revise what they believe." Government has a greater responsibility than implementation of decisions responsive to public wants. Rather, it has a responsibility to engage the public in ongoing dialogue.[34] But it would also presuppose that policy formulation and subsequent analysis will entail a full-blown discussion of communal values. In this vein, it accords with Stephen Macedo's conception of liberalism as an exercise in justification,[35] and Ackerman's conception of liberalism as continuing dialogue.[36] This might presuppose what Dryzek refers to as *discursive democracy.*[37]

By discursive democracy, Dryzek means a set of institutions or some institutional design in which individuals of a community may come forth and make their expectations known and expect that there will be a convergence between theirs and the expectations of others. It is a deliberative scheme that should account for the individual or collective needs and interests of the individual. As such, it is a deliberative scheme that requires that individuals participate in the process. It is a scheme that ultimately rejects the deference to technocratic expertise or what Weber might have referred to as bureaucratic analysis. Consequently, then, it must be viewed as a design that requires the consideration of community values not only in the formulation of policy and its implementation but in its subsequent evaluation as well.[38]

Paul Roth suggests that social scientists would do best to discard the *unity-of-method* approach, holding that no distinction can be made between natural and social science and to adopt a pluralist view of rationalist inquiry. Methodological pluralism, as he calls it, entails pulling together different approaches on a more philosophical plane for the purpose of acquiring more meaningful understanding within the context of specific circumstances. Methodology, like language, has to be culturally relative.[39] All this is to suggest that policy analysis needs to be what Michael Quinn Patton calls utilization-focused. In assessing the effectiveness of policy, the specifics of the circumstances must be taken into account. This then means that no one cannon can be used in all circumstances, but that general methods must be adapted to each individual set of circumstances. The means, then, must be tailored to the specific ends.[40] Patton, however, does not go far enough, for his methodology is still operational within the traditional paradigm of analysis. To a large extent, it assumes that if target groups and their environment are understood, facts can still be separated. Though the specifics are not completely adequate, the framework would certainly be useful if traditional forms of policy analysis were to be combined with normative philosophical inquiries, as MacRae and Goodin suggest. Yet, the question remains, could we even have public discussion? This, of course, differs from neutrality-based measures, which assume that an impartial set of measures can be discovered and applied to all situations. In the end, policy analysis may need to move away from so-called scientific inquiry. Rather, there needs to be more of a philosophical pursuit of truth. The question then is how a particular policy might best assist this process.

Still, this would not obviate the need for general principles, but it would require that they be flexible enough for specific application. That is, the methodology cannot be totally devoid of scientific method. Dryzek suggests the Q methodology, which, while it involves quantification, requires that any statistical analysis be subordinate to a broader analytical and interpretive task.[41] One possible set of criteria for a new methodology of policy analysis might be found in what Stone calls the *rational decision model of analysis.* The focus of policy analysis is on what is called rational methods of decision making. Policy problems are cast as choices between alternative means of achieving a goal. The rational decision model portrays policy problems as choices facing political actors. These choices consist of a sequence of mental operations aimed at arriving at a decision. Goals are defined, alternative means of attaining them are imagined, the consequences are evaluated, and then a choice is made among the alternatives most likely to attain them. In all decision models, decisions are based on whether they maximize total welfare. Actions are evaluated in terms of their consequences, and the standard by which possible actions ought to be evaluated is the stated objective.[42] Yet, the unanswered question is, consequences for what? Though the emphasis on community welfare makes the model unique, it is hard to see how it otherwise differs from what Lindblom refers to as the *root model*, whereby policy makers systematically list alternative policies and make rational judgments based on the possible benefits and consequences of each.[43]

Although Stone's model is still vague, she does clue us into one of the more fundamental problems with the fact-value dichotomy: the absence of policy discussion. By separating facts from values in the name of maintaining the priority of knowledge over politics, traditional policy analysis eliminates the need for public discussion because it effectively defers to policy expertise. Public discussion, after all, is a political enterprise. Nevertheless, Stone's model does attempt to use the framework of the traditional model but factors in values by positing the general welfare as the ends of policy analysis. Yet, it is still difficult to imagine that traditional analysts do not consider their models to be in the ultimate service of some social good or general welfare interest.

The substantive question, then, and one that Stone's model doesn't adequately address, is what we mean by general welfare interest. This idea has to vary from community to community. What still renders it unsatisfactory is that the traditional policy analyst could always counter with the claim that the mere fact that benefits outweigh costs—as revealed through neutral measures—indicates that the general welfare interest is served. The point of a new methodology of analysis is that it isn't served unless that concept embodies the values of the community as defined by the community. And there is no way to determine whether policy will even press against those values unless the philosophic issues that policies are bound to raise are explored.

This isn't to say that Stone's model isn't without application. Although it clearly has application for traditional analysts, it could have application for the normative political theorists as well. Consider for a moment Paul Healy's method of interpretive policy inquiry. This method attempts to derive proposals for social change from decisions of social actors themselves, made in enlightened understanding of the situation. Interpretive policy inquiry conceives its task as inherently normative and moral. This type of inquiry is specifically intended to further understanding as to what it means to live a responsible human life. It attempts to overcome the theory-practice dichotomy in addition to transcending the fact-value dichotomy. Employing this approach, Healy contends that, in addition to technological efficiency, we can make effective policy by improving our understanding of ourselves and our environment.[44] Isn't this then the purpose of policy evaluation?

Healy's approach shares much in common with MacRae's, which he suggests would be a form of what he has called *act-utilitarianism*. Here the application of expert knowledge would be checked by the controls of political responsibility. The object of policy analysis, according to MacRae, is to serve a broader social function. As policy analysis might properly be viewed as a branch of general social science, it ought to "provide guidance to society, through research, reasoned discourse, and education as to what interests should be served in particular circumstances and as to the means to do so."[45] If it is to do this, the specific discipline of policy analysis must continuously examine whether it is effectively carrying out this task. Such an exercise then requires an examination of social values to see whether the ultimate goals of society are being achieved. For to talk of public policy is to talk about the different ways by which the values of the community can be served.[46]

If we are going to bring back values, the twofold nature of value inquiry must be recognized: On the one hand, there are those values that drive the policy in the first place—goals. On the other hand, there are the underpinning values of the community—those that mark its identity and form the cultural set of lenses through which policies will ultimately be viewed. By values, I mean the broad historical traditions of that society. The goals of the policy, then, must be determined in light of those values. But as culturally specific as policy analysis would have to be, there must still be a set of principles to guide the endeavor.

The first principle would be to engage in a philosophical inquiry into the society's underpinning values. An issue that the policy maker would have to raise is whether the policy has implications for the values and traditions of society. Were such a policy to be adopted, the analyst must ask what issues are raised that we need to be mindful of. For instance, in designing a welfare policy, assuming we were to adopt policy A over B, will the result be greater dependency? If this might result, what might be the ramifications for the community's moral fabric? Just what might it mean with regard to the community's values of self-sufficiency and the idea that all members should participate in the common project of society, that is, work? The object of policy ought to be to further those values not hinder them. The implications for the liberal society ought to be clear. A society structuring itself and its policies as a collective expression of itself should have as its goals liberal purposes of individuality and human integrity, as each is developed and nurtured in a strong and cohesive community. If such a society strongly prizes values of independence and self-sufficiency, it should have as the goals of any of its policies the promotion of independence and self-sufficiency. Once these values have been identified, the policy analyst must determine whether the policy acts to further them.

As we are aspiring to have policy conform to the Lockean ideal, we would want to know whether policy serves to foster an inclusive community. Can policy be measured against the criterion of whether it serves to promote the public interest—is it being accountable and responsive to the needs of the community? Liberal policy predicated on the Lockean ideal would need to be such that the following occur: (1) It fosters human agency in that programs may be in place so individuals can develop to their full potential; (2) it allows for individuals to feel comfortable, given the vast diversity in society; policy should ultimately be judged by whether it adds to a general level of mutuality and tolerance or whether it may in fact detract from them; this requires mental operations that go beyond simple cost-benefit analyses; (3) it adds to the common project of society; if a program is so designed that it will provide some benefits to individuals, it imposes a corresponding level of obligations so that a balance between rights and obligations is understood; and (4) it reflects the historical traditions of the community, that is, liberal policy, as such, maintains some consistency with what liberalism has historically and traditionally stood for.

This means that for economic stabilization policies, the question foremost in the minds of policy analysts must be the central economic goals of the community: those policies and measures that will best promote growth and prosperity for all, not just a few. It isn't sufficient to justify the policy on the grounds that it is "efficient" when the effects in many cases may be to compromise human dignity. At some level a serious discussion has to take place, for instance, over the merits of fighting inflation at the expense of employment. The problem, as we saw in chapter 3, is essentially this: the Federal Reserve, operating according to highly technical measures—and, by some standards, neutral ones—has reasoned the following: There is a "natural" rate of unemployment that can serve as a definition of a full-employment economy. When unemployment dips below that natural rate, the result is inflationary pressure, which can be dealt with by raising interest rates so as to control inflation.[47] The by-product of neutrality has been to defer to highly technical models—which in many cases may be completely divorced from empirical reality—and to act accordingly. Yet, there has been no serious engagement of community values to determine just why it is that inflation is so bad that the price to be paid for its control is that members of the community suffer the indignity of being out of work. True enough, fighting inflation may serve the common project, but unless that common project is engaged by the policy analyst, we simply cannot know this to be true. This may well be an example whereby formal statistical models would have a place but within a larger context. What if, for instance, it could be determined through econometric modeling just what the rate of unemployment would be at given time intervals for each half percent below the "natural" rate? Would this not form the basis upon which the community would be able to determine just what its values are? The technocratic approach has assumed the culprit to be inflation, yet the common project of work—that the community might value employment more—hasn't really been considered seriously. The problem is that the overreliance on theory—because it might well be the most neutral means to evaluate a situation—has led to a situation whereby the process is totally isolated from the communities it is intended to serve. The problem of values becomes even more acute when dealing with issues of plant closure and corporatism.

In the realm of welfare policy, the issue again would be what promotes the norms of the community. For instance, what are the implications for a society prizing independence if we have a society offering transfer payments? If the object of policy analysis is to supply information and strengthen the foundations for decision making, this would be a pivotal question in determining whether this policy is appropriate or perhaps another would be more appropriate. Answering the question might then tell us that a more work-oriented policy is appropriate. It does require being able to have a frank and open discussion about substantive values and determining which are of a higher priority. To probe this question is to add a new dimension to the cost-benefit analysis. The costs then get measured in qualitative, as well as quantitative, terms. The questions are no longer simply about costs and their affordability but about whether the costs are really worth the benefits. Though it might be desirable for fewer people to live in poverty, should government sponsor a policy if the effect is to sap individual energy, add disincentive, and ultimately foster greater dependency? The analyst who engages in the narrow cost-benefit analysis of the traditional model will not be concerned with these questions because they are laden with value. But by not asking these questions, what have we really accomplished? We have certainly not learned whether this policy is furthering the social project. On what basis, then, can we determine whether such policies are furthering community purposes, let alone liberal ones?

If independence and self-sufficiency have been at the base of liberalism since its inception, the goals of a welfare policy must be to promote those goals. Similarly, it has to be recognized that a program may be essential merely for the preservation of human dignity. A moral society, in other words, cannot allow its members to starve. A program of general assistance to those who are in need is intended to offer some semblance of dignity to the poor insofar as it serves the purpose of preventing them from starving. Do we know for certain that public charity will not have the opposite effect of undermining their dignity because of the stigma attached to the receipt of charity? Neutral policy can easily answer whether the program has served to feed more people. It cannot easily answer whether such a program hasn't in the process also further undermined their dignity. In attempting to ensure the human dignity of the poor, how can we know whether policy is furthering the goals of mutuality and the common project? The critical issue, then, is weighing the concerns of human dignity against those of mutuality and common project. The policy analyst needs to be able to evaluate policy within these boundaries. These are the criteria by which such policies must be measured. Perhaps the issue is whether the policy analyst can simply evaluate policy in total isolation from the community the policy was intended to affect. In adopting a welfare policy, one must ask, what is the "good" society—as defined by the community—that we are trying to achieve? What are its components? How do specific programs reach these objectives and how do they fall short? In some cases we may only be able to answer by delving into the metaphysical.

Although it is one thing to look at the impact of a policy for particular target groups, it is quite another to look at its impact on society's underpinning philosophic foundations. If liberalism is about justification, the policy analyst has to be able to say whether, given the analysis conducted, the policy can in fact be justified. This problem only became too clear with the public-private partnership, especially as it was tried in Poletown. The basis upon which a partnership must be evaluated is whether it has worked to foster the larger community interest. But policy makers merely viewed the issue within the context of a textbook analysis of what would create more jobs. They assumed that these were the values of the community, and that by generating more jobs the moral fabric of the community would be served. The problem, however, was that they never consulted with the community to determine just what ingredients went into that moral fabric. The lesson from Poletown is that the ramifications of a policy action are always much broader than a neutral model of evaluation would suggest. Moreover, since by all accounts neutrality was ultimately violated in the selection of the policy, there was no real excuse for failing to engage the community and seeking to ascertain just what would be important. Within the context of Lockean philosophy, a red flag should certainly be raised because it was clear that government wasn't being completely accountable and responsive to the community—despite the fact that it thought that it was. Locke's exhortation to be responsive to the community can act both ways, and because it does it is thus necessary to get deeper into the particular values against which policy ought to be measured. Does the partnership further the common project? Does it respect mutuality? And while determining whether it serves these ends, do partnerships work to ensure the integrity and dignity of all members of the community, particularly those who will be most affected by the partnership?

Ultimately, the community interest must be examined with regard to privacy issues. Again, the policy analyst really has to measure policy in terms of what will best achieve a broadly inclusive community, one that ensures the equal dignity of its members but also strives to achieve mutuality and participation in the common project. What we have seen here is that the one who rigidly adheres to neutrality may well be treading on dangerous ground, at least when it comes to the abortion issue. Yet, there are community standards against which such issues as pornography can be measured. Privacy issues are by no means matters that can be relegated to neutral policy analysis in the way that an income transfer program can. They clearly involve a delicate balance between the common project, mutuality, and human agency. Issues that are divisive do ultimately have to be confronted. Neutrality may be one way of avoiding the need to make hard choices, but on sensitive issues it can ultimately prove to be that which leads to the unraveling of the community's moral fabric. If anything, it becomes clear that the policy analyst has to be absolutely clear as to which matters are rightly private and which ones are rightly public. The fact still remains that when it comes to the other policy matters than private ones, we are primarily dealing with public matters. The question is, how do we get from point A to point B?

By no means, then, does this obviate the need for empirical testing. A test of whether this policy is meeting its stated objectives will rest on the confluence between empiricism and normative theory. Certainly we need to know on a basic level that a policy works—that there is a causal relationship between variable A and variable B. But if we are trying to ensure that there will be an intimate connection between policy and the community it serves, we clearly need to know more. Data may well tell us that a policy has effectively led to greater dependency, for instance. But what does that really tell us unless we understand the relationship between this dependency and what the community has long prized? Why is dependency necessarily a bad thing? Is dependency intrinsically bad, or is it bad because of a long history in the United States of prizing independence? We cannot know this if we are divorcing policy analysis from the disciplines of history and philosophy. The point is, empiricism is part of the process, but it is not the entire process. At the same time, however, philosophical inquiry would require more than simply locating the values of society. It would entail philosophical inquiry into the issues in the policy itself. In other words, what are the philosophical implications arising from a particular policy, and what are the ramifications for the society prizing these particular values? It is on this point that an issues-oriented policy approach would be distinguished from, say, Stone's model. Though her model moves in this direction, it doesn't quite reach that point.

Critics, however, might not see much of a difference between this new methodology and the traditional model. Discussions of values, they will argue, are no different from discussions of goals. They may be inclined to argue that the discussion of values has now been shifted from the political arena to the analytical one. They might add that it perhaps breaks the neat separation between politics and administration. And ultimately, it makes the process of evaluation even more complex. More to the point, they will question the viability of arriving at a uniform definition of values. No two people think the same. Observers of the American political scene can surely point to the inability of American political institutions to achieve consensus on annual budgets let alone a set of commonly held values. But more than an inability to achieve consensus, there is simply the problem of ordering our priorities. Who is to say that one value is superior to another, that it ought to be adopted? This inability on a philosophical level to define such values will invariably strengthen the argument for deference to neutral evaluative measures predicated on simple empiricism. For analysts to involve themselves in the search for communal values is only to mire themselves in a definitional morass that is essentially a political problem.

These critics, however, overlook the fact that, as difficult as it may be to agree on specific values, it is possible to locate general currents and traditions that still bind us together as a society, despite apparent differences based on socioeconomic class, gender, race, and ethnicity.[48] As far as the other criticisms are concerned, such a methodology by no means obviates the need to engage in political discourse. By devising a set of measures based on the Lockean ideal—at least in the American context—a specific set of parameters can be established that will balance the interests of the individual with those of the community. A policy that aims to further tolerance, mutuality, and the common project is one that aims to be more specific about what the general welfare interest happens to be. More important, such an approach moves beyond merely factoring some variable—perhaps a dummy variable set to denote the general welfare interest—into a mathematical formula.

To a large extent, such a methodology may represent a broader version of Ackerman's dialogue, in which one must justify one's position in light of one's own conceptions. What it does do, however, is extend the dialogue and make it more complete. Instead of the program being initially justified and then simply deferred to administrative agencies, such a methodology continues the dialogue by requiring continuous justification. In this vein, it might well serve as a corrective to many of the deficiencies that Lowi attributes to the administrative state. Discussion would in fact require that the discussion take place in a more democratic institution. Lowi himself suggests that the best remedy for the abuses of the administrative state would simply have been for Congress to withdraw its delegation of authority and debate the issues as they were supposed to in the first place.[49] This would, after all, further the purpose of liberal justification.

We must presuppose that because of the specialized nature of modern society, there will always be a need for expert policy analysts. This might further presuppose that, educationally, they will need to know more. It does, however, require that specialists be aware of communal values and account for them in their assessment. It requires that, in spite of a plurality of opinion, they locate a commonality, a core that serves to hold the fabric of society together. In short, then, we would be adding another qualification to the policy analysis profession.[50] This, then, is different from the traditional model, which assumes that because values can be separated from facts, analysis can be done solely by specialists totally divorced from the political process. The differences between the two models are illustrated below.

Traditional Analysis

- Definition of goals and objectives
- Empirical measurement of data
- Objective assessment of results: Does the policy work?
- Determination of efficiency through cost-benefit analysis

New Analytical Method

- Definition of society's values
- Derivation of policy goals from those values
- Measurement of data, which can be empirical
- Philosophic inquiry into issues arising from policy
- Philosophic measurement of policy ramifications against philosophic underpinnings, that is, social values
- Qualitative cost-benefit analysis: Do benefits justify social costs?

This methodology is not calling for an abandonment of quantitative approaches. On the contrary, it might be said to accord with what Easton once referred to as the post-behavioral revolution in political science. According to Easton, the essence of this revolution was to make political science relevant to the world in which we live. That was precisely the purpose of modern liberalism as it found expression in Dewey's blueprint for social action: to make those principles in the earlier liberal writings relevant in a world that is forever changing. Research about and constructive development of values are inextinguishable parts of the study of politics.[51] Similarly, they are inextinguishable parts of the study and analysis of policy. And, ultimately, they may be inextinguishable parts of the liberal enterprise. If we are aspiring to the Lockean ideal, the question would be whether there is a Lockean model of education for policy analysts. At issue is what would best serve the public interest. What type of education would enable one to fully develop oneself within one's community? And what type of education would teach the individual the value of mutuality, of meeting one's obligations to the community, not just claiming one's rights. We need to bring philosophy back into the process and recognize that policy is merely the concrete application of philosophical precepts. In this regard, it can never be fully neutral, and liberals end up doing a great disservice when they assume that it can be.

Does this not, in the end, bring us back to what political science historically was: an attempt to understand the relationship between the individual and the state, as well as the individual and society? This was the enterprise of the great political theorists. What has perhaps altered the equation has been the introduction of "policy" into it. But policy is simply a means by which the state expresses itself to its citizens. In the negative, it may be a means by which it offends. In the positive, it may be a means by which it demonstrates accountability and responsiveness to the needs of the community. Neutral measures all too often limit our ability to see beyond the technical concerns and address the larger issues of whether they really do serve the community—and, in this vein, whether they are responsive to the needs of the community. A methodology of policy analysis that serves to ensure that the Lockean ideal is brought to fruition might also be a methodology that engages in the Lockean enterprise.

Implications

The preceding discussion would seem to imply a new role for political theory, that it can be applied to contemporary circumstances for the purpose of deriving greater understanding. The principal mistake within the political science discipline has been to assume that policy, as a scientific endeavor, could simply be studied in virtual isolation from its context. This has perhaps been the unfortunate consequence of the separation of facts from values, that political theory as an esoteric pursuit bore no concrete relevance to the real world in which governments pursue policies, offer programs, and engage in a variety of actions that may assist a variety of different groups at different times, or simply strengthen the hand of one at the expense of the other. Political theory, it was assumed, was merely concerned with the ideal state, what ought to be. Empirical policy, however, was concerned with what was. Yet, how can this so-called ideal state be realized if there is no ideal by which to measure policy? It is supremely ironic that Lockean theory has achieved the status of political philosophy that bears no contemporary relevance, when its view of the ideal is based on experience in the real world—what was observed about the real world that was wrong and what needed to be corrected. This, ultimately, is the goal of the new approach to policy analysis: to utilize the tools of political theory for the evaluation of public policy and, in the process, to make the study of policy meaningful and accessible to those who concern themselves with constructions of the ideal society. The study of policy shouldn't be the sole domain of those who are consumed with the minutiae of the process.

If the purpose of public policy is to further the purposes of the community, those purposes can only be furthered if we truly understand them in philosophical terms. It is imperative, then, that the policy analyst probe communal values, or at least broad social traditions, to discern whether policy is accomplishing social objectives. It isn't merely a question of policy analysis becoming more qualitative and less quantitative. It requires using political theory as a tool of analysis and positing an ideal that contains certain principles by which to measure. At the heart of this approach is the constructive use of political theory as a means of solving social problems.[52] Political theory would then need to be thought of as a paradigm for constructive policy analysis. Instead of political theory being viewed as something detached from the real world, it would be viewed as a response to real world crises.[53] The work of Rawls did much to revitalize political theory as a viable field within the political science discipline. The role of this new methodology would be to carry it a step further and give the theorist a practical role in the world of policy. The new methodology would result in a broader conception of the political science enterprise by bridging the gap between political theory and behavioralism. Only by breaking down some of the artificial distinctions will it be possible to measure policy in such a way that we can determine whether it is consistent with underpinning philosophic foundations. This determination must be a starting point in clearly defining the public welfare.

Many of the problems stem from the fact that many of the policies, though framed with liberal purposes in mind, have only demonstrated a widening gap between those goals and the actual results. If we were to evaluate those policies with those purposes in mind, they might actually represent a greater expression of liberal ideals. Of course, the community would have to decide. But in the final analysis, the issue comes down to whether policy—not only its objectives, but also its actual implementation and effects—can be justified in light of liberal philosophical principles. Moreover, it is imperative that we be able to do this, for if we do not, the end of liberalism will be the result of liberals themselves having failed to transmit a doctrine able to withstand the desires of conservatives, or any enemy of an open society, to exploit liberalism's shortcomings so they can create a society that is ultimately hierarchical and exclusive. For Lowi, the end of liberalism was largely a matter of process. But in today's political climate, the end of liberalism has been more a matter of substance. And yet, the ultimate objective of focusing more on substance is to have a society that is broadly inclusive and binds the community together behind a common project. If it does this, it also has achieved mutuality and tolerance. The role of policy, then, is to be the instrument for the attainment of these objectives.

Notes

Chapter 1. Introduction

1. Louis Hartz, *The Liberal Tradition in America: An Interpretation of American Political Thought Since the Revolution* (New York: Harcourt Brace Jovanovich, 1955); John Patrick Diggins, *The Lost Soul of American Politics: Virtue, Self-Interest, and the Foundations of Liberalism* (Chicago: University of Chicago Press, 1986).

2. Patrick M. Garry, *Liberalism and American Identity* (Kent, Ohio: Kent State University Press, 1992); David P. Barash, *The L Word: An Unapologetic, Thoroughly Biased, Long-Overdue Explication and Celebration of Liberalism* (New York: William Morrow and Co., 1992); F. Forrester Church, *God and Other Famous Liberals: Reclaiming the Politics of America* (New York: Simon & Schuster, 1992).

3. Pat Buchanan quoted in Norman Mailer, "By Heaven Inspired," an account of the Republican convention in the *New Republic*, October 12, 1992, 26.

4. Nancy L. Rosenblum, ed., *Liberalism and the Moral Life* (Cambridge: Harvard University Press, 1989).

5. John Rawls, *Political Liberalism* (New York: Columbia University Press, 1993).

6. Ronald Dworkin, "Liberalism," in *A Matter of Principle* (Cambridge: Harvard University Press, 1985).

7. Theodore J. Lowi, *The End of Liberalism: The Second Republic of the United States* (New York: W.W. Norton, 1979); see also Lowi, *The Personal President: Power Invested, Power Denied* (Ithaca, N.Y.: Cornell University Press, 1985); Lowi, "American Business, Public Policy, Case-Studies, and Political Theory," *World Politics* 16 (1964): 677–715.

8. Lowi, *The End of Liberalism.*

9. Michael J. Sandel, *Liberalism and the Limits of Justice* (Cambridge: Cambridge University Press, 1982), 133.

10. William A. Galston, *Liberal Purposes: Goods, Virtues, and Diversity in the Liberal State* (Cambridge: Cambridge University Press, 1991).

11. See, for example, James Q. Wilson, *The Moral Sense* (New York: Free Press, 1993).

12. See Ruth W. Grant, "Locke's Political Anthropology and Lockean Individualism," *Journal of Politics* 50 (1988): 42–63.

13. See, for example, W. G. Runciman, *Social Science and Political Theory* (Cambridge: Cambridge University Press, 1971); Robert E. Goodin, *Political Theory and Public Policy* (Chicago: University of Chicago Press, 1982); David Easton, "The New Revolution in Political Science," *American Political Science Review* 63 (1969): 1051–61.

14. Frank Fischer, *Politics, Values, and Public Policy: The Problem of Methodology* (Boulder, Colo.: Westview Press, 1980).

15. See, for example, R. Jeffrey Lustig, *Corporate Liberalism: The Origins of Modern American Political Theory* (Berkeley and Los Angeles: University of California Press, 1982).

16. Samuel P. Huntington, *American Politics: The Promise of Disharmony* (Cambridge: Belknap Press, 1981).

17. Kevin Phillips, *The Politics of Rich and Poor: Wealth and the American Electorate in the Reagan Aftermath* (New York: HarperCollins Publishers, 1990); see also Jonathan Rieder, *Canarsie: The Jews and Italians of Brooklyn Against Liberalism* (Cambridge: Harvard University Press, 1985).

18. See Bruce A. Ackerman, *Social Justice in the Liberal State* (New Haven: Yale University Press, 1980).

19. See, for example, Martin J. Sklar, *The United States as a Developing Country: Studies in U.S. History in the Progressive Era and the 1920s* (Cambridge: Cambridge University Press, 1992); and *The Corporate Reconstruction of American Capitalism, 1890–1916: The Market, the Law, and Politics* (Cambridge: Cambridge University Press, 1988).

20. See Stein Ringen, *The Possibility of Politics: A Study in the Political Economy of the Welfare State* (Oxford: Claredon Books, 1987).

21. See David Osborne, *Laboratories of Democracy* (Boston: Harvard Business School Press, 1988).

Chapter 2. The Lockean Ideal

1. John Locke, *Two Treatises of Government*, ed. Peter Laslett (Cambridge: Cambridge University Press, 1988), 2:350–51.

2. Gordon J. Schocket, "Introduction" to *Life, Liberty, and Property: Essays on Locke's Political Ideas*, ed. Schocket (Belmont, Calif.: Wadsworth Publishing, 1971).

3. See Daniella Gobetti, *Private and Public: Individuals, Households, and Body Politic in Locke and Hutchens* (London: Routledge, 1992), 56.

4. Sir Robert Filmer, *Patriarcha and Other Writings*, ed. Johanne P. Sommerville (Cambridge: Cambridge University Press, 1991), 6–7, 9.

5. John Dunn, *The Political Thought of John Locke: An Historical Account of the Argument of the "Two Treatises of Government"* (Cambridge: Cambridge University Press, 1969), 44.

6. Richard Ashcraft, *Revolutionary Politics: Locke's Two Treatises of Government* (Princeton: Princeton University Press, 1986).

7. Ashcraft, *Revolutionary Politics*, 338, 391.

8. See Louis Hartz, *The Liberal Tradition in America: An Interpretation of American Political Thought Since the Revolution* (New York: Harcourt Brace Jovanovich, 1955).

9. Ruth W. Grant, *John Locke's Liberalism* (Chicago: University of Chicago Press, 1987); Richard E. Flathman, *Willful Liberalism: Voluntarism and Individuality in Political Theory and Practice* (Ithaca, N.Y: Cornell University Press, 1992); W. von Leyden, *Hobbes and Locke: The Politics of Freedom and Obligation* (New York: St. Martin's Press, 1982).

10. Grant, *John Locke's Liberalism.*

11. See Ian Shapiro, *The Evolution of Rights in Liberal Theory* (Cambridge: Cambridge University Press, 1986).

12. Judith N. Shklar, "The Liberalism of Fear," in *Liberalism and the Moral Life*, ed. Nancy L. Rosenblum (Cambridge: Harvard University Press, 1989).

13. Andrzej Rapaczynski, *Nature and Politics: Liberalism in the Philosophies of Hobbes, Locke, and Rousseau* (Ithaca, N.Y.: Cornell University Press, 1987), 25, 50.

14. Von Leyden, *Hobbes and Locke*, 71–72.

15. Shapiro, *The Evolution of Rights in Liberal Theory*; see also Rapaczynski, *Nature and Politics: Liberalism in the Philosophies of Hobbes, Locke, and Rousseau.*

16. Von Leyden, *Hobbes and Locke*, 100.

17. J. W. Gough, *John Locke's Political Philosophy* (Oxford: Clarendon Press, 1956), 1–4.

18. Grant, *John Locke's Liberalism*, 6.

19. W. von Leyden, "John Locke and Natural Law," in *Life, Liberty, and Property: Essays on Locke's Political Ideas*, ed. Gordon J. Schocket (Belmont, Calif.: Wadsworth Publishing, 1971).

20. See Rapaczynski, *Nature and Politics: Liberalism in the Philosophies of Hobbes, Locke, and Rousseau.*

21. J. P. Day, "Locke on Property," in *Life, Liberty, and Property: Essays on Locke's Political Ideas*, ed. Gordon J. Schocket (Belmont, Calif.: Wadsworth Publishing, 1971).

22. See, for example, Glen O. Robinson, "Evolving Conceptions of 'Property'

and 'Liberty' in Due Process Jurisprudence," in *Liberty, Property, and Government: Constitutional Interpretation Before the New Deal*, ed. Ellen Frankel Paul and Howard Dickman (Albany: State University of New York Press, 1989).

23. Locke, *Two Treatises*, 2:350–51.

24. Isaac Kramnick, *Republicanism and Bourgeois Radicalism: Political Ideology in Late Eighteenth-Century England and America* (Ithaca, Cornell University Press, 1990), 7.

25. Paine, quoted in Kramnick, *Republicanism and Bourgeois Radicalism*, 154.

26. C. B. Macpherson, *The Political Theory of Possessive Individualism: Hobbes to Locke* (London, Oxford University Press, 1964).

27. C. B. Macpherson, "The Social Bearing of Locke's Political Theory," in *Life, Liberty, and Property: Essays on Locke's Political Ideas*, ed. Gordon J. Schocket (Belmont, Calif.: Wadsworth Publishing, 1971).

28. Locke, *Two Treatises* 2:412.

29. Shapiro, *The Evolution of Rights in Liberal Theory;* M. Seliger, *The Liberal Politics of John Locke* (London: George Allen & Unwin, 1968).

30. See, for example, John Rawls, *A Theory of Justice* (Cambridge: Harvard University Press, 1971); Ronald Dworkin, "Liberalism," in *A Matter of Principle;* Ackerman, *Social Justice in the Liberal State.*

31. Richard Ashcraft, *Locke's Two Treatises of Government* (London: Allen & Unwin, 1987), 100.

32. Ruth W. Grant, "Locke's Political Anthropology and Lockean Individualism," *Journal of Politics* 50 (1988): 42–63; and *John Locke's Liberalism.*

33. See, for example, Hans Aarsleff, *The Study of Language in England, 1780–1860* (Minneapolis: University of Minnesota Press, 1983).

34. John Locke, *An Essay Concerning Human Understanding*, ed. Peter H. Nidditch (Oxford: Oxford University Press, 1975), 1:48.

35. Locke, *Two Treatises*, 1:142.

36. J. G. A. Pocock, *The Ancient Constitution and the Feudal Law: A Study of English Historical Thought in the Seventeenth Century* (New York: W.W. Norton, 1967), 189.

37. Gobetti, *Private and Public: Individuals, Households, and Body Politic in Locke and Hutchens*, 56.

38. Locke, *Essay*, 1:48.

39. Locke, *Essay*, 1:69.

40. Locke, *Two Treatises*, 1:161.

41. Locke, *Two Treatises*, 2:304.

42. Shapiro, *The Evolution of Rights in Liberal Theory*, 87.

43. Locke, "Of Conquest," *Two Treatises*, 2:384–97; Pocock, *The Ancient Constitution and the Feudal Law.*

44. Hans Aarsleff, *From Locke to Saussure: Essays on the Study of Language and Intellectual History* (Minneapolis: University of Minnesota Press, 1982).

45. Dunn, *The Political Thought of John Locke*, 39.

46. Locke, *Two Treatises* 2:269; Grant, *John Locke's Liberalism.*

47. Grant, *John Locke's Liberalism*, 68.

48. Locke, *Essay*, 2:392.

49. Locke, *Essay*, 3:431–32.

50. See Steven B. Smith, *Hegel's Critique of Liberalism: Rights in Context* (Chicago: University of Chicago Press, 1989); Charles Taylor, *Hegel and Modern Society* (Cambridge: Cambridge University Press, 1979).

51. Smith, *Hegel's Critique of Liberalism*, 233.

52. Daniel Bell, *Communitarianism and Its Critics* (Oxford: Oxford University Press, 1993), 43, 90–95.

53. See, for example, John Durham Peters, "John Locke, the Individual, and the Origins of Communication," *Quarterly Journal of Speech* 75 (1989): 387–99.

54. Locke, *Essay*, 3:402.

55. Locke, *Two Treatises of Government*, 2:318.

56. Alasdair MacIntyre, *After Virtue: A Study in Moral Theory* (Notre Dame, Ind.: University of Notre Dame Press, 1984), 222.

57. Locke, *Essay*, 3:443.

58. Locke, *Essay*, 3:476.

59. Locke, *Essay*, 3:506.

60. Locke, *Two Treatises*, 2:272.

61. Dunn, *The Political Thought of John Locke*, 48.

62. Stephen Holmes, *The Anatomy of Antiliberalism* (Cambridge: Harvard University Press, 1993), 193.

63. See Richard C. Sinopoli, *The Foundations of American Citizenship: Liberalism, the Constitution, and Civic Virtue* (Oxford: Oxford University Press, 1992), 41.

64. Grant, *John Locke's Liberalism*, 136.

65. Locke, *Two Treatises*, 2:406.

66. Locke, *Two Treatises*, 2:270–72.

67. Seliger, *The Liberal Politics of John Locke*, 62.

68. Shapiro, *The Evolution of Rights in Liberal Theory*, 117.

69. Locke, *Two Treatises*, 2:350.

70. Jeremy Waldron, *The Right to Private Property* (Oxford: Oxford University Press, 1988), 120–28, 138.

71. Locke, *Two Treatises*, 2:302.

72. Waldron, *The Right to Private Property*, 139, 216.

73. Ashcraft, *Revolutionary Politics*, 264–66.

74. Gough, *John Locke's Political Philosophy*, 81–84.

75. Locke, *Two Treatises*, 2:290.

76. John Christman, *The Myth of Property: Toward an Egalitarian Theory of Ownership* (Oxford: Oxford University Press, 1994), 52.

77. Thomas Pangle, *The Spirit of Modern Republicanism: The Moral Union of the American Founders and the Philosophy of Locke* (Chicago: University of Chicago Press, 1988).

78. Seliger, *The Liberal Politics of John Locke*, 180.

79. Nathan Tarcov, *Locke's Education for Liberty* (Chicago: University of Chicago Press, 1984), 26, 132.

80. Waldron, *The Right to Private Property*, 158.

81. Pangle, *The Spirit of Modern Republicanism*; see also Edward J. Erler, "The Great Fence to Liberty: The Right to Property in the American Founding," in *Liberty, Property, and the Foundations of the American Constitution*, ed. Ellen Frankel Paul and Howard Dickman (Albany: State University of New York Press, 1989).

82. Richard I. Aaron, *John Locke* (Oxford: Clarendon Press, 1971), 286.
83. Locke, *Two Treatises*, 137.
84. See Tarcov, *Locke's Education for Liberty.*
85. Roberto Mangabeira Unger, *Law in Modern Society: Toward a Criticism of Social Theory* (New York: Free Press, 1976).
86. Grant, *John Locke's Liberalism*, 130, 135, 174, 203.
87. Michael Walzer, *Obligations: Essays on Disobedience, War and Citizenship* (Cambridge: Harvard University Press, 1970); Hanna Pitkin, "Obligation and Consent—I," *American Political Science Review* 59 (1965): 990–99; and "Obligation and Consent—II," *American Political Science Review* 60 (1966): 39–52.
88. Gough, *John Locke's Political Philosophy*, 19.
89. Ashcraft, *Locke's Two Treatises of Government*, 46.
90. Rawls, *A Theory of Justice*, 135.
91. Von Leyden, *Hobbes and Locke.*
92. Locke, *Two Treatises*, 2:332.
93. See Ronald Dworkin, *Taking Rights Seriously* (Cambridge: Harvard University Press, 1977).
94. L. W. Sumner, *The Moral Foundations of Rights* (New York: Clarendon Press, 1987).
95. Gary C. Bryner, "Constitutionalism and the Politics of Rights," in *Constitutionalism and Rights*, ed. Gary C. Bryner and Noel B. Reynolds (Provo, Utah: Brigham Young University, 1987).
96. Sandel, *Liberalism and the Limits of Justice.*
97. Locke, "A Letter Concerning Toleration," in *John Locke: A Letter Concerning Toleration in Focus*, ed. John Horton and Susan Mendus (London: Routledge, 1992), 18.
98. Locke, "A Letter Concerning Toleration," 20.
99. *Texas v. Johnson*, 491 U.S. 397, 414 (1989).
100. John Stuart Mill, *On Liberty*, ed. Currin V. Shields (Indianapolis: Bobbs-Merrill, 1956), 7.
101. *Texas v. Johnson*, 414.
102. Locke, *A Letter Concerning Toleration*, 20.
103. Mill, *On Liberty*, 8.
104. Mill, *On Liberty*, 13.
105. *Texas v. Johnson*, 429.
106. Locke, "A Letter Concerning Toleration," 17.
107. J. W. Gough, "The Development of Locke's Belief in Toleration," in *John Locke: A Letter Concerning Toleration in Focus*, ed. John Horton and Susan Mendus (London: Routledge, 1992), 60.
108. See, for example, Charles Reich, "The New Property," *Yale Law Journal* 73 (1964): 733–87.
109. Gough, *John Locke's Political Philosophy*, 45.
110. John Dewey, *Liberalism and Social Action* (New York: Capricorn Books, 1963); see also Charles W. Anderson, *Pragmatic Liberalism* (Chicago: University of Chicago Press, 1990).
111. Robert B. Westbrook, *John Dewey and American Democracy* (Ithaca, Cornell University Press, 1991), 432–38.

Chapter 3. Economic Stabilization

1. Lustig, *Corporate Liberalism: The Origins of Modern American Political Theory*; Martin J. Sklar, *The Corporate Reconstruction of American Capitalism, 1890–1916: The Market, the Law, and Politics* (Cambridge: Cambridge University Press, 1988); James Weinstein, *The Corporate Ideal in the Liberal State: 1900–1918* (Boston: Beacon Press, 1968).

2. See Marver H. Bernstein, *Regulating Business by Independent Commission* (Princeton: Princeton University Press, 1955).

3. See Michael D. Reagan, *Regulation: The Politics of Policy* (Boston: Little, Brown, 1987).

4. See Weinstein, *The Corporate Ideal in the Liberal State.*

5. See Huntington, *American Politics: The Promise of Disharmony*, esp. his discussion of creedal passion periods, 85–129.

6. See, for example, Harry N. Scheiber, "The Jurisprudence—and Mythology—of Eminent Domain in American Legal History," in *Liberty, Property, and Government: Constitutional Interpretation Before the New Deal*, ed. Ellen Frankel Paul and Howard Dickman (Albany: State University of New York Press, 1989), 221.

7. See, for example, Andrew F. Brimmer, "Monetary Policy and Economic Activity: Benefits and Costs of Monetarism," *American Economic Review* 73, no. 2 (May 1983): 1–12.

8. See, for example, Alan Wolfe, *America's Impasse: The Rise and Fall of the Politics of Growth* (New York: Pantheon Books, 1981).

9. Michael D. Reagan, "The Political Structure of the Federal Reserve System" *American Political Science Review* 55 (1961): 64–76.

10. Employment Act of 1946, *Statutes at Large* 60 (1946): 23.

11. Reagan, "The Political Structure of the Federal Reserve System."

12. *Loan Association v. Topeka*, 87 U.S. (20 Wall.) 655 (1874); see also Charles Fairman, *History of the Supreme Court of the United States: Reconstruction and Reunion 1864–88* (New York: Macmillan, 1971), 6:1101–12.

13. Rawls, *A Theory of Justice.*

14. Lowi, "American Business, Public Policy, Case-Studies, and Political Theory," 677–715.

15. See, for example, William Greider, *Secrets of the Temple: How the Federal Reserve Runs the Country* (New York: Touchstone Books, 1987).

16. See, for example, William Julius Wilson, *The Truly Disadvantaged: The Inner City, the Underclass, and Public Policy* (Chicago: University of Chicago Press, 1987).

17. Ackerman, *Social Justice in the Liberal State.*

18. See John T. Woolley, *Monetary Politics: The Federal Reserve and the Politics of Monetary Policy* (Cambridge: Cambridge University Press, 1984).

19. See Grieder, *Secrets of the Temple.*

20. See, for example, G. William Donhoff, *The Power Elite and the State: How Policy Is Made in America* (Hawthorne, N.Y.: Aldine de Gruyter, 1990); Thomas R. Dye, *Who's Running America? The Conservative Years* (Englewood Cliffs, N.J.; Prentice-Hall, 1986).

21. See Milton Friedman, "The Role of Monetary Policy," *American Economics*

Review 58 (March 1968): 1–17; Friedman, "Unemployment versus Inflation?" *Institute for Economic Affairs* lecture no. 2, occasional paper 44 (London: IEA, 1975); Edmund S. Phelps, "Phillips Curves, Expectations of Inflation and Optimal Unemployment over Time," *Economica* 34 (August 1967): 254–81; and Phelps, *Inflation Policy and Unemployment Theory: The Cost-Benefit Approach to Monetary Planning* (London: Macmillan, 1972).

22. Bruce A. Ackerman, *Private Property and the Constitution* (New Haven: Yale University Press, 1977).

23. Dworkin, *Taking Rights Seriously.*

24. Rawls, *A Theory of Justice.*

25. See Laurence H. Tribe, *American Constitutional Law*, 2nd ed. (Mineola, N.Y.: Foundation Press, 1988).

26. *Pennsylvania Coal Co. v. Mahon*, 260 U.S. 57; L. Ed. 322, 326 (1922).

27. See, for example, Joseph L. Sax, "Some Thoughts on the Decline of Private Property," *Washington Law Review* 58 (1983): 481.

28. *Penn Central Transportation Co. v. New York City*, 438 U.S. 104 (1977).

29. Tribe, *American Constitutional Law*, 597.

30. See Woolley, *Monetary Politics.*

31. See Grieder, *Secrets of the Temple.*

32. Woolley, *Monetary Politics*, 152.

33. Oren M. Levin-Waldman, *Plant Closure, Regulation, and Liberalism: The Limits to Liberal Public Philosophy* (Lanham, Md.; University Press of America, 1992).

34. Joseph A. Schumpeter, *Capitalism, Socialism and Democracy* (New York: Harper and Row, 1975).

35. Philip L. Martin, *Labor Displacement and Public Policy* (Lexington, Mass.: D.C. Heath, 1983).

36. U.S. General Accounting Office, *Plant Closings: Limited Advance Notice and Assistance Provided Dislocated Workers* (Washington, D.C.: U.S. GAO, July 1987).

37. Diane E. Herz, "Worker Displacement Still Common in the late 1980's: Even During a Period of Rapid Growth—From 1985 Through 1989—4.3 Million Persons Were Displaced from Their Jobs," *Bureau of Labor Statistics Bulletin* (Washington, D.C.: U.S. Department of Labor, June 1991), 2382.

38. "Worker Displacement During Early 1990s," Bureau of Labor Statistics News Release, September 14, 1994.

39. See John S. Hekman and John S. Strong, "Is There a Case for Plant Closing Laws?" *New England Economic Review*, July–August 1980; Richard B. McKenzie, *Fugitive Industry: The Economics and Politics of Deindustrialization* (San Francisco: Pacific Institute for Public Policy Research, 1984).

40. Mary Jane Bolle, "Plant Closing Legislation: Worker Adjustment and Retraining Notification Act (WARN)," *CRS Issue Brief* (Washington, D.C.: Congressional Research Service, 1991); Herz, "Worker Displacement Still Common in the Late 1980's"; Barry Bluestone and Bennett Harrison, *The Deindustrialization of America: Plant Closings, Community Abandonment, and the Dismantling of Basic Industry* (New York: Basic Books, 1982).

41. Bluestone and Harrison, *The Deindustrialization of America.*

42. See esp. Robert Z. Lawrence, *Can America Compete?* (Washington, D.C.: Brookings Institution, 1984); Levin-Waldman, *Plant Closure, Regulation, and Liberalism*, esp. chap. 2.

43. See R. Jeffrey Lustig, "The Politics of Shutdown: Community, Property, Corporatism," *Journal of Economic Issues* 19 (1985): 123–52.

44. See, for example, Peter Bachrach and Aryeh Botwinick, *Power and Empowerment: A Radical Theory of Participatory Democracy* (Philadelphia: Temple University Press, 1992); Samuel Bowles and Herbert Gintis, *Democracy and Capitalism: Property, Community and the Contradictions of Modern Social Thought* (New York: Basic Books, 1987).

45. Also based on a survey which I administered to state dislocated worker units, among the twenty-five states that did respond, there was general agreement that the legislation was weak precisely because it lacked a mechanism for enforcement and compliance.

46. Lawrence E. Rothstein, *Plant Closings: Power, Politics and Workers* (Dover, Mass.: Auburn House, 1986); William D. Ford, "Coping with Plant Closings," *Labor Law Journal* 36 (1985): 323–26.

47. See, for example, Edward J. Blakely and Philip Shapira, "Industrial Restructuring: Public Policies for Investment in Advanced Industrial Societies," *Annals of the American Academy of Political and Social Science* 475 (September 1984): 96–109.

48. See, for example, Nancy R. Folbre, Julia L. Leighton, and Melissa R. Roderick, "Plant Closings and Their Regulation in Maine, 1971–1982," *Industrial and Labor Relations Review* 37 (January 1984): 185–96; John T. Addison and Pedro Portugal, "The Effect of Advance Notification of Plant Closings on Unemployment," *Industrial and Labor Relations Review* 41, no. 1 (October 1987): 3–16; Douglas O. Love and William D. Torrence, "The Value of Advance Notice of Worker Displacement," *Southern Economic Journal* 55 (January 1989): 626–43; Stephen Nord and Yuan Ting, "The Impact of Advance Notice of Plant Closings on Earnings and the Probability of Unemployment," *Industrial and Labor Relations Review* 44 (July 1991): 681–91.

49. See Levin-Waldman, *Plant Closure, Regulation, and Liberalism*, 145–52.

50. Martin, *Labor Displacement and Public Policy*.

51. Oren M. Levin-Waldman, "Dilemmas of Plant Closing Policy in Liberal Society: Equality, Rights, Justice," *Public Affairs Quarterly* 4 (January 1990): 333–53.

52. Theodore J. Lowi, "Liberal and Conservative Theories of Regulation," in *The Constitution and the Regulation of Society*, ed. Gary C. Bryner and Dennis F. Thompson (Provo, Utah: Brigham Young University, 1988).

53. Roberto Mangabeira Unger, *Knowledge and Politics* (New York: Free Press, 1975), 134.

54. Dworkin, *Taking Rights Seriously*, 272–73.

55. John Stuart Mill, quoted in Sumner, *The Moral Foundations of Rights*, 136.

56. See, for example, McKenzie, *Fugitive Industry*; Hekman and Strong, "Is There a Case for Plant Closing Laws?"

57. See Mary Ann Glendon, *Rights Talk: The Impoverishment of Political Discourse* (New York: Free Press, 1991); Sax, "Some Thoughts on the Decline of Private Property."

58. See Cass R. Sunstein, *After the Rights Revolution: Reconceiving the Regulatory State* (Cambridge: Harvard University Press, 1990).

59. Michael Walzer, *Spheres of Justice: A Defense of Pluralism* (New York: Basic Books, 1983), 75, 79.

60. Rawls, *A Theory of Justice*, 152.

61. Sandel, *Liberalism and the Limits of Justice*; see also Taylor, *Hegel and Modern Society*; MacIntyre, *After Virtue: A Study in Moral Theory*; Smith, *Hegel's Critique of Liberalism: Rights in Context.*

62. On the distinction between partial democracy and full democracy, see Kenneth M. Dolbeare, *Democracy at Risk: The Politics of Economic Renewal* (Chatham, N.J.; Chatham House, 1986); see also Robert A. Dahl, *A Preface to Economic Democracy* (Berkeley: University of California Press, 1985); Joshua Cohen and Joel Rogers, *On Democracy: Toward a Transformation of American Society* (New York: Penguin Books, 1983).

63. See Charles E. Lindblom, "The Science of Muddling Through," *Public Administration Review* 17 (1959): 79–88; Lindblom, *The Intelligence of Democracy: Decision Making Through Mutual Adjustment* (New York: Free Press, 1965).

64. Kerry Schott, *Policy, Power and Order: The Persistence of Economic Problems in Capitalist States* (New Haven: Yale University Press, 1984), 19.

65. Leo Panitch, "The Development of Corporatism in Liberal Democracies," *Comparative Political Studies* 10 (1977): 61.

66. Philippe C. Schmitter, "Still the Century of Corporatism?" *Review of Politics* 36 (1974): 107–98.

67. Panitch, "The Development of Corporatism in Liberal Societies," 66.

68. Gerhard Lehmbruch, "Liberal Corporatism and Party Government," *Comparative Political Studies* 10 (1977): 94.

69. Martin A. Schain, "Corporatism and Industrial Relations in France," in *French Politics and Public Policy*, ed. Philip G. Cerney and Martin A. Schain (London: Methuen, 1980).

70. David C. Cameron, "Social Democracy, Corporatism, Labour Quiescence and the Representation of Economic Interest in Advanced Capitalist Society," in *Order and Conflict in Contemporary Capitalism*, ed. John H. Goldthorpe (Oxford: Oxford University Press, 1984), 146.

71. See Stanley C. Brubaker, "Can Liberals Punish?" *American Political Science Review* 82 (1988): 821–36.

72. Charles E. Lindblom, *Politics and Markets: The World's Political Economic Systems* (New York: Basic Books, 1977).

73. Panitch, "The Development of Corporatism in Liberal Democracies."

74. Lehmbruch, "Liberal Corporatism and Party Government."

75. See for example, David Wilmoth, "Regional Economic Policy and the New Corporatism," *Sunbelt/Snowbelt: Urban Development and Regional Restructuring*, ed. Larry Sawers and William K. Tabb (New York: Oxford University Press, 1984).

76. See Glen W. Miller, *American Labor and the Government* (New York: Prentice-Hall, 1948); Harry A. Millis and Emily Clark Brown, *From the Wagner Act to Taft-Hartley: A Study of National Labor Policy and Labor Relations* (Chicago: University of Chicago Press, 1950).

77. Bachrach and Botwinick, *Power and Empowerment.*

78. Philippe C. Schmitter, "Modes of Interest Intermediation and Models of Societal Change in Western Europe," *Comparative Political Studies* 10 (1977): 7–38.

79. Schott, *Policy, Power and Order,* 42.

80. Schain, "Corporatism and Industrial Relations in France."

81. Bluestone and Harrison, *The Deindustrialization of America;* Samuel Bowles, David M. Gordon and Thomas E. Weisskopf, *Beyond the Wasteland: A Democratic Alternative to Economic Decline* (New York: Doubleday, 1983); Roger W. Schmenner, "Every Factory has a Life Cycle," *Harvard Business Review* 62 (1983): 121–29.

82. See Martin Carnoy and Derek Shearer, *Economic Democracy: The Challenge of the 1980s* (White Plains, N.Y.: M. E. Sharpe, 1980).

83. See Sanford Levinson, *Constitutional Faith* (Princeton: Princeton University Press, 1988).

84. *Youngstown Sheet and Tube Co. v. Sawyer,* 343 U.S. 579 (1952).

Chapter 4. Welfare Policy

1. J. Donald Moon, ed., *Responsibility, Rights, and Welfare: The Theory of the Welfare State* (Boulder, Colo.; Westview Press, 1988), 3–7.

2. Ringen, *The Possibility of Politics: A Study in the Political Economy of the Welfare State.*

3. Hugh Heclo, "General Welfare and Two American Political Traditions," *Political Science Quarterly* 101 (1986): 179–96.

4. See, for example, Herbert McCloskey and John Zaller, *The American Ethos: Public Attitudes Toward Capitalism and Democracy* (Cambridge: Harvard University Press, 1984).

5. Hugh Heclo, "The Political Foundations of Antipoverty Policy," in *Fighting Poverty: What Works?* ed. Sheldon Danziger and Daniel Weinberg (Cambridge: Harvard University Press, 1986).

6. Robert E. Goodin, *Reasons for Welfare: The Political Theory of the Welfare State* (Princeton: Princeton University Press, 1988).

7. Charles Murray, *Losing Ground: American Social Policy, 1950–1980* (New York: Basic Books, 1984).

8. Edward C. Banfield, *The Unheavenly City Revisited* (Boston: Little, Brown, 1974), 112–13.

9. Richard B. Freeman and Harry Holzer, eds., *The Black Youth Employment Crisis* (Chicago: University of Chicago Press, 1986); Roy H. Kaplan and Curt Tausky, "Work and the Welfare Cadillac: The Function of and Commitments to Work Among the Hard-Core Unemployed," *Social Problems* 19 (1972): 469–83.

10. See, for example, Linda Gordon, *Pitied but Not Entitled: Single Mothers and the History of Welfare 1890–1935* (New York: Free Press, 1994).

11. See, for example, Demetra Smith Nightingale and Robert H. Haveman, eds., *The Work Alternative: Welfare Reform and the Realities of the Job Market* (Washington, D.C.: Urban Institute Press, 1995); Robert H. Haveman, *Starting*

Even: An Equal Opportunity Program to Combat the Nation's New Poverty (New York: Simon & Schuster, 1988); Henry J. Aaron, *Why Is Welfare So Hard to Reform?* (Washington, D.C.: Brookings Institution, 1973).

12. Lawrence M. Mead, *Beyond Entitlement: The Social Obligations of Citizenship* (New York: Free Press, 1986); and for a liberal analysis, see Wilson, *The Truly Disadvantaged: The Inner City, the Underclass, and Public Policy*; Mickey Kaus, *The End of Equality* (New York: New Republic/Basic Books, 1992).

13. Lawrence M. Mead, *The New Politics of Poverty: The Nonworking Poor in America* (New York: Basic Books, 1992).

14. Mead, *Beyond Entitlement.*

15. Murray, *Losing Ground*, 197.

16. Robert Nozick, *Anarchy, State, and Utopia* (New York: Basic Books, 1974), 169.

17. Richard A. Epstein, "The Uncertain Quest for Welfare Rights," in *The Constitution and the Regulation of Society*, ed. Gary C. Bryner and Dennis F. Thompson (Provo, Utah: Brigham Young University, 1988), 34.

18. See Goodin, *Reasons for Welfare*; Walzer, *Spheres of Justice: A Defense of Pluralism.*

19. See Frances Fox Piven and Richard A. Cloward, *The New Class War: Reagan's Attack on the Welfare State and its Consequences* (New York: Pantheon Books, 1982).

20. See Mary Jo Bane and David T. Ellwood, *Welfare Realities: From Rhetoric to Reform* (Cambridge: Harvard University Press, 1994).

21. John E. Schwarz, *America's Hidden Success: A Reassessment of Public Policy from Kennedy to Reagan* (New York: W.W. Norton, 1988), 24–25. See also Forrest Chrisman and Alan Pifer, *Government for the People: The Federal Role: What It Is, What It Should be* (New York: W.W. Norton, 1987).

22. See Maurice MacDonald and Isabel V. Sawhill, "Welfare Policy and the Family," *Public Policy* 26 (Winter 1978): 89–119.

23. "Remarks of the President at Howard University, June 4, 1965," cited in Lee Rainwater and William L. Yancy, *The Moynihan Report and the Politics of Controversy* (Cambridge: MIT Press, 1967), 125–32.

24. See Kramnick, *Republicanism and Bourgeois Radicalism: The Political Ideology in Late Eighteenth-Century England and America.*

25. See Frances Fox Piven and Richard A. Cloward, *Regulating the Poor: The Functions of Public Welfare* (New York: Pantheon Books, 1971).

26. Rainwater and Yancy, *The Moynihan Report: The Politics of Controversy.*

27. Lowi, *The End of Liberalism*, 225.

28. Rainwater and Yancy, *The Moynihan Report and the Politics of Controversy.*

29. Kaus, *The End of Equality*; Christopher Jencks, *Rethinking Social Policy: Race, Poverty, and the Underclass* (Cambridge: Harvard University Press, 1992).

30. Nathan Glazer, *The Limits to Social Policy* (Cambridge: Harvard University Press, 1988), 28–29.

31. See Daniel P. Moynihan, *The Politics of a Guaranteed Income: The Nixon Administration and the Family Assistance Plan* (New York: Random House, 1973); Henry Aaron, *Why Is Welfare So Hard to Reform?* Note that the initial FAP proposal of the Nixon administration called for a guaranteed income of $1,600.

32. Goodin, *Reasons for Welfare.*

33. See Robert Kuttner, *The Economic Illusion: False Choices Between Prosperity and Social Justice* (Philadelphia, University of Pennsylvania Press, 1987), 240.

34. See Blanche Bernstein, "Shouldn't Low-Income Fathers Support Their Children?" *Public Interest* 66 (1982): 55–71.

35. See, for example, Theresa Funiciello, *Tyranny of Kindness: Dismantling the Welfare System to End Poverty in America* (New York: Atlantic Monthly Press, 1993).

36. Reich, "The New Property," 733–87.

37. Joan Higgins, "Public Welfare: The Road to Freedom?" *Journal of Social Policy* 11 (1982): 177–99.

38. Goodin, *Reasons for Welfare,* 196.

39. Jeremy Waldron, "Welfare and the Images of Charity," *The Philosophical Quarterly* 36 (1986), 463.

40. Waldron, "Welfare and the Images of Charity," 471–73.

41. Rogers M. Smith, *Liberalism and American Constitutional Law* (Cambridge: Harvard University Press, 1985).

42. Some of the material that follows is drawn from my article, "Liberals' Opposition to Workfare: A Misunderstanding of their Philosophic Tradition," *Public Affairs Quarterly* 8 (1994): 341–57.

43. *Dandridge v. Williams,* 397 U.S. 471 (1969).

44. *Dandridge v. Williams,* 486.

45. *New York State Department of Social Services v. Dublino,* 413 U.S. 413 (1972).

46. *Lavine v. Milne,* 424 U.S. 577 (1975).

47. *Slaughter-House Cases,* 83 U.S. (16 Wall.) 36 (1872).

48. Glendon, *Rights Talk: The Impoverishment of Political Discourse,* 144.

49. See Robert K. Fullinwider, "Citizenship and Welfare," in *Democracy and the Welfare State,* ed. Amy Gutmann (Princeton: Princeton University Press, 1988), 262.

50. Lawrence M. Mead, "Social Programs and Social Obligations," *Public Interest* 69 (1982): 23; see also Mead, "Expectations and Welfare Work: WIN in New York City," *Policy Studies Review* 2 (1983): 648–62.

51. Kaus, *The End of Equality,* 18–20, 127, 135.

52. Mead, *Beyond Entitlement,* 257.

53. Fullinwider, "Citizenship and Welfare," 273–74.

54. Blanche Bernstein, "The Case for Work Requirements," in Blanche Bernstein and Leonard Goodwin, "Do Work Requirements Accomplish Anything?" *Public Welfare* 32 (1978): 38–39.

55. Kaus, *The End of Equality.*

56. M. E. Hawkesworth, *Theoretical Issues in Policy Analysis* (Albany: State University of New York Press, 1988).

57. Ken Auletta, *The Underclass* (New York: Vintage Books, 1982).

58. Banfield, *The Unheavenly City Revisited.*

59. See Michael B. Katz, *The Undeserving Poor: From the War on Poverty to the War on Welfare* (New York: Pantheon Books, 1989).

60. Mead, *The New Politics of Poverty,* 29; see also Nathan Glazer, "Making Work Work: Welfare Reform in the 1990s," in *The Work Alternative: Welfare Reform*

and the Realities of the Job Market, ed. Demetra Smith Nightingale and Robert H. Haveman (Washington, D.C.: Urban Institute Press, 1995).

61. Michael Walzer, *Obligations: Essays on Disobedience, War and Citizenship* (Cambridge: Harvard University Press, 1970), 28, 148.

62. Leonard Goodwin, "The Case Against Work Requirements," in Blanche Bernstein and Leonard Goodwin, "Do Work Requirements Accomplish Anything?" *Public Welfare* 32 (1978): 38–39.

63. See David Osborne, "Massachusetts: Redistributing Economic Growth," *Laboratories of Democracy* (Boston: Harvard Business School Press, 1988), 197–98.

64. Auletta, *The Underclass.*

65. Goodwin, "The Case Against Work Requirements."

66. Lawrence M. Mead, "Expectations and Welfare Work: WIN in New York State," *Polity* 18 (1985): 224–52.

67. Mead, *The New Politics of Poverty.*

68. Stephen Holmes, "Liberal Guilt: Some Theoretical Origins of the Welfare State," in *Responsibility, Rights, and Welfare: The Theory of the Welfare State*, ed. J. Donald Moon (Boulder, Colo.: Westview Press, 1988), 100–01.

69. Fullinwider, "Citizenship and Welfare"; Mead, *Beyond Entitlement;* Auletta, *The Underclass.*

70. Judith N. Shklar, *American Citizenship: The Quest for Inclusion* (Cambridge: Harvard University Press, 1991), 97.

71. Katz, *The Undeserving Poor.*

72. Walzer, *Spheres of Justice: A Defense of Pluralism*, 278.

73. Walzer, *Spheres of Justice.*

74. Fullinwider, "Citizenship and Welfare"; Mead, *Beyond Entitlement.*

75. James R. Kluegel and Elliot Smith, *Beliefs About Inequality: Americans' Views of What Is and What Ought to Be* (Hawthorne, N.Y.: Aldine de Gruyter, 1986).

76. Fay Lomax Cook and Edit J. Barrett, *Support for the American Welfare State: The Views of Congress and the Public* (New York: Columbia University Press, 1992).

77. Dennis F. Thompson, *John Stuart Mill and Representative Government* (Princeton: Princeton University Press, 1976), 98–99.

78. Michael Krouse and Michael S. McPherson, "The Logic of Liberal Equality: John Stuart Mill and the Origins of Welfare State Liberalism," in *Responsibility, Rights, and Welfare: The Theory of the Welfare State*, ed. J. Donald Moon (Boulder, Colo.; Westview Press, 1988).

79. Shapiro, *The Evolution of Rights in Liberal Theory*, 95.

80. Richard E. Flathman, *Toward a Liberalism* (Ithaca, N.Y.: Cornell University Press, 1989); Rapaczynski, *Nature and Politics: Liberalism in the Philosophies of Hobbes, Locke, and Rousseau.*

81. See Walzer, *Obligations.*

82. Flathman, *Toward a Liberalism.*

83. Mead, "Expectations and Welfare Work."

84. Mead, *Beyond Entitlement*, 119.

85. See David L. Kirp, "The California Work/Welfare Scheme," *Public Interest* 83 (1986): 34–48.

86. Testimony of Dennis J. Boyle, in *Implementing the Family Support Act of*

1988, Hearing before the Subcommittee on Social Security and Family Policy of Committee on Finance, U.S. Senate, S. Hrg 101-323 (Washington, D.C.: GPO, 1989), 26.

87. See Osborne, "Massachusetts: Redistributing Economic Growth."

88. Demetra Smith Nightingale, Douglas A. Wissoker, Lynn C. Burbridge, D. Lee Bawden, and Neal Jeffries, *Evaluation of the Massachusetts Employment and Training (ET) Program* (Washington, D.C.: Urban Institute Press, 1991).

89. Kirp, "The California Work/Welfare Scheme," 48.

90. Or so these were the stated objectives as put forth by Sen. Daniel P. Moynihan, architect of this reform, in his prepared statement, *Implementing the Family Support Act of 1988*, 122.

91. Testimony of Constance Horner, *Implementing the Family Support Act of 1988*, 6.

92. See *Engel v. Vitale*, 370 U.S. 421 (1962); and *Abington School District v. Schempp*, 374 U.S. 203 (1963).

93. John Horton and Susan Mendus, eds., *John Locke: A Letter Concerning Toleration in Focus* (London and New York: Routledge, 1992).

94. *Griswold v. Connecticut*, 381 U.S. 479, 513 (1965).

95. Flathman, *Toward a Liberalism.*

96. *Roe v. Wade*, 410 U.S. 113 (1972).

97. *Harris v. McRae*, 448 U.S. 297, 318 (1979).

98. Goodin, *Reasons for Welfare.*

99. See Adam B. Seligman, *The Idea of Civil Society* (New York: Free Press, 1992).

100. Rawls, *A Theory of Justice*; Ronald Dworkin, "Liberalism," in *Public and Private Morality*, ed. Stuart Hampshire (Cambridge: Cambridge University Press, 1978); Ackerman, *Social Justice in the Liberal State.*

Chapter 5. Public-Private Partnership

1. Barton J. Bernstein, "The Continuation of Corporate Capitalism" in *The New Deal: The Historical Debate*, ed. Richard Kirkendall (New York: John Wiley, 1973).

2. Westbrook, *John Dewey and American Democracy*, 432–38.

3. See, for example, Jordan A. Schwarz, *Liberal: Adolf A. Berle and the Vision of an American Era* (New York: Free Press, 1989).

4. Wolfe, *America's Impasse: The Rise and Fall of the Politics of Growth.*

5. See, for example, Ronald Inglehart, "Post-Materialism in an Environment of Insecurity," *American Political Science Review* 75 (1981): 880–900.

6. Osborne, *Laboratories of Democracy.*

7. See Katherine C. Lyall, "Public-Private Partnerships in the Carter Years," in *Public-Private Partnerships: Improving Urban Life*, ed. Perry Davis, *Proceedings of the Academy of Political Science* 36, no. 2 (1986): 4–13.

8. Lindblom, *Politics and Markets: The World's Political Economic Systems.*

9. James O'Connor, *The Fiscal Crisis of the State* (New York: St. Martin's Press, 1973).

10. See Seymour Martin Lipset, *The First New Nation: The United States in Historical and Comparative Perspective* (New York: W.W. Norton, 1979).

11. See, for example, Robert Goodman, *The Last Entrepreneurs: America's Regional Wars for Jobs and Dollars* (New York: Simon & Schuster, 1979); see also Peter K. Eisinger, *The Rise of the Entrepreneurial State: State and Local Economic Development Policy in the United States* (Madison: University of Wisconsin Press, 1988).

12. See Lynn Bachelor, "Reindustrialization in Detroit: Capital Mobility and Corporate Influence," *Journal of Urban Affairs* 4:3 (summer 1982): 35–50.

13. Lowi, *The End of Liberalism*; see also Lowi, *The Personal President: Power Invested, Power Denied.*

14. Sunstein, *After the Rights Revolution*, 12–13, 102.

15. Sunstein, *After the Rights Revolution.*

16. Lindblom, *Politics and Markets*; Brubaker, "Can Liberals Punish?"

17. See, for example, Thomas Byrne Edsall, *The New Politics of Inequality* (New York: W.W. Norton, 1984); G. William Domhoff, *The Power Elite and the State: How Policy Is Made in America* (Hawthorne, N.Y.; Aldine de Gruyter, 1990).

18. See, for example, Martin Carnoy and Derek Shearer, "Towards a Democratic Alternative: Neo-Liberals vs. Economic Democrats," in *American Economic Policy: Problems and Prospects*, ed. Gar Alperovitz and Roger Skurski (Notre Dame, Ind.: University of Notre Dame Press, 1984).

19. Fred Block, *Revising State Theory: Essays in Politics and Postindustrialism* (Philadelphia: Temple University Press, 1987), esp. chap. 3.

20. Dworkin, *Taking Rights Seriously.*

21. See Bachelor, "Reindustrialization in Detroit."

22. Glendon, *Rights Talk: The Impoverishment of Political Discourse*, 109–20.

23. Bowles and Gintis, *Democracy and Capitalism.*

24. See Carnoy and Shearer, *Economic Democracy: The Challenge of the 1980s.*

25. See, for example, Walzer, *Spheres of Justice: A Defense of Pluralism.*

26. Paul Peterson, *City Limits* (Chicago: University of Chicago Press, 1981).

27. Glendon, *Rights Talk: The Impoverishment of Political Discourse*

28. Jon Elster, "Is There (or Should There Be) a Right to Work?" in *Democracy and the Welfare State*, ed. Amy Gutmann (Princeton: Princeton University Press, 1988), 70.

29. See Bachelor, "Reindustrialization in Detroit."

30. See, for example, Pitkin, "Obligation and Consent—I" and "Obligation and Consent—II."

31. "Proceedings Had before the Honorable Thomas D. Lambrose . . . on . . . February 28, 1980," *United Steel Workers of America v. United States Steel Corporation*, cited in Staughton Lynd, "The Genesis of the Idea of a Community Right to Industrial Property in Youngstown and Pittsburgh, 1977–1987," in *The Constitution and American Life*, ed. David Thelen (Ithaca, N.Y.: Cornell University Press, 1988).

32. Lynd, "The Genesis of the Idea of a Community Right to Industrial Property."

33. Walzer, *Obligations: Essays on Disobedience, War, and Citizenship.*

34. James Madison, *Federalist Paper* No. 10, in *The Federalist Papers: Hamilton, Madison, Jay*, ed. Clinton Rossiter (New York: Mentor Books, 1961).

35. Robert B. Reich and John D. Donahue, *New Deals: The Chrysler Revival and the American System* (New York: Time Books, 1985).

36. See Chalmers Johnson, "Introduction: The Idea of Industrial Policy," in *The Industrial Policy Debate*, ed. Johnson (San Francisco: ICS Press, 1984).

37. See Lustig, *Corporate Liberalism: The Origins of Modern American Political Theory.*

38. Lee Iacocca, *Iacocca* (New York: Bantam Books, 1984).

39. Reich and Donahue, *New Deals.*

40. Chrysler officials would often cite the precedents of New York City and the Lockheed Corporation. See Iacocca, *Iacocca.*

41. See, for example, *The Industrial Policy Debate*, ed. Johnson.

42. See, for example, Thomas C. Schelling, *Choice and Consequence: Perspectives of an Errant Economist* (Cambridge: Harvard University Press, 1984).

43. Dolbeare, *Democracy at Risk: The Politics of Economic Renewal.*

44. See Bachrach and Botwinick, *Power and Empowerment: A Radical Theory of Participatory Democracy.*

45. Lowi, *The End of Liberalism*, 298–300.

46. Lowi, "American Business, Public Policy, Case-Studies, and Political Theory."

47. See Lester C. Thurow, *The Zero-Sum Society: Distribution and the Possibility for Economic Change* (New York: Basic Books, 1980).

48. James L. Sundquist, *Constitutional Reform and Effective Government* (Washington, D.C.: Brookings Institution, 1986); James MacGregor Burns, *The Power to Lead: The Crisis of the American Presidency* (New York: Simon & Schuster, 1984).

Chapter 6. Privacy Issues

1. Rawls, *Political Liberalism.*

2. *Palko v. Connecticut*, 302 U.S. 319 (1937).

3. See Flathman, *Toward a Liberalism*; and *Willful Liberalism: Voluntarism and Individuality in Political Theory and Practice.*

4. Flathman, *Toward a Liberalism.*

5. Aaron, *John Locke*; see also Gough, *John Locke's Political Philosophy.*

6. See, for example, William Lee Miller, *The First Liberty: Religion and the American Republic* (New York: Paragon House, 1988).

7. *Engel v. Vitale*, 370 U.S. 421, 424, 429 (1962).

8. *Engel v. Vitale.*

9. *Abington School District v. Schempp*, 374 U.S. 203, 205 (1963).

10. *Abington School District v. Schempp*, 222.

11. *Abington School District v. Schempp*, 226.

12. *Lemon v. Kurtzman*, 403 U.S. 602 (1971).

13. *Everson v. Board of Education*, 330 U.S. 1, 18 (1947).

14. *Lemon v. Kurtzman*, 612-13.

15. *Engel v. Vitale*, 431–32.

16. *Pierce v. Society of Sisters*, 268 U.S. 510 (1924); and *Meyer v. Nebraska*, 262 U.S. (1922); *Meyer* specifically involved the rights of parents to teach their children the German language.

17. See, for example, Michael Walzer, "Liberalism and the Art of Separation," *Political Theory* 12 (1984): 315–30.

18. See Dworkin, *A Matter of Principle.*

19. See, for example, William M. Sullivan, *Reconstructing Public Philosophy* (Berkeley: University of California Press, 1986).

20. Levinson, *Constitutional Faith.*

21. *Wallace v. Jaffree,* 472 U.S. 38, 40 (1985).

22. *Wallace v. Jaffree,* 59.

23. *West Virginia Board of Education v. Barnette,* 319 U.S. 624, 642 (1943).

24. *Wisconsin v. Yoder,* 406 U.S. 205, 211, 215 (1972).

25. *Wisconsin v. Yoder,* 228.

26. *Wisconsin v. Yoder,* 245–46.

27. *Brown v. Board of Education,* 347 U.S. 483 (1953).

28. Walzer, "Liberalism and the Art of Separation."

29. *Edwards v. Aguillard,* 476 U.S. 1103; 96 L. Ed. 2d 510, 521 (1987).

30. Justice Scalia dissenting, *Edwards v. Aguillard,* L. Ed., 551–52.

31. See, for example, Nat Hentoff, *Free Speech for Me—But Not for Thee: How the American Left and Right Relentlessly Censor Each Other* (New York: HarperCollins, 1992).

32. Gough, "The Development of Locke's Belief in Toleration."

33. Walzer, *Spheres of Justice: A Defense of Pluralism.*

34. See Robert H. Bork, *The Tempting of America: The Political Seduction of the Law* (New York: Free Press, 1990); John Hart Ely, "The Wages of Crying Wolf: A Comment on *Roe v. Wade,*" 82 *Yale Law Journal* 920 (1973).

35. *Pierce v. Society of Sisters; Meyer v. Nebraska.*

36. *Griswold v. Connecticut,* 381 U.S. 479 (1965).

37. *Eisenstadt v. Baird,* 405 U.S. 438, 453 (1971).

38. *Roe v. Wade,* 410 U.S. 113, 153 (1972).

39. *Roe v. Wade,* 155.

40. See Laurence H. Tribe, *Abortion: The Clash of Absolutes* (New York: W.W. Norton, 1990).

41. *Roe v. Wade,* 179.

42. *Lochner v. New York,* 198 U.S. 45 (1905).

43. Ely, "The Wages of Crying Wolf."

44. Bork, *The Tempting of America.* Similarly, many see the abortion issue as cultural as well. See, for example, Peter Skerry, "The Class Conflict over Abortion," *Public Interest* 52 (1978): 69–84.

45. *U.S. v. Carolene Products Co.,* 304 U.S. 144, 153 (1937).

46. See, for example, Roger Wertheimer, "Understanding the Abortion Argument," *Philosophy and Public Affairs* 1 (1971): 67–95.

47. See, for example, Mary C. Segers, "Tolerance and the Abortion Controversy" in *Legislating Morality: Private Choices on the Public Agenda,* ed. Kim Ezra Shienbaum (Rochester, Vt.: Schenkman Books, 1988).

48. See, for example, Ronald Dworkin, *Law's Empire* (Cambridge: Harvard University Press, 1986); Laurence H. Tribe, *Constitutional Choices* (Cambridge: Harvard University Press, 1985).

49. Michael J. Perry, "Abortion, the Public Morals, and the Police Power: The

Ethical Function of Substantive Due Process," *UCLA Law Journal* 23 (1976): 689, 706.

50. Tribe, *Constitutional Choices*, 11.

51. *Maher v. Roe*, 432 U.S. 464 (1976).

52. *Harris v. McRae*, 448 U.S. 297, 318 (1979).

53. *City of Akron v. Akron Center for Reproductive Health Inc.*, 462 U.S. 416 (1982).

54. *Thornburgh v. American College of Obstetricians and Gynecologists*, 476 U.S. 747, 754 (1985).

55. *Webster v. Reproductive Health Services*, 109 Supreme Court Reporter 3040, 3050 (1989).

56. See Dworkin, *A Matter of Principle*.

57. *City of Akron v. Akron Center for Reproductive Health Inc.*, 453–60.

58. See, for example, Michael Kinsley, "Life Terms," *New Republic*, 2 pts., July 15, 22, 1991.

59. Tribe, *Abortion*, 233.

60. Jed Rubenfeld, "The Right to Privacy," *Harvard Law Review* 102 (1989): 737, 791. Also there are those who argue that such laws also effectively force women to be good samaritans against a tradition in American law which presumes that individuals do not have to be good samaritans. See, for example, Donald H. Regan, "Rewriting *Roe v. Wade*," *Michigan Law Review* 77 (1979): 1569; Judith Jarvis Thomson, "A Defense of Abortion," *Philosophy and Public Affairs* 1 (1971): 47–66.

61. Mary Ann Glendon, *Abortion and Divorce in Western Law: American Failures, European Challenges* (Cambridge: Harvard University Press, 1987), 35, 53.

62. See, for example, Arthur Maass, *Congress and the Common Good* (New York: Basic Books, 1983).

63. Kenneth L. Karst, "Forward: Equal Citizenship Under the Fourteenth Amendment," *Harvard Law Review* 91 (1977), 1, 6.

64. Cass R. Sunstein, "Public Values, Private Interests, and the Equal Protection Clause," *Supreme Court Review*, 1982, 127–66.

65. See Judith A. Baer, *Equality Under the Constitution: Reclaiming the Fourteenth Amendment* (Ithaca, N.Y.: Cornell University Press, 1983).

66. John Hart Ely, *Democracy and Distrust: A Theory of Judicial Review* (Cambridge: Harvard University Press, 1980), 83.

67. *Slaughter-House Cases*, 36.

68. See Sotiros A. Barber, *On What the Constitution Means* (Baltimore: Johns Hopkins University Press, 1984).

69. *Bowers v. Hardwick*, 478 U.S. 186 (1986).

70. See, for example, Cass R. Sunstein, "Sexual Orientation and the Constitution: A Note on the Relationship Between Due Process and Equal Protection," *University of Chicago Law Review* 55 (1988): 1161.

71. *Cruzan v. Director, Missouri Dept. of Health*, 110 Supreme Court Reporter 2841 (1990).

72. *Cruzan v. Director, Missouri Dept. of Health*, 2854.

73. *Stanley v. Georgia*, 394 U.S. 557, 564, 565 (1968).

74. *Paris Adult Theatre I v. Slaton*, 413 U.S. 49 (1972).

75. *Miller v. California*, 413 U.S. 5, 24 (1973).

76. *Miller v. California*, 30.

77. *Miller v. California*, 40–41.

78. Galston, *Liberal Purposes: Goods, Virtues, and Diversity in the Liberal State.*

79. See John W. Kingdon, *Agendas, Alternatives, and Public Policies* (Boston: Little, Brown, 1984).

Chapter 7. Toward a New Methodology of Policy Analysis

1. See, for example, Susan B. Hansen, "Public Policy Analysis: Some Recent Developments and Current Problems," in *Political Science: The State of the Discipline*, ed. Ada W. Finifter (Washington, D.C.: American Political Science Association, 1983).

2. See, for example, Theda Skocpol, *Social Policy in the United States: Future Possibilities in Historical Perspective* (Princeton: Princeton University Press, 1995).

3. See, for example, David Johnston, "Human Agency and Rational Action," in *The Economic Approach to Politics: A Critical Reassessment of the Theory of Rational Action*, ed. Kristen Renwick Monroe (New York: HarperCollins, 1991).

4. See Anthony Downs, "Social Values and Democracy," in ibid.

5. See Fischer, *Politics, Values, and Public Policy: The Problem of Methodology.*

6. See Charles W. Anderson, "The Place of Principles in Policy Analysis," *American Political Science Review* 73 (1979): 711–23.

7. See Douglas Torgeson, "Between Knowledge and Politics: Three Faces of Policy Analysis," *Policy Sciences* 19 (1986): 33–59.

8. See Mark Warren, "Max Weber's Liberalism for a Nitzschean World," *American Political Science Review* 82 (1988): 31–50.

9. See, for example, Laurence H. Tribe, "Policy Science: Analysis or Ideology?" *Philosophy and Public Affairs* 2 (1972): 66–110.

10. See Mark P. Petracca, "The Rational Actor Approach to Politics: Science, Self-Interest, and Normative Democratic Theory," in *The Economic Approach to Politics: A Critical Reassessment of the Theory of Rational Action*, ed. Kristen Renwick Monroe (New York: HarperCollins, 1991).

11. See Stuart S. Nagel, *Policy Studies: Integration and Evaluation* (New York: Praeger Press, 1988).

12. See, for example, Peter H. Rossi, Howard E. Freeman and Sonia R. Wright, *Evaluation: A Systematic Approach* (Beverly Hills, Calif.: Sage Publications, 1979).

13. See Duncan J. MacRae, *The Social Function of Social Science* (New Haven: Yale University Press, 1976).

14. See Nagel, *Policy Studies.*

15. See Schelling, *Choice and Consequence: Perspectives of an Errant Economist.*

16. MacRae, *The Social Function of Social Science*, 133–36.

17. William L. Hays, *Statistics*, 3rd ed. (New York: Holt, Rinehart and Winston, 1981), 245.

18. Fischer, *Politics, Values, and Public Policy*, 2.

19. Deborah A. Stone, *Policy Paradox and Political Reason* (New York: HarperCollins, 1988), 14.

20. See Max Weber, *The Methodology of the Social Sciences* (Glencoe, Ill.; Free Press, 1949).

21. See, for example, Schwarz, *America's Hidden Success: A Reassessment of Public Policy from Kennedy to Reagan*; Chrisman and Pifer, *Government for the People: The Federal Role: What It Is, What It Should Be.*

22. See, for example, Mead, *Beyond Entitlement: The Social Obligations of Citizenship*; Murray, *Losing Ground: American Social Policy, 1950–1980*; Banfield, *The Unheavenly City Revisited.*

23. See Hawkesworth, *Theoretical Issues in Policy Analysis.*

24. Fischer, *Politics, Values, and Public Policy.*

25. Weber, *The Methodology of the Social Sciences*, 56.

26. Robert E. Goodin, *Political Theory and Public Policy* (Chicago: University of Chicago Press, 1982).

27. See MacIntyre, *After Virtue: A Study in Moral Theory*; Sandel, *Liberalism and the Limits of Justice*; Taylor, *Hegel and Modern Society.*

28. Lowi, *The End of Liberalism.*

29. Karl R. Popper, *The Open Society and Its Enemies*, vol. 1: *The Spell of Plato* (Princeton: Princeton University Press, 1966).

30. See Mead, *The New Politics of Poverty: The Nonworking Poor in America.*

31. Gary King, Robert O. Keohane, and Sidney Verba, *Designing Social Inquiry: Scientific Inference in Qualitative Research* (Princeton: Princeton University Press, 1994).

32. MacRae, *The Social Function of Social Science.*

33. Mark Sagoff, "Values and Preferences," *Ethics* 96 (January 1986): 301–16.

34. Robert B. Reich, introduction to *The Power of Public Ideas*, ed. Reich (Cambridge: Ballinger Publishing, 1988), 6.

35. Stephen Macedo, *Liberal Virtues: Citizenship, Virtue, and Community in Liberal Constitutionalism* (Oxford: Claredon Press, 1990).

36. Ackerman, *Social Justice in the Liberal State.*

37. See John S. Dryzek, *Discursive Democracy: Politics, Policy, and Political Science* (Cambridge: Cambridge University Press, 1990).

38. Dryzek, *Discursive Democracy.*

39. Paul A. Roth, *Meaning and Method in the Social Sciences: A Case for Methodological Pluralism* (Ithaca, N.Y.: Cornell University Press, 1987).

40. Michael Quinn Patton, *Utilization-Focused Evaluation* (Beverly Hills, Calif.: Sage Publications, 1978).

41. Dryzek, *Discursive Democracy*, 173.

42. Stone, *Policy Paradox and Political Reason.*

43. See Lindblom, "The Science of Muddling Through"; Lindblom, *The Intelligence of Democracy: Decision Making Through Mutual Adjustment.*

44. Paul Healy, "Interpretive Policy Inquiry: A Response to the Limitations of the Received View," *Policy Sciences* 19 (1986): 381–96.

45. MacRae, *The Social Function of Social Science*, 306.

46. MacRae, *The Social Function of Social Science.*

47. See, for example, Friedman, "The Role of Monetary Policy"; Friedman, "Unemployment versus Inflation?"; Phelps, "Phillips Curves, Expectations of Infla-

tion and Optimal Unemployment over Time"; Phelps, *Inflation Policy and Unemployment Theory: The Cost-Benefit Approach to Monetary Planning.*

48. See, for example, William Galston, "Civic Education in the Liberal State, in *Liberalism and the Moral Life,* ed. Nancy L. Rosenblum (Cambridge: Harvard University Press, 1989); see also Macedo, *Liberal Virtues;* John Rawls, *Political Liberalism* (New York: Columbia University Press, 1993).

49. Lowi, *The End of Liberalism.*

50. See, for example, Yehezkel Dror, *Design for Policy Sciences* (New York: American Elsevier, 1971).

51. Easton, "The New Revolution in Political Science."

52. See Runciman, *Social Science and Political Theory;* Goodin, *Political Theory and Public Policy.*

53. See, for example, Sheldon S. Wolin, "Political Theory as a Vocation," *American Political Science Review* 63 (1969): 1062–82.

Index